PEACEABLE FRUIT

*For the Nurture of
Covenant Youth*

PEACEABLE FRUIT

*FOR THE NURTURE OF
COVENANT YOUTH*

taken from the following context in Hebrews, Chapter 12: "Now no chastening for the present seemeth to be joyous, but grievous: nevertheless afterward it yieldeth the peaceable fruit of righteousness unto them which are exercised thereby."

by Gertrude Hoeksema

REFORMED FREE PUBLISHING ASSOCIATION
Grand Rapids, Michigan

(Distributed by Kregel Publications)

Copyright © 1974 by Gertrude Hoeksema. All rights reserved.
Published by the Reformed Free Publishing Association, P.O.
Box 2006, Grand Rapids, Michigan 49501.

This book, or parts thereof, may not be reproduced in any form without permission in writing from the Publisher.

Library of Congress Catalog Card Number 73-91780

ISBN 0-8254-2821-1

Printed in the United States of America

**to
my children**

CONTENTS

Foreword 9
Acknowledgments 11
Introduction 13
On Washing 16

1. *Who* Is the Child.......................... 19
   A covenant child: in the line of the promise, in the organic line of believers. A distinct individual: totally depraved, redeemed in Christ. A gift from God: in the line of salvation, with the potential adult within him.

2. *What* Is the Child......................... 33
   Created in God's image: rational, moral, responsible. An image bearer: has lost God's image, retains only remnants. Personality of the child: interaction of person—"I," nature, intellect, will; environment. Personality and emotions. Personality and sin and grace.

3. Preparation for the Child.................... 57
   Questions to be answered: meaning of "be fruitful and multiply," how many children?, fatalism versus responsibility. Period of preparation: physical, mental, spiritual.

4. Birth of the Child.......................... 73
   Paradoxes: all ours and all God's, natural birth and a wonder, perfect and imperfect child, fear and trust. Why bring forth covenant seed: improper motives, positive motives.

5. The Child from Birth to Nine Months............ 83
   Routine. Communication. Training: attitude, practical examples. Consistency. Results: for parents, for child.

6. The Child from Nine Months to Two Years........ 107
   Characteristics: a unique individual, new independence, curious, active. Suggestions for: time use, teaching and training. Spiritual atmosphere.

7. The Child from Two to Five Years............... 133
   New awareness: of physical coordination, of environment, by his questions. Activities: for helping, varied crafts, proper habits. Preparation in behavior: for visits to doctor or grocery store, for emergencies, for church-going.

8. The Child from Two to Five Years (continued)..... 159
   Discipline—handling: positive atmosphere, relaxed attitude. His disobedience: proper chastening, motivation for obedience, spiritual undercurrent. His speech: learned by example, correct speech, respectful speech. Spiritual growth: prayer, worship.

9. The Kindergartner 191
   His training toward freedom. Our choice of school. His readiness. His abilities. Our attitude toward his time. His relationship to classmates.

10. The Child's Early Primary Years................. 213
    School life: Extension of the home—teacher and the early primary; relationships between parents, teacher, child; his abilities; his characteristics. Home: still most important, first evidences of outside influences on our child, new kinds of problems, positive guidelines, spiritual development.

11. The Child in Later Primary Years................ 245
    Changes: physical, mental, psychological. Development in handling the child. Correcting specific faults at this age. Growth in spiritual understanding: church, catechism, in life's perspective.

12. The Early Adolescent......................... 271
    Characteristics: physical, peculiarities at this age, traits. Development: transitional period—independence, abilities, responsibilities. Guidance: kinds, positive instruction.

13. The High School Adolescent.................... 299
    Independent age: mistaken ideas of independence; equality, skepticism, lack of foresight; proper idea of independence, under parental authority, with guidance. New responsibilities: kinds, motivation. Forward-looking teenager.

FOREWORD

One finds very little resource material, written from a Scriptural or a Reformed perspective, about the child. When parents or teachers want to study child psychology or when they need answers to their questions about dealing with the child, they can go only to books which are, for the most part, humanistic or evolutionistic, or to books which are generally Christian in outlook, but with many of whose ideas they cannot agree. Both parents and teachers have expressed the necessity for a theoretical and practical study of the child from a distinctively Scriptural and Reformed viewpoint. This need I have tried, in a measure, to fill, particularly from a practical perspective.

In this study of the covenant child, based on textbook research and varied experience, I have tried to combine the technical and the practical. In order to keep the book at a popular reading level, I have included only the minimum of technical terms, and have woven them into a story; most of the technical aspect is confined to chapters one and two.

In order to achieve more than an abstract theoretical treatise on the covenant child, I have followed the hypothetical life of a boy in a covenant home, from pre-birth through his high school years. This boy, whom I have named Tim, has his own physical characteristics and a definite personality, and in many aspects will resemble our own children. When I used concrete examples in Tim's life, they were based on actual experiences, the details of which I may have altered slightly. This study does not touch on all aspects of Tim's life. Tim lives in a small family, in an urban setting. Life in a larger family or in a rural community would, in some respects, be different. But, by way of narrative and illustration, I have tried to lay down basic principles governing the life of a godly family. These principles could be adapted and modified to fit circumstances in any covenant family.

In these last days, the need of a Scriptural, spiritually sensitive training for our children is urgent; for, almost imperceptibly, the philosophy of this age creeps into our lives and we live along with the world in our family lives. Though we find ourselves with many more leisure hours than our parents had, we are so busy filling them with "this-worldly" pleasures, that we have no time for quiet spiritual talks with our children. Another danger that creeps into our thinking is that the church and the Christian day schools are diligent and adequate teachers for our children; therefore we tend to neglect our covenantal duties of instructing our seed in the fear of the Lord. Slowly, if we are not spiritually watchful, our homes become arenas of worldly joys and activities instead of citadels of godliness. This manual points to some of the weaknesses, brings you and me up short when we fail to do our covenant duties, and shows us the Scriptural way to lead our family in the paths of righteousness.

May this study help us better to understand our children, and spur us on to train them devotedly, to the end that our covenant God may receive all the glory.

ACKNOWLEDGMENTS

The author wishes to thank the publishers listed below for permission to include material from their publications in this book:

The Banner of Truth for articles by A. N. Martin in *The Banner of Truth;* The Christian Reformed Publishing House for an editorial in *The Banner* by L. DeKoster; Wm. B. Eerdmans Publ. Co. for *Human Development, Learning and Teaching,* by C. Jaarsma; Harcourt, Brace, Jovanovich, Inc. for *Psychology, Its Principles and Applications,* by T. L. Engle; J. H. Kok, Kampen for *Moeder, Zeg Me Eens,* by Gera Kraan, and *Het Christelijk Leven in Huwelijk en Gezin* and *Zedelijke Opveoding,* by G. Brillenburg Wurth; Prentice-Hall, Inc. for *Child Psychology,* by A. T. Jersild; Review and Herald Publ. Ass'n for an article in *Liberty Magazine* by R. Nixson; Zondervan Publ. House for *Principles of Personality Building for Christian Parents,* by C. B. Eavey, and *The Home Beautiful,* by J. R. Miller; Webster/McGraw Hill for *Psychology for Living,* by H. Sorenson and M. Malm.

The author also acknowledges the following sources:

Child Psychology, by M. W. Curti, David McKay Co., Inc., *Christian Counseling,* by G. Brillenburg Wurth, Presb. and Ref. Publ. Co., and *Talks to Teachers on Psychology,* by W. James, Henry Holt.

Photography by Richmond Studio, Grandville, Mich.

A word of thanks to my husband, Homer C. Hoeksema, professor of theology at the Protestant Reformed Seminary; to Mr. Donald Doezema; and to the Rev. Herman Hanko for the many hours they spent helping and advising me.

INTRODUCTION

If thy children will keep my covenant and my testimony that I shall teach them, their children shall also sit upon thy throne for evermore.
—Psalm 132:12

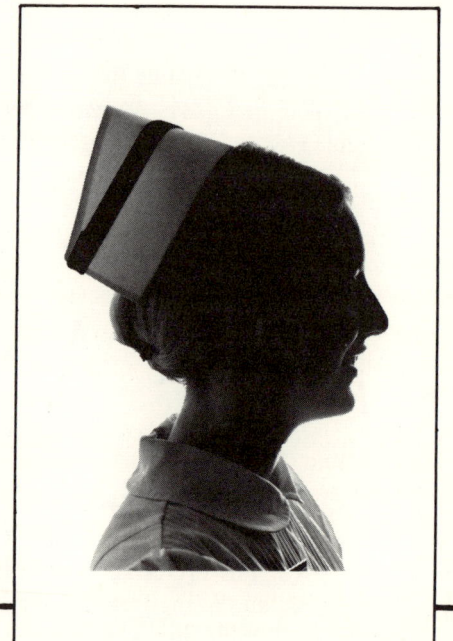

In the brief period of being hospitalized for a serious illness, one often has unique personal conversations with his nurses or fellow patients. During one of my hospital conversations, after my nurse remarked that what was different about me was that I had "faith," she asked me what was so special about my religion to make my reactions noticeably different. Was it "grace or something?" she wanted to know.

Understandably, I was not prepared for this question. Why was our Reformed and specifically our Protestant Reformed development of the truths of Scripture so dear to me? I thought for a while. Was it the belief in God's sovereignty, His beautiful decrees, justification by faith, particular grace, or a dedicated life of sanctification? It was all of these, I was sure. But I gave the nurse none of these answers. "If I would choose one precious Biblical truth which has had a powerful influence on my life, as it was taught me by the theologians of our churches, it would be the doctrine of the covenant," I finally said.

"The covenant? What's that?" my nurse, with a background in England, wanted to know.

How should I explain God's covenant so that she could understand more than superficially what it meant to me? From my sickbed I told my nurse what I remembered from a brief lifetime of listening and studying. I told her that our covenant belief is rooted in the idea that our God is triune, a **God** of fellowship and communion in Himself, and that this **triune** covenant God in His eternal purpose determined to establish a relationship of friendship between Himself and a people He chose. The negative side of this is that we do not believe in a lone or lonely "Supreme Being" way up there, but rather a God and Father Who communicates with Himself and through His Son and Spirit with us, His people. This meant that God would create a people, creatures like Himself, made in His image. His people had to be made like Him, for friendship presupposes likeness. But these creatures would not be parties, much less *equal* parties in this covenant relation of friendship. It would always be a relationship of Creator and creature, a relationship of humble sorrow for sin, grateful deliverance, and lives of thanks, from the creatures to their Creator. I wished I could quote her something from the beautiful writings of Herman Hoeksema, such as the following, taken from a personal letter to a pastor beginning his labors, and quoted in the *Banner of Truth*.[1]

By this truth (the covenant) I do not mean an agreement between God and man, or between God and the sinner, nor a mere way of salvation, but the eternal relation of friendship and fellowship between God and the elect in Christ Jesus, according to which He saves them from sin and death and gives unto them eternal life and as a fruit of which they love Him with all their heart and mind and soul and strength.

    Then I went on to tell my nurse about all the beauties of the covenant. I told her about God's part in the covenant. I told her about the promises culminating in *the* promise. I told her that *the* promise was Christ, the Son of God in the flesh, the suffering Savior, the risen Lord, the salvation of His people. Then I backtracked and told her that God showed Noah that the Lord would save, not only a *people,* but a whole *creation* which that people would inherit. Next I tried to get my nurse to see *how* God established that covenant. I went to Adam and Eve in Paradise and told her that God promised already then that the seed of the woman would inherit the promise of the covenant, and that God renewed this promise to **Abraham** *and to his seed.*

We talked about Abraham's seed then; and I tried to show my nurse that it was a *spiritual* seed, chosen by grace. But God did not choose this seed helter-skelter. Instead, God chooses His covenant people along organic lines, and establishes this covenant with believers and their seed throughout all nations. This is the true seed of Abraham, chosen by God in the line of continued generations.

I had told my nurse a lot already, and I was tired; but I could not stop yet. I had to tell her the implications of our belief that God establishes His covenant along the line of continued generations. I told her about our part in the covenant. I told how we lived as covenant parents who promised at baptism to instruct our children in the doctrines of the covenant to the utmost of our power, that our whole way of life centered on teaching our children in every sphere of their lives in the knowledge that these children are God's children, and therefore the church of tomorrow. All of our lives and those of our children are controlled by the spiritual assurance that we are God's covenant people.

There was so much more I could have told my nurse. I had only scratched the surface in describing the rich covenant promises in store for us and for our children. I had not told her anything at all about our children, their natures, their persons, their minds and wills, souls and spirits. Nor had I showed her how we tried to teach and train our children in their early home training, their church, catechism, Sunday School and Christian day school instruction. And how could I expect her to learn and remember it all, when even we, who have learned it all from infancy, often lose sight of and neglect our high calling in God's covenant?

Often in the years following this conversation with my nurse I have thought about us and our children. Since that conversation I have studied our children in God's Book, in textbooks, and firsthand, by watching them closely. And I felt the urge to write about the covenant children I love. I want to write not merely a treatise on the child, nor a psychology textbook in the usual sense of the word, nor a mere manual for training him, but rather a systematic Biblical approach to the covenant child, to find out who he is, what he is, and how he is prepared for his mature years. This means, of course, that we as parents know the Biblical approach to our covenant responsibilities, and bow before God's Word as it tells us what to do, knowing that His covenant will stand fast with us forever.

NOTES

1. The Banner of Truth Trust, London, Eng., No. 88, p. 42.

ON WASHING

I watched God wash the world today.
With sudden shower hard and clean.
He scrubbed the sloping, sandy beach,
And pelted rocks and stones with sheen.

I watched Him freshen feathered birds
And wash the dusty, woolly sheep;
He splashed the green and yellow fields,
And rinsed the rising hillside steep.

I watched Him bathe the blades of grass,
And wash the pansy's pretty face;
Each leaf He laved with sparkling drop
And edged each tree with sequined lace.

I watched a cov'nant child in church,
By solemn father gently held,
Baptized with sprinkled water, sign
That stains of sin were all dispelled.

I watched with eyes of faith and saw,
Through God's own Word, the reason why.
God washed a special, chosen world
In precious blood. It made Christ die.

I'll watch and wait until I'll be
Among the saints arrayed in white
Who washed their robes in the Lamb's own blood,
To dwell by living fountains bright.
                              G. H.

1
WHO IS THE CHILD

Notwithstanding she shall be saved in childbearing, if they continue in faith and charity and holiness with sobriety.
—I Timothy 2:15

I F YOU WERE WATCHING MY NEIGHBOR AND ME AS WE WERE talking together in our backyards, when suddenly a bright-eyed child darted past our feet in her play, and I asked, "Who is that child?" you would probably have heard my neighbor tell me in astonishment, "Why, that's Kathy. You know Kathy."

Yes, I know that is Kathy. But that was not what I was really asking. I wanted to know *who* she is. I had to know all about her, not only *who* but also *what* she is if I was in any way going to share a part of my life with her. Using this hypothetical, dark-haired, sparkling-eyed Kathy as our model in these first two chapters, let us try to find out all about her.

Again I asked, "Who is she? Who is the child?" I said to my neighbor, "Go with me, if you will, to try to find the answers in the library. We will ask the librarian to direct us to the Psychology Section, and there we will search the crowded shelves for books by learned authors, which will tell us who this child is."

We wanted answers to questions such as, "What is this child's origin? Why does she act as she does? What does it mean that she is a person?"

The table of contents of the first book which we eagerly pulled from the shelf listed these chapter headings: "The Nervous System," "Neutral Action," "Sensation," "Selection and Control," "Perception."[1] We shook our heads. This was not quite what we were looking for; Kathy is more than a neuro-sensory being. We pulled down another book and read: "Development of Overt Sensory-Motor Adjustments," "Native Factors in Emotion and Motivation," "Perceptual-Motor Learning: The Conditioned Response," "Perceptual-Motor Learning: Complex Habits."[2] No, this book seemed to stress Kathy's development as mechanical.

"Here," I told my neighbor as I pulled down a third volume, "is a work by a psychologist of world renown. It is titled, *Talks to Teachers on Psychology: And to Students on Some of Life's Ideals*. Again we thumbed through the table of contents and saw, "The Stream of Consciousness: our mental life is a succession of conscious fields," "The Child as a Behaving Organism: mind as pure reason and mind as practical guide," "The Necessity of Reactions," "The Laws of Habit: habit due to plasticity of organic tissues."[3]

My neighbor and I looked at each other and shook our heads again. Because we are covenant people, trained to live a God-centered and Scripturally oriented life, we began to realize that we had come to the wrong place to find out who the child is. Most authors of books on studies of children base their psychology on what they see and observe about the child; they see him as a physical, a neurological or a behavioral entity, according to the particular school of thought they favor. They tell us what *they* see of the child and how *they* interpret what they see.

But perusing a table of contents is not a fair way to judge an author, my neighbor argued, so we sat down at one of the tables in the library and studied these books. We read that the authors concern themselves only with the tangible: the child and his environment. Scientifically they dissect the child and analyze his physical being, his neurological functions, his intellectual responses. Now this in itself is not wrong, my neighbor and I agreed. But when the authors of these books on child psychology apply their findings, they tell us that mechan-

Who Is the Child / 21

ical training, called conditioning, will often produce proper behavior, for our child is a behaving organism; they teach us to be careful how we treat his impulses for fear of neural damage; and they show us how to redirect his frustrations (sins?) so that our child meets society's standards of living.

By this time we knew why this was the wrong place to try to find the answers to our questions. The authors of these books were secular, worldly, unregenerate men, devoid of grace. They did not start at the right place. And if they do not start at the right place—if *they* do not know who the child is how can they tell *us?*

My neighbor, being by nature more timid than I, asked me to tell the librarian that we could not use these books. So I told the librarian that we were still interested in psychology books about children, but could she suggest some with a Biblical approach? There are not many, she told us, but perhaps this book by C. Jaarsma is what we were looking for.

"Part One treats the person and personality," my neighbor whispered to me. "The person is the *who,* isn't it? We had better read this part."

We read the pages about the Christian theory of the person, and found a Scriptural approach to the fall of man, the nature of man, the doctrine of sin and grace. But my neighbor scratched his head. "His concepts are fuzzy, indefinite to me," he said. "Jaarsma writes general Biblical truths but not, in my opinion, very pertinent to a Christian theory of the person, and not organized so that I can pinpoint *who* the child is. Wait a minute, though. Here is his summary at the end of the chapter. It is called 'The Whole-Person-in Life.' This may help us."

We settled down to read again. I noticed my neighbor was re-reading the last part. It read:

> The person is the ego operative in psychosomatic functioning. The person, in turn, expresses himself in life through his dimensions of personality.
> When a person communicates in the dimensions of life according to consciously accepted ends, he is a personality. When ends and the direction of communication of a person

fail to constitute a field of related activity, he is without personality. An infant, comparatively speaking, is without personality. Likewise a person has lost contact with his in-life relationship when end and relationship fail to constitute a field of meaning. The latter is true of extreme forms of abnormality in the mentally ill. Personality is strong when the in-life relationship is well established, weak when it lacks adequate field relationship. Personality is bad when the in-life relationship of the dimensions of life violate standards of righteousness, good when they are valued as right. A person communicates in the dimensions of life, and it is in the in-life relationship that these dimensions are formed according to consciously chosen direction of the person. We speak, therefore, of the whole-person-in-life.[4]

Neither of us said anything. I think we were both asking ourselves questions. Is this the conclusion reached by a search of the Scriptures about the person? Does this author satisfactorily define the person of the covenant child? Can we not find a truly satisfying Scriptural answer to the question with which we started: who is Kathy, who is the child?

My neighbor and I quietly put the psychology books on the shelf and went home. "There is nothing wrong with studying the child," my neighbor maintained, "provided it is a Christian study, based strictly on the Bible." *That* was what we had to do—go first to the Bible. Here we would find the answer to our question.

Kathy is a covenant child, born in the generation of believers. Both of us already knew that, of course. With that information we went to God's Word to find out who this covenant child really is. Genesis 3:15 tells us: "And I will put enmity between thee and the woman, and between thy seed and her seed; it shall bruise thy head, and thou shalt bruise his heel." This child is the seed of the woman in the natural sense, to be sure, but particularly in the spiritual sense. She is a child of a seed that is at enmity with the devil, a seed that has the promise of salvation in Christ. As this seed developed, God showed them more of His promise: to Abraham He promised to establish His covenant for an everlasting covenant, in Genesis 17:7. Through the history of His people, God spelled out the blessings of His promise more clearly, until Christ came. Now, this child Kathy shares with us the promise of Acts 2:39: "For the promise is unto you, and to your children, and to all that are afar off, even as many as the Lord our God shall call."

My neighbor and I read more Biblical truths about the seed of the promise. We saw that though all the children of the saints in the Old Testament were in the line of covenant generations and all lived in the sphere of the covenant, not all of them were chosen by God to be His own. We read about Cain and Esau and Absalom, all born from believing parents, all brought up in the sphere of the church, but who showed by their lives that they were truly of the spiritual seed of the devil. We read, too, that "they are not all Israel that are of Israel," Romans 9:6. We could not look into this child's heart and determine whether the Lord had chosen her to salvation. But we need not be over-anxious about the problem, either. The Lord takes care of that. What we must know is that the Lord, as a usual rule, saves His own, in the seed of the woman, in the line of believers and their seed, in the way of His covenant promises; and before our own consciousness we view *our* children as His children, unless they show by their lives that they are not.

However, my neighbor and I had more questions. Why may we believe that this child is a child of God's covenant promise? Is she not an individual, with physical, mental, and spiritual traits all her own? And is not this child responsible *individually* to the calling of God? Certainly, she is called as an individual to live a godly life of sanctification. God teaches us, too, that we and our children will be judged individually. "For we must all appear before the judgment seat of Christ; that everyone may receive the things done in his body, according to that he hath done, whether it be good or bad," II Corinthians 5:10.

But we do not forget that this Kathy is not just *any* individual, placed at random in the history of God's creation. God chose the organic line of the covenant in which to place this child, the child with the promise. There was only one place where she would fit, according to God's design, and that was in the organic line of the household of her believing parents.

For the Lord saw fit, in His eternal counsel, to call elect, believing parents and to use them, as the spiritual line of Abraham, to continue the seed of the church and to teach that seed the truth of His Word.

Tied in with this thought is the beautiful concept that the covenant child, any covenant child, in his exact place in the organic line of believers and their seed, has his exact place in the body of Christ. "From whom the whole body fitly framed together and compacted by that which every joint supplieth, according to the effectual working in the measure of every part, maketh increase of the body unto the edifying of itself in love," Ephesians 4:16. There are many special privileges, spiritual pleasures, and grave responsibilities for us and for all our children as we live in that organic line of God's covenant promise.

For, my neighbor and I found, this covenant child in the organic line of believers, chosen by God, redeemed by Christ, is a regenerated, reborn child. We looked at Kathy in the light of Ephesians 4:22-24, which says: "That ye put off concerning the former conversation the old man, which is corrupt according to the deceitful lusts; and be renewed in the spirit of your mind; and that ye put on the new man, which after God is created in righteousness and true holiness."

We saw Kathy, on the one hand, as a child whose old nature is under the domination of sin, "which is corrupt according to the deceitful lusts." We saw her as a child who could easily go along with cheating, lying, stealing, and disobedience; as a child who would not be quick to admit her fault. We saw her as the rotten sinner we know ourselves to be. In her center, on the other hand, completely surrounded by her whole sinful nature, the Lord has put into her a new heart; and the issues of this heart are pure, for they proceed from the life of Christ. This new life, "created in righteousness and true holiness," must express itself through the wickedly corrupt old nature. Though Kathy is too young to comprehend it all, *we* know, of course, that this is the conflict of sanctification. We see her, as we see ourselves, wanting to and not wanting to do the right; and, even though we know her youthful mind cannot fully comprehend it all, we tell her that she *really* wants to do the right. Then we tell her why. It is because of the new heart which the Lord has given her, and with which He wants her to serve Him just perfectly. She is, we trust, one of His own who likes nothing better than to serve the Lord she loves with all her heart and with all her soul, and with all her mind, and with all her strength. Next we ask her why, if she wants to to serve the Lord perfectly, she doesn't do it. If she cannot answer our question (many very small covenant children can), we explain that we all were born full of sin and wickedness, and all we see around us is evil. And we like that, too. Then our wicked nature tells us to forget God's law for a while and to lie, or cheat, or kill someone with our tongue. And we like to sin. We enjoy it. This is the way we might explain to Kathy the conflict between our old nature and our new life in Christ.

When Kathy has given in to the horrible monster of sin and brazenly disobeys and lies (and we have seen her do it) then we have to tell her who she is—a corrupt sinner who enjoys her sin. We tell her, too, that there is nothing she can do about it *all by herself*. Only her Father in heaven can make her sorry for that sin, and take it away in His grace because He loves her, and wash her clean again in Christ's blood. For when we called Kathy a corrupt sinner we have told only half the story: Kathy, the covenant child, is also a repentant sinner and a saved sinner. Even while she sins, she is a reborn child of light who loves her Savior and loves to serve Him.

Kathy probably will not ask how it is possible that God works grace in her heart so that then she is sorry and asks God to forgive her. She is a covenant child. She just believes it. She has the faith of a little child. The one question she might ask would be, "How can I be a better girl?" Our answer would be to teach her to fight hard the sins that surround her, and to pray each day that she may do the right. For she has the same struggle as Paul, and she will say with him every day of her life, "For the good that I would I do not, but the evil which I would not, that I do," Romans 7:19.

During our search in the library we saw that many textbooks or treatises on child psychology stress that child psychology is different in approach and application from applied psychology in general, that the problems of the child are different from the problems of the man. We agreed that there was danger in such an assertion. The child is the potential man or woman. There really is no separate child psychology. It is true that physically, psychologically, mentally, and emotionally the child must be treated according to his limited or growing capacities and receptivity. But basically he is an individual in the beginning stages of his development, not a separate entity called a "child." He has the same body, the same mind, and the same will as he will have when his growth and development are complete. This means that from the time he is the smallest infant he is the potential man or woman with his place prepared for him on this earth. All that we do for and with the child we do for and with the man-that-will-be.[5] Applying this truth to Kathy, we know that when she was a baby, she had all the faculties and powers she ever will have; and as she dashes carefree and happily across the lawn, this sprightly child is the potential mature woman.

This process of growing up, the books on the library shelves told us, was a normal process. From babyhood to old age this process, called the learning process or the developmental process, happened according to the laws of development, and this was a good and healthy progress. I had seen my neighbor shake his head as he closed his book in the library. Now he suggested that we look at Kathy in her process of development through the eyes of faith.

"The development of the human race, and even the development of the covenant seed is not good and healthy," he told me. "It is abnormal, blurred, tainted with sin. Because of this, Kathy's believing parents know they are by nature a corrupt stock who produce a corrupt offspring."

For proof he showed me the confessions. The Third and Fourth Heads of Doctrine of our Canons, which tells us that at the fall man, who was originally made in the image of God, "forfeited these excellent gifts; and on the contrary, entailed on himself blindness of mind, horrible darkness, vanity and perverseness of judgment. . . . " Further, our creed tells us that in man (that is, in us and in our child) there remain only "the glimmerings of natural light." To make matters even worse for our child, "this light, such as it is, man in various ways renders wholly polluted, and holds it in unrighteousness. . . . "

We looked at pretty, dashing Kathy again. What a sorry picture our Canons paint of that child. Scripture paints that picture, too. With all her burden of sin, this child, the potential woman, grows up to be the imperfect woman, listening to and obeying her imperfect parents, who are burdened with the same sins she has.

If this were the whole picture of the child as she grows to maturity, her outlook (and ours) would be bleak indeed. Together parents and child would grope and fumble through the formative years, without direction, without incentive, without hope. But shining through this picture is Christ, the Light of the world, Who has come to make us perfect in Him. For as soon as we tell our covenant children how imperfect they are, we can also tell them, "Whosoever is born of God doth not commit sin," I John 3:9a, and "I delight in the law of God after the inward man," Romans 7:22. These truths are at the same time the hope and the assurance of the covenant parent.

We walked out to the backyard, my neighbor and I. As Kathy climbed up on his back, we reviewed together some of our conclusions about *who* she was—who all our covenant children are.

"We believe that our children are chosen by God, not as individuals scattered here and there over the world, but in the organic line of believing parents," he started.

"But our children are individual persons, each with his own physical, mental, and spiritual traits, and are individually responsible to the Judge of heaven and earth," I added.

"Regenerated, too," he said as Kathy peeked around the side of his face in wonder at his big, solemn words; "imperfect, yet perfect; corrupt by nature, redeemed by grace."

"She doesn't look like the woman she will be, but it's all there in potential," I said as I pinched her lithe leg.

With that, she jumped down and ran off again. "She isn't happy with us today," my neighbor murmured. "We aren't talking her language. But I think we have a start in knowing *who* she is."

He thought awhile, rubbing his head. Then he said slowly, "You would think that the main concern of covenant parents would *never* be their children's temporal needs: you know, that they have proper vitamins, rest, nourishment, that they learn how to be well-groomed and comfortable in social gatherings, that they be properly educated and trained for a job. That *should* not be the main concern of covenant parents. And I don't see how it *can* be if they truly see who their children are."

"Then their concern will be. . . . "

"To train their children for the kingdom of our Lord Jesus Christ. To train them to be other-worldly; to help them to set infinite values on spiritual gifts, and to know that they are only stewards for the material ones. They will teach them what path the Lord wants them to walk, for tomorrow they will be confessing members of God's church on earth, running swiftly their pilgrim's way on the road to glory. Covenant parents may not forget that they are molding the church of tomorrow!"

And with that my neighbor acted as if he were going home. "We aren't finished," I said. "If we ask, 'Who are our covenant children?' we have one more answer. They are gifts from God."

We went to Scripture again and saw how parents in Old Testament times accepted their children as gifts from their Father. Eve said of her first child, "I have gotten a man from the Lord," Genesis 4:1. Leah said, "Now will I praise the Lord: therefore she called his name Judah," Genesis 29:35. These examples of God's people who gave thanks for the children God gave them could be multiplied. We as God-fearing parents do that, too. Even many people of the world acknowledge the Lord's hand in giving children, although they do not receive their children in faith nor with humble thanksgiving.

But, we asked ourselves, is that all that God's people do? When parents give thanks, is their thanksgiving deeper than a mere superficial, "Thank you, Lord"? Hannah's thanks at the birth of Samuel encompassed a deeper concept. She prayed, "My heart rejoiceth in the Lord . . . because I rejoice in thy salvation." Hannah saw salvation in the birth of her son, salvation for herself, too. How?

She saw salvation as the children of Israel before her had

seen God's salvation. God taught them already when they were in the wilderness that their salvation was linked with the children that God would give them. For God's purpose is to save people through Christ so that He may be glorified. This people is not merely a group of individuals, but a unity, and this people is saved in God's wisdom in the line of the believing seed. This organic unity of people perpetuates itself not only by believing parents bringing forth covenant seed, but also by their faithful instructing of that seed in the doctrines of salvation. This people of God, all through the history recorded in Scripture, had a promise, a promise of a Savior, of the resurrection of the dead, of life everlasting. But, particularly in the Old Testament times, the parents did not clearly see all the elements of the fulfillment of that promise, for their vision through revelation was limited; but they looked for their salvation in the loins of their children, who would ultimately bring forth the Christ. That is why, after the giving of the law at Sinai, the instruction in God's law was so vital for the children of the nation of Israel. Deuteronomy 4:10 is but one of the many examples: "Gather me the people together, and I will make them hear my words, that they may learn to fear me all the days they shall live upon the earth, and that they may teach their children." This beautiful idea, of God's people keeping His commandments *with their children,* so that they, with their children, may live forever before Him, occurs again and again in God's Word.

What was true for God's people in Bible times is true in an even richer sense for us now. We, too, receive our children as gifts from God, to train them as covenant children and prepare them for their place in God's kingdom. In distinction from Old Testament Israel, we have a broader perspective. We see God's plan of salvation being realized in us and in our children. Because God fulfilled the prophecy of Isaiah, "For unto us a child is born, unto us a son is given," and sent the Great Gift of His Son, we and our children no longer have to look forward in hope for the birth of God's Son. We have that salvation in His cross.

Now we and our children look forward to the final realization of God's promise: the full measure of the growth of the body of Christ until the end of time, when we shall enjoy God's fellowship in the church triumphant in glory forever. And, both of us thought, we could view with more understanding this text: "Notwithstanding she shall be saved in childbearing, if they continue in faith and charity and holiness with sobriety."

This continuing "in faith and charity and holiness with sobriety," applied to our children, is the way in which God works with His people. For our God always uses means. God's people "continue" these graces of faith and charity and holiness in their children by *teaching* them to their covenant seed. Is it not easy, then, for us to understand the tremendously important truth that covenant instruction is the God-ordained *means* of perpetuating the covenant? From the beginning of time God has used the means of covenant parents who have diligently taught the covenant seed, for His purpose of bringing many sons unto glory. What a precious privilege for us!

Does that mean, then, that non-parents have no blessings, my neighbor wanted to know. Surely they personally do not enjoy the blessings of parenthood. But, taken in the broader sense, in whatever contact they have with God's people and His covenant children, they also surely share, in the place in life which God has provided for them, in the covenant blessings with all of God's people.

My neighbor went home, asking, "Will knowing *who* our child is make us more humble, more diligent, more thankful?"

NOTES

1. W. B. Pillsbury, *The Essentials of Psychology* (New York: Macmillan, 1917).
2. M. W. Curti, *Child Psychology* (New York: Longmans, Green and Co., 1940).
3. W. James, *Talks to Teachers on Psychology* (New York: Henry Holt, 1910).
4. C. Jaarsma, *Human Development, Learning, and Teaching* (Grand Rapids: Wm. B. Eerdmans, 1961), pp. 50, 51.
5. This was also the view of Herman Hoeksema in Unpublished Catechetics Notes, p. 8.

2
WHAT IS THE CHILD

Keep thy heart with all diligence, for out of it are the issues of life.
—Proverbs 4:23

T̲HE NEXT MORNING I HEARD A KNOCK AT THE BACK DOOR. There stood my neighbor again, with an armful of books which he dumped unceremoniously on the kitchen table as I invited him in.

"We didn't finish," he began abruptly.

He saw me raise my eyebrows.

"Finish talking about Kathy," he explained. "I think we learned a lot yesterday about *who* she is. But there are so many questions left. We don't know *what* she is, how she is all put together. . . . You know," he broke off, "what 'makes her tick.'

"So last night I went back to the library and took out some of those psychology books we looked at yesterday. Read them till after midnight.

"I wanted to know some more, not just about Kathy, but about children in general, and covenant children in particular: what makes them act the way they do, how they develop habits, what makes them learn, how they set their goals in life. . . ."

His series of questionings trailed off as he busily leafed through one of the books. "Here! Read what James says the life of the child is."

I read:

Man . . . has been evolved from infra-human ancestors, in whom pure reason hardly existed, if at all, and whose mind, so far as it can have had any function, would appear to have been an organ for adapting their movements to the impressions received from the environment. Consciousness would thus seem in the first instance to be nothing but a sort of super-added biological perfection.[1]

Farther on I read: "All our life, so far as it has definite form, is but a mass of habits—practical, emotional, intellectual—systematically organized for our weal or woe, and bearing us irresistibly toward our destiny, whatever the latter may be."[2]

My neighbor, explaining that he had read these pages last night, told me that, according to James, the child comes into the world a *tabula rasa,* a blank sheet, and over this sheet stream fields of consciousness, sensations, images, thoughts, memories. This stream of consciousness, flowing relentlessly over the child, must be channeled, guided by a parent or teacher so that everything in this stream may be turned into *practical* good for the child. The parent and teacher do this by properly molding his behavior so that the child may attain his ideals in life.

"Now, what do you think of that?" he asked, disdainfully. But, without giving me time to answer, he pointed to a paragraph in another book. "Read this," he ordered.

The child does not come trailing clouds of glory, with ideas of truth and beauty gained in his happy play by the shores of that immortal sea which brought him hither, although that poetic statement of a not uncommon belief makes a strong appeal to anyone who has watched a wide-eyed 'thoughtful' baby grow up through the delightful first months into the inevitably more or less naughty years of early childhood. Neither does he come into the world burdened by original sin. It has become a truism to say that the child is neither good nor bad, neither moral nor immoral. He is simply non-moral.³

"Don't you see?" my neighbor was saying. "If a child is not good nor bad, if he is simply non-moral, then it must be that there are no fixed moral standards to which he must conform, no laws of ethics which he must obey. We believe that God's law is the moral standard, and in relation to it we are either disobediently immoral, or obediently moral. Never can we be neutral—you know, "non-moral"—nor are we ever bound by a so-called moral code, made by man.

But if his parents believe that there is no God Who insists on obedience to His moral law, how do they explain some of the standards that exist? Here is what the author thinks:

The line between social and ethical conduct is hard to draw. In general we may say that ethical conduct is socially approved conduct. It is the sort of conduct which in a given social group is called right. Unethical conduct would be the converse of this. In a broader sense ethical conduct or behavior would include any activities to which judgments of right or wrong would customarily be attached.⁴

If children are non-moral creatures, my neighbor and I told one another, if they are subject merely to standards that are socially approved by their given society, then children are no more than behaving organisms, greatly influenced and conditioned by their environment. This is the child which these two psychologists portray: a physical, functioning human being, without soul and spirit, without God, without Christ, and without salvation.

My neighbor was rubbing his head again. "I don't know why I even took these books out of the library. What a hopeless, ungodly philosophy these men have," he bemoaned, "and to think they are leaders in the field of child psychology; and that amounts to their being leaders in the future of the human race."

"We're more interested in the future of the church on earth," I reminded him, walking to my bookshelf. I had suddenly remembered a book which might help my neighbor.

Sitting down with him again at the table, I opened the book.

Principles of Personality Building for Christian Parents was the title. "This may help us," I said. "It was written by an evangelical author, and we won't find the crass biological, evolutionistic approach of the ungodly in it."

The room was quiet as we read for a while. The author *did* make an attempt to base his views of the Christian child in the Christian family on Scripture. But then we read: "On the whole, children with warped and twisted personalities are not born thus. The circumstances under which the child grows up have most to do with the determination of his personality."[5] Again, "Recent studies indicate that personality is largely the product of the interaction between parents and child."[6] And, "The parent, like the gardener, works with God, serving as an agent through whom God may accomplish what He wills to do."[7]

Abruptly, we both looked up. Neither of us could accept these statements. True, they were not so blatantly humanistic and ungodly as the other quotations we had read. We *knew* a Christian cannot view man as a biological creature who can improve his behavior and his morals by improving his environment. Yet we did not, at first, expect these statements from an evangelical author. But as we sat there at the table, we discussed how this worldly philosophy that man is not completely bad crept into the church. It came through the well-known doctrine of Pelagianism, that insidious theory that teaches that a child may choose for the right, may choose for his own destiny, and in effect choose what he is and will be. If that error of Pelagianism were true, it would follow, of course, that, since the child is free to choose, he makes the best choices under the best conditions, in the most favorable environment. And the next logical step is to say that the child's personality is molded to a large degree by his environment: and we are able to help God (to be His agents) to accomplish His purpose—God's work, surely—but ours, too, by providing the proper circumstances in which to bring up the child.

We talked about still another view of the child. We tried to look at him through the theory of common grace, the teaching which allows man's (or the child's) sin to be restrained so that man is not as bad as he might be, so that he may do good without being reborn by the Spirit; he can, say the proponents of common grace, improve the lot of man by the civic good which he can do. He is not, even in his natural sphere, completely bad.

"No," my neighbor said, thoughtfully, "we are on the same wrong track we were on yesterday. None of these books and none of these theories tell the Christian *what* the child really is. These are the same theories that my wife reads in her magazines. You know, those articles on child care that the ladies read first. And, to tell you the truth, I never saw till this minute just why those articles were so bad."

"Why? What kind of articles?" I asked, puzzled that suddenly we were discussing magazine articles.

"Oh, you know the kind. *Educate* your child. Train his mind and then he will be a success. Or, *listen* to your child. His ideas and desires are just as important as yours are. And don't *repress* him. If he has his heart set on a ten-speed bike, try to scrape the money together to get him one. This bike may be fulfilling one of his basic needs. Oh, yes, and don't *frustrate* him. Let him do his own thing. He may grow away from you and have emotional problems later in life, and *you* will be to blame. Enough examples?" he laughed.

"Enough."

"But don't you see," he went on seriously, "why worldly psychologists talk as they do. They proceed from the theory that our child's basic wants, needs, and desires are *good*. It follows, then, that all we have to do is heed and cultivate these basically good intents, and give our child the culture and education necessary to develop his inner desires and he will turn out to be the emotionally well-adjusted adult."

"Let's start over," he suggested, "and see *what* the child is from a Reformed, Scriptural perspective."

We took out the Bible and read Genesis 1:27: "So God created man in his own image, in the image of God created He him." Man (the first man, Adam) was created a perfect creature of God, with powers and gifts which we could scarcely imagine to be possible. For he had true knowledge of God, true righteousness, and holiness.

But Adam fell. He lost his perfect powers and gifts, for he

lost God's image. Because Adam was our head and the father of the human race, we fell in him. Adam turned his back to God and became a servant of the devil. Sin became his master. And as a result, all of us and our children are born totally depraved and by nature ugly workers of iniquity. Scripture tells us what we and our children are: "Behold, I was shapen in iniquity; and in sin did my mother conceive me," Psalm 51:5. From Christ's mouth we hear that, "Ye are of your father the devil, and the lusts of your father ye will do," John 8:44. And, "All we like sheep have gone astray; we have turned everyone to his own way," Isaiah 53:6.

My neighbor was nodding his agreement heartily, yet sadly. "Scripture has nothing to say about how good or beautiful our children are when they are born, nor even how non-moral. We're bad, all bad."

"And our sin and our children's sin isn't only in the deed, but in our whole corrupt natures. We are so corrupt that we are dead to anything holy and good," I added. "I have a paper here somewhere that explains it. Here, read this":

This corruption is an hereditary disease, to be traced back through birth and generation to the first sin of Adam as its original source. In paradise, not merely the human nature of Adam but the nature of the whole race was corrupted. This corruption of the entire race through the sin of Adam must be explained from the fact that God did not make mankind a multitude of individuals, but an organism, the father and root of which was the first man, Adam. And this corruption of the organism of the human race must in turn be traced, as far as its judicial ground is concerned, to the fact that God also created the race a legal corporation, with Adam as its legal, representative-head, so that the whole race is guilty with a communal guilt in the one man Adam. . . . An imputed guilt, therefore, and an inherited depravity and corruption as its consequence, is the heritage of every child of Adam that is ever born, Christ, the Son of God, excepted.[8]

We knew that when we accept Scripture's teaching about our words and deeds, we part company with worldly philosophy.

For then it is no more a question of point of view. It is a question of unbelief or faith. Unbelief begins with a *tabula rasa* or an inherently good man, and faith begins with one who is totally depraved. Unbelief says sin is the result of imitating a bad example, or the influence of an evil environment, and faith says it is the result of God's, "Ye shall surely die."

"But faith says more about the child," my neighbor added. "God does not leave us and our children with that 'Ye shall surely die.' "

So we studied some more and learned that though fallen man has lost God's image, he has not lost his *reason*. He is a personal being, still possessing a rational, moral nature, and capable of standing in a personal, conscious relationship to his God. His nature, therefore, is adapted to bear the image of God. He cannot, of course, become the image-bearer of God of or by himself. This is where the last part of the text from Isaiah 53:6 comes in: "And the Lord hath laid on him [Christ] the iniquity of us all." Only through the cross, where all our guilt and corruption were taken away, and where we were turned around from being servants of the devil to servants of the Most High, is this image of God restored in man. The cross of Christ is the objective basis for our restoration; and the Holy Spirit as the Spirit of Christ works in our hearts and applies this restoration. We call it the work of regeneration. Ephesians 4:23, 24 describes this restoration: "And be renewed in the spirit of your mind; and that ye put on the new man, which after God is created in righteousness and true holiness."

"That is what those unbelieving authors don't understand," I broke in at this point. "They *can't* understand it, either. Not because they are so ignorant. But because they do not have God's gift of faith."

"Understand what?"

"That the child, though hopelessly dead in sin, is at the same time a new and holy creature in Christ. On the one hand, he sins continually and is responsible before God for these sins; and, on the other hand, he struggles daily to become the perfect man of God, thoroughly furnished to all good works."

"I'm glad, though, that the Lord left us to be rational, thinking creatures," my neighbor said. "Otherwise I couldn't even learn about what we and our children are."

"The paper we were just reading treats the subject of these remnants of the light man originally had. Shall we look at it again?" I asked.

My neighbor began to read aloud:

We must remember that even apart from the spiritual, ethical operation of sin in man's nature, the operation of death extends to that very nature itself. The effect of the wrath of God is felt in the very physio-psychical nature of man. The result is that man has only remnants of natural light.[9]

"Listen to this, too:"

And that means that the fall not only caused him to become depraved in a spiritual, ethical sense, something that dare never be forgotten in the education of a child, but he is also deprived of all his excellent gifts even from a natural point of view and has only a few remains thereof.[10]

"It says here that these remnants, though very small in comparison to those with which Adam was blessed, are the capital which man possesses and with which he works and with which he sins. Do you want me to read you a list of those remnants we have?"

I nodded.

He read:

1. Some knowledge of God . . . which simply means that the natural man knows that God is and that He is to be served and glorified. 2. Some knowledge of things natural, which again is never to be confused with true knowledge, the knowledge of God. 3. Ability to discern the difference between good and evil. 4. A regard for virtue and external orderly deportment, according to which he attempts to walk outwardly as much as possible in the way of the law of God.[11]

"There's Kathy," he added, almost in the same breath.

Laughing and shrieking, she was chasing a squirrel through the backyard. We shoved our books aside and went to the window to watch her happy face.

"I'm seeing her better already," my neighbor mused, "and if I were her parent, I don't know if I would be very happy with what I see. For, knowing *what* Kathy is does not make her education and upbringing any easier. At best it is often a disappointing and laborious process. Do you know why? Because as covenant parents, her parents see her as totally depraved, as having only small remnants of natural light, and at the same time as being redeemed and a new creature, by grace, in Christ. But by nature, she does not even have a receptivity for spiritual instruction, and her parents are unable to instill it. And then just think of these papers we read. All of our children will have to struggle to learn; some will have a few more gifts than others. Because she retains only remnants of natural light, Kathy might be a slow learner, a dull pupil who needs her parents' and teachers' constant, diligent, and consecrated labor all her lifetime of learning. Her parents are totally depraved, too, which makes it harder for them to exercise patience and sympathy, prayer and love, as they train Kathy."

He sighed and walked to the door; and while I prepared coffee, my neighbor joined Kathy in chasing the squirrel.

* * *

"No, I'm not going home," he said to my unspoken question after we had had our cup of coffee in the backyard. Kathy was still sitting on his shoulder eating the cookie she had begged from him. "You just said she had quite a personality. And I was reading in those books all about what personality is. Why don't you bring those books out here? It's such nice weather."

"I thought we weren't going to. . . ," I protested.

"Get them anyway," he laughed. "Won't hurt to see what they say."

So I brought them out while my neighbor made himself comfortable in a lawn chair.

"Here is a definition," he said: " 'Personality is that unique group of characteristics which describes the individual in relation to other people.'[12] That means how Kathy acts toward you and me, I think. In this book I found some more. How about, 'Personality is a product of growth. It is not an unchangeable something implanted in the child at birth. It does not have preformed or unvarying characteristics.'[13] Or, 'Personality is not a thing; it is a product of interaction between a living organism and the environment in which that organism lives.'[14] Or, 'Any individual becomes what he is in personality through the process of growth and learning.'[15] Should we agree with any of that?"

"Are you an environmentalist?" I asked, not unkindly. "Do you believe that a carefully controlled environment will produce a better personality, and the better the personality, the better the child? Isn't that the theory of evolution applied to the growing child? It seems to me to be Pelagianism in practice. We can do our part to make the environment favorable so as to change a crude child into a gracious personality."

"No, but . . . but . . . , " he stammered. "Look at Kathy. Surely the time and place of her life, the home and personalities with which she is surrounded affect her somehow. If her personality is not made by her environment, is she born with it? . . . Am I asking the wrong questions?"

In spite of myself, I smiled.

"Oh, I know. We have to start all over again," he said.

I started. I told him that we should define the child's person and his nature before we answered all his questions. And I told him that, based on Scripture, I thought we could define a person as "an individual in a rational, moral nature." It is the *person* who is self-conscious, who can say "I." The child, even when a baby, is a person even though we must wait for him to say "I." And surely we know that the child is an individual, different from other children and from any other individual.

However, the child is more than the person, the "I." He has a body, soul, and spirit. And these are properties, not of the self-conscious "I," but rather are aspects of the *nature*. Now we can broaden the definition of the child as a person to "an individual in a rational, moral nature, *body, soul,* and *spirit.*"

This definition is longer only because it has explained the term *nature*.

"Whew!" my neighbor sighed as he rubbed his forehead. "It's too hard to understand when we just look at definitions," I sympathized. "Let's look at us and at Kathy.

"We'll look at you first," I began. "Your person and nature belong together; in fact, your whole nature is perfectly adapted to your person. You 'fit.' That's the way God made you. A man's nature and bodily characteristics fit with his person, and a woman's with hers. But no person in this world could live in another's body or with another's nature. Just imagine your timid nature united with Kathy's unique person. What a misfit! What a monstrosity!"

He laughed. But almost immediately I saw his lips silently repeating the definition: "an individual in a rational, moral nature."

"Oh, I see," he said slowly. "An *individual!* My *person* gives individuality to my whole nature, body and soul. . . . My appearance, too, do you think?"

I nodded, but before I could open my mouth to speak, he was eagerly going on. "That's why I'm different from anyone else, even down to my fingerprints. My person, my individuality, shows up even at the tips of my fingers. No one has a set of fingertips like *I* do. And we all have noses. But mine is—"

"Longer than most," I prompted. "And, speaking of noses, when someone hits you on the nose, you don't say only, 'He hit my nose.' You say, 'He hit *me.*' You and the characteristics of your physique and of your nature are inseparable. It's easier now, isn't it, to see the connection between the 'me' (the person) and the body, soul, and spirit which house the person.

"And think of children born with abnormalities," I went on. "Is it not striking that mental defects such as mongoloidism are noticeable in the bodily features almost from birth? The 'I' of a mongoloid child lives in a mongoloid's body and has a mongoloid's nature. And I think the converse is true. A body defect, such as a stroke later in life, greatly affects the *person,* the 'I' of the afflicted one."

My neighbor nodded, but I could see that he was not listening intently any more. He was watching Kathy as she daintily brushed the cookie crumbs from her dress. Repeating the definition to himself once more, and scrutinizing Kathy as if he were labelling her, he nodded for me to go on. "The person has personality?" he wondered.

I explained that this individual in a rational, moral nature is placed by the Lord in an environment which He has prepared for him. Following from that, the definition of personality would be "the characteristics of the individual person revealed and expressed through his nature in the particular environment which the Lord creates for him."

"Too hard to understand," my neighbor protested.

"How about this?" I persisted. "The elements of personality are the *person,* which the Lord created, the *nature,* which the Lord provided to house the person, and the *surroundings* which the Lord in His providence prepared."

"Scriptural proof?" he asked curtly.

"Yes. Isaiah 43:21: 'This people have I formed for myself.' *God* formed us, not *environment* formed us. Also Psalm 139:15 and 16: 'My substance was not hid from thee, when I was made in secret, and curiously wrought in the lowest part of the earth. Thine eyes did see my substance, yet being unperfect; and in thy book all my members were written, which in continuance were fashioned, when as yet there was none of them.' We would be foolish to say that our surroundings do not affect us, for it is reality to admit that they do. Scripture says that events refine us. 'For thou, O God, hast proved us: thou hast tried us, as silver is tried . . . thou laidst affliction on our loins. Thou hast caused men to ride over our heads; we went through fire and through water: but thou broughtest us out into a wealthy place,' Psalm 66:10-12."

But I knew that my neighbor wanted some examples from Scripture, examples of people and personalities. We agreed, before we opened the Bible, that our environment affects us. What we wanted to know was whether it changes our personalities. We found David to be a poetic personality. As a shepherd he could quietly express himself on the hills of Judea. When he fled from Saul, and even in the land of the Philistines, he still expressed himself in psalmody. At perhaps the lowest point of his life, after he had sinned with Bathsheba, his poetic personality did not change, and Psalm 51 was born.

Peter had an impetuous personality. He wanted to build three tabernacles on the Mount of Transfiguration, he wanted to follow Christ though all others would forsake Him and to defend Christ to the death in the garden. Then came his impetuous denial. After he had fallen and was restored, his personality was still impetuous. He was the first to speak at Pentecost.

The terms *personality* and *character* are closely related, and oftentimes are used interchangeably. Our personalities have a spiritual side; our characters reside in a nature that is at the same time both depraved and sanctified. Neither David's nor Peter's personalities (characters) changed, although both personalities were purged and sanctified, and after their falls into gross sin, were redirected, as chastened personalities, to the service of God.

For a moment I thought my neighbor had dozed off in the comfortable lawn chair. But he hadn't, for he opened his eyes and asked an unexpected question.

"Do you think Kathy has a determined, resolute character?"

"You know her better than I do."

"Well, I think she has. That's not good, is it?"

"Why not?"

"You see," he explained, with a hint of embarrassment, "we live right next door, and can't avoid hearing her family talk sometimes. Just yesterday Kathy did not want to wear her rubbers after all that rain we had. And you know how her mother is—you might say, domineering. Kathy stamped her little foot and said she was going out without them. The last thing I heard was her mother shouting, 'No rubbers, no outside play! The last thing you'll do while I'm boss is disobey me, young lady.' And she snatched her out of the doorway while Kathy was still shouting, 'I am! I am!' Now, that's not good, is it?"

"Kathy wasn't very good right then, and maybe her mother wasn't either," I began. "But. . . . "

"Don't tell me," he interrupted. "All of a sudden I know the answer to my own question. Kathy has a determined character or personality. Her mother has a character with qualities of leadership. They were born with them. They'll always have them. Taken strictly by themselves, the personality qualities of leadership and wilfulness are good, if properly directed. The problem lies in what they *do* with their traits. Kathy's resoluteness became stubborn disobedience. Her mother's leadership at least bordered on bossiness. Both were using their personalities sinfully, each trying to attain a selfish goal."

"And her mother may not say, 'I can't help it. She's just a wilful kid.' Nor will she say about herself, 'I can't help it. We clash. I'm bossy.' "

"I'm bossy!" came a small echo from behind the lawn chair.

"No, you're not. You're determined, Kathy," he said, as he swooped her up. "But you have covenant parents and they will teach you to use your determined character to God's glory."

"Me?" she asked, not understanding.

* * *

"While I take Kathy along to the library to bring back these books," my neighbor was saying, "you think about her nature."

"What about her nature?" I asked.

"Isn't that what we have left to talk about? We know about her person and personality. But you said her person exists in a rational, moral nature, body, soul, and spirit. And I never was so able to understand the soul and spirit part."

"Isn't it striking," I said to my neighbor after he came back, "that the part of the child that we see and care for, the body, is not mentioned in the creation story? Genesis 2:7b says, '. . . and man became a living soul,' not '. . . and man became a living body.' "

We had already learned that these two entities, body and soul, are inseparably intertwined and interwoven into the fabric of his being. We cannot determine where one stops and the other starts. We do not have to. But we can say something about each.

The soul is the faculty which makes us intelligent and willing creatures, for the two powers of the soul are the *intellect* and the *will*. Our soul also has two sides, the physical, closely tied to our body, so closely that no one knows where the one stops and the other starts. There is also the intangible, psychical side, which we call our mind and our will. Our ability to think (psychical side) presupposes the necessity of our brain (physical side). But no one can tell the exact interrelation. Destroy the brain, and the thinking and willing is gone, too.

"I'm not sure I understand," my neighbor muttered, "but while we let the subject rest a little while, shall we discuss something easier? I think you forgot one of the powers of the soul. You mentioned two, the intellect and the will. What about the emotions?"

"Now I know you have been reading too many of those books," I chided. "I have read some of the definitions of emotions myself, such as 'the complex of bodily sensations which accompany the internal responses,'[16] 'a stirred-up state that moves the organism to action of some kind,'[17] or as 'feeling-tone.'"[18]

"I read them, too," my neighbor commented. "And I thought they were rather hazy. The people who wrote those definitions place the emotions as the agent which translates the cold outside world into terms of personal, aesthetic, sensuous feeling."

"Through the influence of Rousseau and the French Revolution," I explained, "almost every psychologist has placed the emotions next to the intellect and will as another faculty of the soul. And they place the faculties of the soul in this order of importance: intellect, emotions, will. They believe in a *tri*chotomy of soul-faculties. I believe it is Scriptural to speak of a *di*chotomy of soul-powers, and leave out the emotions."

I knew what my neighbor would say. He would say that he was sure that we and the child have feelings, that we react to all the stimuli in our lives, that we love, hate, fear, or become angry. We agreed that no one could deny that we have feelings, emotions, moods. But the danger of believing with Rousseau that emotion is a faculty which stands by itself is that, as a result, the emotions will not be governed by the intellect or will. If emotions are a separate faculty of the soul, part of the child's behavior will be based on arbitrary feelings, raw emotions, undisciplined temperament, which arise, it is supposed, from the urges or repressions of its inner humanity. It is supposed to follow logically that the child cannot help these feelings and therefore is not responsible for them. And if he is not responsible for them, we have no right to chasten the child for his wild outbursts of undisciplined temperament.

"But we believe that we and our children are responsible to God for everything we do, so Rousseau's trichotomy cannot be accepted by covenant parents," my neighbor said. "That leaves us with the two soul-powers, intellect and will, again. Where do our feelings come in?"

"Let us try to put our feelings into the category where they belong," I said, "and view feeling as the pleasurable or displeasurable, agreeable or disagreeable reaction of the will upon the sensations presented to it by the intellect."[19]

But my neighbor did not understand. We decided that an illustration might help, and we talked about Kathy when she was very small, under a year old. . . . It is feeding time. She is hungry, and has all the sensations of hunger: a hollow stomach, a dry mouth and throat, and a general feeling of discomfort. Her intellect interprets these sensations as a need of nourishment. Now the will of the child begins to act on these sensations presented to her by way of her intellect. She longs for food. She wills to have it. She wants our attention, so her whimpering becomes a howl. So far she had only displeasurable feelings and reactions. When she hears the bottle being prepared, she reacts to this perception with hope and joy; and after she has had her nourishment, she wills to be content. She may not will this entirely consciously, but physically satiated, she wills it. . . . This was an oversimplification of the complexities of Kathy's nature, we knew. None of these actions and perceptions exists alone, but all are interrelated and interdependent. "There never is a pure sensation or perception, nor a pure feeling or emotion. All the powers and faculties of the soul, in fact, of the body, act simultaneously and in unison."[20]

We discussed the feelings and emotions of the child as she grows older, too. When my neighbor carries Kathy on his back up and down the backyard, she wills to act favorably and she wills to be happy. If her mother calls her for lunch in the middle

What Is the Child / 49

of a good time, she wills to be angry and she may even will to have a temper tantrum. We began to understand how our emotions and those of our children take on a spiritual dimension, for their wills are involved. In whatever our children do, they stand with their wills in an ethical relationship to God, whether they will sin or will the good.

Both of us understood that, in our thinking and willing we are always responsible before God. But how would we teach our children that our feelings don't "just come," but are controlled by our thinking and willing, and that our children are responsible for their emotions? It was then that I remembered a story which a friend had told me, and I told the story to my neighbor. It went something like this.

My friend's school-age boy had come home again in a silent mood. It seemed to be getting a habit with him. He was not angry or sullen, just depressed.

"What happened?" his parents asked him.

"Nothing. I just don't feel very peppy," he said.

When his friend called for him, he said, "No, I don't feel like playing ball." And at the dinner table he didn't laugh at the jokes, much less tell his own.

His parents talked with him after dinner, and he assured them nothing had happened at school. He even got a "B" in that history test. As parents, they had probably almost decided to drop the matter of this boy's unhappy moods. They could not find any reason for his feeling the way he did.

But this did not mean that there *was* no reason. As he went silently up to bed, unasked, too early, he stubbed his toe on the bottom step. They had lived in this house two months already, and he should know by now that the bottom step is a bit higher than the other steps. They heard him mutter, "Crummy step. Crummy house. No-good neighborhood. Dumb kids." Then his parents knew. Then they understood. After moving into this house, he had had new sensations, many new ones, crowding into his mind. (That was his intellect.) He reacted to these sensations with dislike. (Now his will entered in.) He willed to dislike all the aspects of his new surroundings and showed it by being "moody."

"I hope his parents didn't say, 'Poor boy! He can't help it.

He just doesn't like it here,' " my neighbor blurted out. "I hope they told him that if they believed that they moved into this home for the good of the family, then it was his calling to be happy here. I hope they told him that it is always God Who directs our lives and that we have to change *our* wills to fit His. If that boy was one of God's own children, I know what he did, too. He prayed that his will would be God's will; and then his unhappiness would change to contentment."

We found that the Scriptures support the idea that the mind and will guide and govern the feelings. We read the book of Proverbs. The whole tenor of this book of practical criteria for our lives is based on "understanding and will." "He that handleth a matter wisely shall find good; and whoso trusteth in the Lord, *happy* is he," Proverbs 16:20. *"Happy* is the man that findeth wisdom, and the man that getteth understanding," Proverbs 3:13. "He that is slow to anger is better than the mighty; and he that ruleth his spirit than he that taketh a city," Proverbs 16:32.

Still, all our problems in understanding how our minds and wills govern our emotions did not disappear. We thought of the emotion of fear. Does our will enter this emotion? Sometimes it does, as when we *will* to do something (swim across a lake without a life jacket) and *know* that it could be disastrous (we could tire or cramp and drown). Whether we swim it or not, we have fear. But fear need not always be a conscious act of our will. It may be a spontaneous, involuntary reaction, such as running, or pulling our hand away from a hot stove. For our willing is not always conscious. God's is.

"That's not so easy to understand," my neighbor was objecting again. "I can believe that emotions are not a third faculty of the soul, equal to and separate from the intellect and the will. If the emotions were based only on arbitrary feelings and undisciplined urges, for which we are not responsible, what problems we would have in the training of our children! They wouldn't be responsible before God, either. Besides, the Bible is on our side. I can see from the passages we read that the intellect and the will enter into our emotional reactions. What I don't understand is exactly how.

"But, . . " and he paused awhile, "our feelings are always

with us . . . some kinds of feelings. Come to think of it," and he was rubbing his head again, "I really never stop to think whether my intellect is presenting sensations for me to react to, or that I *will* to react in a certain way. And I'm *sure* that Kathy doesn't."

I opened my mouth to agree, but he continued talking. "Emotions are powerful things. They're real, you know. And they're real to our covenant children. Don't you think the Bible talks a lot about our feelings?"

"Ours, too, but God's first. The Bible reveals the powerful emotions of our almighty God," I reminded him. "Just to mention a few, how about His *anger* ('Therefore the Lord was very angry with Israel,' II Kings 17:18), *love* ('Yea, I have loved thee with an everlasting love,' Jeremiah 31:3), *pity* ('Like as a father pitieth his children, so the Lord pitieth them that fear him,' Psalm 103:13), *mercy* ('For as the heaven is high above the earth, so great is His mercy toward them that fear Him,' Psalm 103:11), *grief* ('He is despised and rejected of men; a man of sorrows and acquainted with grief,' Isaiah 53:3)."

"And we, as God's creatures, reflect in a creaturely way, these emotions," my neighbor added. "Think of David, of Job, of Paul. God's people experience the whole range of emotions, from ecstatic happiness to abject grief."

"Think of Kathy."

"I *am* thinking of her. She's the kind of child who lets you know about her feelings. She's happy, she's sad, she's angry," he was half muttering to himself, "and I can't quite understand the depths of it all yet, but one thing I know: she's responsible for her emotions. She can serve God with them, and she can sin with them. I can't find the answers to all my questions about how her mind and will, consciously or unconsciously, govern her emotions, but this discussion has helped me to see how closely intertwined her whole being is—her body, intellect, will, feelings. . . . It helps one to know how to handle her with a bit more understanding. And maybe I'll never completely understand. . . . "

"What are you saying?" I asked, straining to hear.

"I need a break," my neighbor answered. "I'm going to take a walk and think it over. And I'll try to find Kathy. Perhaps if I study her in the light of what we've been discussing, I'll understand it even better."

An hour later I found them in her sandbox. Kathy was sifting sand and chattering to her silent neighbor, who was absorbed in watching her.

"More talk?" Kathy asked as I approached.

"A little," I answered. Then I turned to my neighbor, "I've been thinking of that text in Deuteronomy 6:15, ' . . . love the Lord thy God with all thy soul.' That leads us to the spiritual aspect of our soul, which we have not talked about, and which is sometimes called our 'spirit' in Scripture. Sometimes Scripture treats man's whole being as his soul. 'My soul shall make her boast in the Lord,' Psalm 34:2; or 'The soul that sinneth, it shall die,' Ezekiel 18:4b. However, throughout Scripture we read of one area that stands at the core of our spiritual life, in relation to God first, and also in relation to our fellow man. That is our *heart*."

Our talk concentrated on the heart of the covenant child, in whom we were so interested. His heart is his physical center, the pulse beat of his life. The heart, from the spiritual viewpoint, is also the center of his being and gives direction to the life of the soul. It is the child's *heart* that is reborn, whose pulse beat throbs with the new lifeblood of regeneration. The Bible teaches that just as out of the unregenerate heart "proceed evil thoughts, murders, adulteries, fornications, theft, false witness, blasphemies," Matthew 15:9, so out of the renewed heart of children of the covenant comes the confession, "With my whole heart have I sought thee," Psalm 119:10. Only because the child has a renewed heart which seeks after God is there hope for parents in the otherwise hopeless task of training him. For the grace of God has entered his heart and made pliable what was by nature hard. With his reborn heart the covenant child will turn to his parents, listen to them, and obey them, because he is "doing the will of God from the heart," Ephesians 6:6.

"We've had a hard day," my neighbor said abruptly, "but I'm glad we had our talk."

"Finished?" Kathy eagerly took the cue, as she dumped a pail of sand over his foot.

"Shall we wind it up? You know: come to some conclusions, and pull all the ends of our talk together."

"Then let's do it simply," I said. "Scripture often presents the most profound truths so clearly. We've taken the covenant child apart and analyzed each part. Now let's look at all these parts as wonderfully woven into one complete whole. Scripture, after all, describes the whole man in simple, brief terms. Genesis 2:7 says, 'And the Lord God formed man of the dust of the ground, and breathed into his nostrils the breath of life; and man became a living soul.' That's what we are, and what Kathy is: the dust of the ground, and an in-breathed living soul, a marvelous creation."

"And did the thought ever come to you," my neighbor added, "that when Jesus was on earth and commanded us to love the Lord with all our hearts, and with all our souls, and with all our minds, and with all our strength, that He was joining all of our faculties together—body, soul, mind, and heart—and telling us that all these separate powers must unite so that the whole man of God will love his Lord? I think that is the way the Bible teaches us to look at our children, too," he said, "as a wonderfully fashioned whole, from the hand of our all-wise Father."

He was mumbling again. "Body, soul, spirit, person and nature, intellect and will, and . . . what am I forgetting?" he asked, raising his voice.

"Heart."

"Heart," he repeated, looking straight at Kathy's chest. "Heart, the center of her being. Well, I don't know if I will ever fully comprehend God's wonderful creation, the covenant child, in all its fulness and richness, but I have a beginning. And now I understand this text better, too: 'Keep thy heart with all diligence, for out of it are the issues of life.' "

* * *

In the next chapters we will leave my neighbor and Kathy for a time, and apply these principles with which they have helped us to our practical lives as parents.

NOTES

1. James, op. cit., pp. 23, 24.
2. Ibid., p. 64.
3. Curti, op. cit., p. 400.
4. Ibid., p. 387.
5. C. B. Eavey, *Principles of Personality Building for Christian Parents* (Grand Rapids, Mich.: Zondervan Publ. House, 1952), p. 14.
6. Ibid., p. 15.
7. Ibid., p. 18.
8. H. C. Hoeksema, Unpublished paper, *The Effects of Sin on the Person.*
9. Ibid., p. 7.
10. Unpublished Catechetics notes, p. 8.
11. Ibid., pp. 7, 8.
12. Jaarsma, op. cit., p. 24.
13. Eavey, op. cit., p. 11.
14. Ibid., p. 13.
15. Ibid., p. 291.
16. Curti, op. cit., p. 104.
17. Eavey, op. cit., p. 189.
18. Jaarsma, op. cit., p. 111.
19. H. Hoeksema, op. cit., p. 15.
20. H. Hoeksema, op. cit., p. 16.

3
PREPARATION FOR THE CHILD

Lo, children are an heritage of the Lord: and the fruit of the womb is his reward.
—Psalm 127:3

IF YOU ARE AN OLDER PERSON, GO BACK WITH ME IN TIME to your early years of married life. If you are still in your teens, travel ahead with me to the day that, God willing, will come for you—your wedding day. If you are making plans for marriage, or are one of those young married couples with small children, stay with me. You are living in a happy time of life, perhaps the happiest!

Taking as our premise that we all have been brought up in covenant homes by believing parents, we know intellectually, but overwhelmingly more so from experience, *why* and *what* a covenant child is, because we remember our own unique youth. For, as we look back upon our tender years, were they not distinctly happy? Did not the joy of the assurance of our safe-keeping in the arms of our Redeemer run as a strong thread through those years? Were not our very difficulties often our great comforts: our difficulties of saying *no* to the enticements of our companions, and our comforts that came with the peace of keeping God's law in sanctification? Even through the problems of our childhood, our disobedience and punishments, our quarrels and bitternesses, or our dread of being called "different," we could feel, could we not, the basic undercurrent that buoyed all our lives, the peace and contentment that comes with the growth in grace of God's covenant children.

Now we stand at the beginning of our maturity, the climax of our lives. Although we will never stop learning or growing in grace, our formal training is ended. We want to plan for our future, to make a home of our own, to have a family, to continue the organic line of God's covenant in this world.

Because this discussion centers on the child, we will pass over the area of dating, the problems and joys of courtship, the choice of our mate, our wedding, and, finally, the relationship of husband and wife. Presupposing again that we are covenant children who have grown up to be consecrated young people, we will marry in the Lord and consecrate our lives together in His service. We will pray that we may establish a home together that will be a fitting place to nurture the covenant seed.

Often before marriage, and certainly soon after, we begin to talk about the family we want. Flippantly, if we are the wife, we may say, "I want to work a year at least before we start a family." Or together we may say, "We love children. But they mustn't be too close. For them and ourselves it is better to have a breathing spell of a few years between each." Possibly our thoughts run this way: "We're going to start a family immediately. We'll have at least six, maybe eight kids. We believe in 'the more, the merrier!'"

This talk, fellow believing Christians, is borrowed from the world, and the philosophy behind it comes straight from hell. When we as Christians think these thoughts and mouth these words, we take the devil's ideas as our own, namely, that we would be as God, knowing good and evil. I do not think we mean it when we say it, but we are saying that our future and that of our family is in our own hands, and that we will have the final word in regulating our family size and spacing. We want to be the ultimate judges, and consider ourselves qualified ones, at that.

These ideas of the world are so common and so commonly accepted as permissible, if not downright good, that we as believers often find ourselves nodding our heads in agreement. We say, "Yes, we should space our children wisely (?) in order to give them educational and economic advantages. We don't want too many, and it may be well to control their birth. And if zero-population growth is feasible for their well-being, we may have to tighten our birth control measures."

Is this what the Lord meant when He said, "Be fruitful and multiply, and replenish the earth," Genesis 1:28? When the ungodly hear these words of the Lord, their reaction, also regarding the control over their families, stems only from unbelief. They cannot hear and obey this word of God. The people of God, on the other hand, listening to these words from Genesis, view the size and spacing of their families with the eyes of faith. What do the words of Jehovah in this first chapter of Genesis mean for us as believers today in this modern twentieth century? Do we interpret these words as a *must* or a *may?* How fruitful should we be? How much should we multiply? Who decides? Dr. G. Brillenburg Wurth, in *Het Christelijk Leven In Huwelijk en Gezin,*[1] sheds a worthwhile light on this subject. Much of what he writes could profitably be quoted, and I wish, for the benefit of our generation, that his work had been written and published in the English language. But since it is not, I will translate and quote some of his thoughts.

Dr. Wurth is asking how we as covenant people should view God's statement to be fruitful and multiply.

Again in this (statement) the particular nobility of man as created in God's image comes out. Although for us it is going too far, to find, with Brunner, the image of God as such in man's responsibility, that responsibility indeed forms an inherent and integral part of the image of God. It also concerns this side of humanness, namely, the keeping in existence of the species. In connection with his creation in God's image, it bears the character of a task for the fulfillment of which God makes man sacredly answerable.

Now we have already, in a certain sense, given an answer to the exegetical question whether the divine word 'be fruitful and multiply' must be explaind as an imperative or as an indicative or future; in other words, whether God here *commands* man to be fruitful and multiply or whether

He only declares that it *shall* take place. Grammatically both are possible. But it seems to us, that, as it is continually in God's revelation, when it concerns man, those two, imperative or indicative (future) form no actual contrast.

Of course—we will come back to this later in another context—it does make some difference whether one hears in this divine word a blessing or a command. In connection with the concrete question of the number of children, some have onesidedly laid all the emphasis upon the *command* character, and then want to read here the obligation to produce a maximum number of children while others, objecting to that, with emphasis assure us: yes, but this is no command, but a blessing. God is not prescribing something here: He only promises that He will take care that the human race remains in existence.

But once again, we understand only the deep sense of this word, and what God means by it exactly comes out when we allow the divine double-sense of this word to come to its own as much as possible.

Throughout his work, Dr. Wurth emphasizes the *attitude* of God's child (as the Christian parent), the attitude of warm reverence for God's Word. Also in the context of this statement, the author asks us not to accept God's commands coldly and dogmatically. Thus being fruitful and multiplying may never be a distasteful duty for the devout parent; nor may the covenant parent shrug his shoulders fatalistically and mutter that what shall be, shall be. After Dr. Wurth states that "to be fruitful and multiply" is both a command and a blessing, he comes back to this subject later in his book. There, before he asks his next question, he warns us to ask it with him in a spirit of earnest trust. His question is, "Who has, in last instance, the say in determining how large our family shall be?"[2] In beginning his answer, Dr. Wurth says that we powerless creatures, especially in the sphere of procreation, must look to God's all-wise sovereign decrees in the first place, and then to His providential Fatherly care over us, His children. He says that, in wedded life, though children *can* be born, *we* cannot by ourselves accomplish the birth of a child. For:

Between coitus and conception there is not only a temporal but also an essential distinction. The first is the act of us men; the second, however, falls outside of our competence and remains—let us never forget it—ever a creative wonder of God.

And thus, in the deepest degree, the question of the number of children in our marriage is solved. As Christians, it behooves us in believing humility to leave this above all else to the all-wise decree of God for our lives. He will give us as many children as He knows is good for us.

And fundamentally we should also live so in wedlock, that with respect to the birth as well as the later life and upbringing of our children, we can leave the results of our intercourse as man and wife to Him and His Fatherly care.

Also in these things, faith is the opposite of reckoning. Rationalization is in every respect, also with a view to the question of marriage and the forming of a family, the curse of our modern world. But faith and rationalization exclude one another. Faith dares, looking at God's commandment, to leave the outcome principally to God. It is convinced that with God there is infinitely much more possible than we in our human short-sightedness and anxiety often think possible.

In this connection, there are many families in which the mother is sometimes not at all strong, and the economic circumstances are all but rosy; and nevertheless the number of children is rather high. It appears repeatedly that as they live out of a believing trust in God, much more is possible than one would think possible on rational grounds. There it appears that there are also irrational, unaccountable factors in life which are sometimes more important than rational ones.

It seems to us, therefore, that the opposing of the spirit of neomalthusianism [family planning, G.H.] also in our Christian circles ought to be sought much more from this point of view than in that of the legalistic morality, from the viewpoint of which questions such as this are frequently discussed.

The hard, severe commandment without anything more is powerless here. Especially for the church there is in particular a pastoral task. The evil of a control over birth lies even more in the religious than exclusively in the ethical sphere. The real cause of it is unbelief, or at least, little faith; and it can only actually be conquered if we begin to see the joy, the glory of the fact that also with a view to family formation we *may* live out of that faith, which in obedience to God, 'goes out, not knowing where it shall come,' and which dares to think big, very big, of what God's loving care signifies in the life of His children.

Only, however much this aspect of our problem may be of importance, it would nevertheless be very incorrect if we fail to realize that there are also still other aspects. There is no possibility that God's providence cancels out our human responsibility. In other words, faith in providence is not the same as fatalism, and it does not seem superfluous in this connection to underscore this with emphasis. There is an insidious spirit of rationalism with respect to family formation in many modern marriages and many marriages motivated by the modern spirit. But also in some Christian circles there also rules a kind of marriage fatalism which certainly deserves serious rejection—no less.

What do we mean when we speak of 'marital fatalism'? Indeed, we think of the silent, although often inwardly grumbling trust, by which the birth of a child or a whole series of children is accepted, because a person simply cannot or may not do anything about it; but so that one nevertheless endures it as a necessity rather than that one freely accepts it as a joy and blessing.

Such an attitude over against the increase of a family is no more pious than the first attitude. Of course, it can happen in the best believing marriages that one, for whatever reason, initially may look against the birth of a child, while one later happily and thankfully receives it as a gift from God. However, what we here have in mind is much rather that despicable phenomenon, that one certainly does not prevent the birth of a child, but indeed inwardly curses against it, together with all the detrimental consequences which it must have for the entire sphere of marriage and family.

But not only do we want to warn negatively against such

a marriage fatalism. Also positively we would stress that family formation bespeaks, besides a question of believing trust, also a question of responsible calling.

It is not unknown to us that the term 'responsible parenthood' is suspect in the ears of many, and that not unjustly! For it is often used by the proponents of neomalthusian practices. It speaks for itself that, understood in that sense, we reject it as decisively as possible.

But in itself the thought expressed by the term is completely proper. Also parenthood is—and that repeatedly anew—a task which must be freely accepted by us in joyful responsibility. That does not mean, of course, that in every intercourse the desire for a child is the only rightful motive. Then coitus after conception or after the beginning of menopause would have to be considered impermissible; and there is certainly no ground at all for this.[3]

Continuing this subject of responsible parenthood in forming a family, and stressing his theme of believing trust, Dr. Wurth tells godly parents that they must always be aware that they should be able to shoulder the consequences of sexual intercourse. Is it a fruit of faith, then, to have as many children as is physically possible? Is it "responsible parenthood" before God? Dr. Wurth says he would never dare say that, although at the same time he states that he is a hearty advocate of "the large family." He sees many benefits in a large family that a small family simply could not yield.

The practical advantages of opportunities for service to others and a spirit of selflessness on the part of both parents and children, though great, cannot compare to the spiritual blessings of bringing covenant children into the world and nurturing them, for Scripture teaches that children are a blessing from the Lord. If we receive the fruit of the womb as His reward, we as covenant parents will not look upon their care as a mere duty or even a burden, nor will we dream of great careers in this world for our children. Instead, Dr. Wurth insists, we should always have before us the spiritual approach to parenthood that, should the Lord give us children, we *may* labor, exactly in training our children, in the kingdom of God. If it is a privilege instead of a task to raise a godly family, even a large godly family, then our work with our families will not proceed from a cold observance of the laws of God, but will proceed from the joy and thanks which spontaneously arise in our hearts for the rich blessings He has seen fit to give us, His humble servants.

Dr. Wurth, aware that in recent times even Christian parents listen to the philosophy that large families are not good for anyone, sees more danger of covenant parents listening to this kind of humanistic reasoning than that covenant parents will try to have just as many children as they can possibly have, regardless of consequences. There is a danger in both extremes, as there usually is in extremism. But both these attitudes stem from the same rationalism, namely, that *we* are the masters of our fate, that we may bring as many children as we can into the world, even if we do not know how we can responsibly train them, or we may prevent the birth of as many children as we want, to suit our whims. Recognizing all these factors which confront the godly parent, Dr. Wurth, still pleading for spiritually minded parents to raise up children for the Lord, treats some remaining problems:

But is the responsibility for parenthood only positive or can there also be a negative side? Could there be circumstances in which a husband and wife, exactly in responsibility, think that they should prevent the increase of the family?

We will leave out of consideration the question of the method by which one reaches that end. It is our purpose here only to determine motives. Are there such justifiable motives for preventing conception, and if so, what are they? We purposely put the question in that form, and rather not speak, as is often done, of 'birth control.' First of all, there is really no possibility of a controlling of birth by us men, but at best a regulation of marital intercourse in connection with possible conception. But above all we feel the objection that the term 'birth control' brings us into that sphere of thinking in which people go about figuring beforehand how long a time they can have children, and then in as far as they have that in their own hands, independently go about determining the number of children.

Therefore we would rather ask in what circumstances, on the ground of which motives, it is, at a given moment, permissible to prevent conception.

In recent times, also in Christian circles, we are in general more agreed that there can be such motives. Especially important is the so-called medical indication. When a trustworthy physician sees in a new pregnancy a great threat to the life of the mother, a believing husband and wife will earnestly ask themselves whether in these circumstances they nevertheless may risk it that they may expect a child.

We warn at once against a too superficial acceptance of such a medical indication. Also in this respect we may as Christians still live more out of the faith that God is powerful sometimes to put to shame our fears, which according to first appearances seemed justified. False anxiety is also in this respect sin.

But that means least of all that we would recklessly cause our men to put the life of their wives in the balance. There is undeniably a divine mandate to 'multiply,' but that nevertheless finds its limitation in the divine commandment of love of the neighbor, which also in marriage 'worketh no ill to his neighbor' (Rom. 13:10).

However, could there be for us as Christians, besides this serious, trustworthy medical indication, still other motives for prevention of birth that are considered acceptable?

Also here, even as with divorce, we would warn against arbitrarily stating one or two possible exceptions. Every legalistic casuistry in that spirit runs the danger of violating the conscience and of introducing arbitrariness. Is there, for example, an essential difference between the medical and the social indication?

Of course, the question instantly will arise: but may financial worries then be a reason why people desire no more children in their marriage? And in the light of what we have said about the faith relationship in marriage, the answer is immediately given. In the nature of the case it cannot be that people who live out of faith think that they should give up the blessing of children out of monetary considerations. But we may be reminded that a social indication is still somewhat different from an economic or financial one. When we speak here of 'social indication,' then we think of that entire complex of factors, for example the moral or psychical weakness of the wife, who may be socially or educationally unequipped for her task as mother in the household; which can cause a family such a condition of inner turmoil that the birth of more children can no longer be considered responsible.

Where the boundaries lie is never to be judged by an outsider. After proper enlightenment of those concerned, Christian ethics and caution of spirit must have the courage to take over the ultimate decision themselves. That does not mean that one arbitrarily opens the door to every excuse to escape the divine calling to family formation. To prevent that evil it is good that husband and wife, before the face of God, ask themselves, among other things, whether declining of the fulfillment of this calling, be it temporary or permanent, will bring them grief. And in general it also applies here that each in his own conscience must be fully assured with respect to his calling (Rom. 14:5), but with the full emphasis on the 'being assured.' In other words, one may not decide to refuse further procreation unless husband and wife together have arrived at the full conviction that they would do wrong, would commit sin against God, by doing differently.

But then one must also dare to leave such a decision to believers in their marriage. That is the demand of that freedom in Christ which has nothing in common with a light brushing aside of the commandments of God, but which indeed in last instance in its decisions knows itself to be answerable only to God.[4]

We as covenant parents or potential covenant parents will feel at home with the Biblically oriented principles of Dr. Wurth. More than that, we will also feel the bond of spiritual sensitivity which guides his thoughts on our godly conduct as husband and wife. If we read Dr. Wurth's interpretations of the attitudes of godly parents with our hearts as well as with our heads, our starting point in raising a family will be one of true piety, and our life's outlook will be one continual question, "Lord, what wilt *Thou* have us to do?"

* * *

The preparation for a new child in the family will roughly into three categories: the physical, the mental, and the spiritual. The physical, less important than the other two elements, nonetheless urges us to remember that our bodies are the temples of the Holy Ghost, which we have of God, and we are not our own (I Cor. 6:19). The very fact that a believing mother knows that she is sheltering, not only a new life, but a new covenant life, will be the incentive, for her and for her husband, to care meticulously for her physical needs.

The whole physical well-being of the mother (and very possibly of the father, too) hinges on her mental and spiritual attitude. If husband and wife are enthusiastic and happy about the arrival of a new child and are contented because they know the Lord leads them, they tend to minimize the problems and troubles that arise. Dr. J. R. Miller in *The Home Beautiful* says it is these attitudes of husband and wife which build the character of the home for the future family.

It must be a home in which children will grow up for true and noble life, for God and for heaven. Upon the parents the chief responsibility rests.... If it be happy they must be the authors of the happiness. Its tone, its atmosphere, its spirit, its influence, it will take from them. They have the making of the home in their own hands, and God holds them responsible for it.[5]

Miller believes that happiness and beauty are companion attitudes in the home of a Christian married couple. He says:

Every home can at least be made bright, clean, sweet and beautiful, even if bare of ornament and decoration. It is almost impossible for a child to grow up into loveliness of character, gentleness of disposition and purity of heart amid scenes of slovenliness, untidiness, repulsiveness and filthiness. But a home clean, tasteful, with simple adornments and pleasant surroundings, is an influence of incalculable value in the education of children.[6]

And again:

The home life should be made bright and full of sunshine. The courtesy of the true home is not stiff and formal, but sincere, simple and natural. Children need an atmosphere of gladness. . . . No child can ever grow up into its richest and best development in a home which is gloomy and unhappy. No more do plants need sunshine and air than children need joy and gladness.[7]

Though what Miller says is true, he could probably have further defined the joy and gladness of God's children as founded in the joy of knowing the care of their heavenly Father, and founded in the gladness of the rich blessings of their salvation in Christ. Only we as God's children know true happiness, because our Father sends us only good—in love which we know better each day. So when we discover that we are pregnant when we had really planned not to be, or are not pregnant when we wanted more than anything in the world to be, what do we do? Grumble a little? Probably. But not for long. Not if we are devout parents, living our lives to God's glory. Before we know it, we are praying for grace to be glad with what the Lord gave us or didn't give us. Our basic contentment and downright happiness will be caught by our covenant spouse; and as we raise our family, we will understand from experience the words of Psalm 128: "Thy wife shall be as a fruitful vine by the sides of thine house; thy children like olive plants round about thy table. Behold, that thus shall the man be blessed that feareth the Lord."

As the time of the birth of the child nears, both father and mother will prepare to sacrifice their own selfish interests.

Self is no longer the center. There is a new object to live for, an object great enough to fill all their life and engross their highest powers. It is only when children come that life becomes real, and that parents begin to learn to live. We talk about training our children, but they train us first, teaching us many a sacred lesson, stirring up in us many a slumbering gift and possibility, calling out many a hidden grace and disciplining our wayward powers into strong and harmonious character.[8]

When parents prepare physically and mentally for the arrival of their baby, do they tend to neglect the most important part of their preparation, their spiritual readiness? Do they dedicate their lives anew to God's service and pray that they may train their future child in His fear? For:

Some things God gives often: some He gives only once. The seasons return again and again, and the flowers change with the months, but youth comes twice to none.[9]

And:

O that God would give every mother a vision of the glory and splendor of the work that is given to her when a babe is placed in her bosom to be nursed and trained! Could she have but one glimpse into the future of that life as it reaches on into eternity, could she look into its soul to see its possibilities, could she be made to understand her own personal responsibility for the training of this child, for the development of its life, and for its destiny—she would see that in all God's world there is no other work so noble and so worthy of her best powers, and she would commit to no other the sacred and holy trust given to her.[10]

I hasten to add that this vision is not only for the mother, but for both parents. The path into this future lies along the way of prayer, personal prayers, parental prayers, always prayers for strength and courage and grace to be fit instruments to bring up children for the Lord. And the purpose in this sacred and holy trust is the glory of God! For, "lo, children are an heritage of the Lord: and the fruit of the womb is his reward," Psalm 127:3.

70 / Peaceable Fruit

NOTES

1. Wurth, op. cit., pp. 74, 75.
2. Ibid., p. 255.
3. Ibid., pp. 256-258.
4. Ibid., pp. 259-262.
5. J. R. Miller, *The Home Beautiful* (Grand Rapids: Zondervan, 1912), p. 60.
6. Ibid., p. 68.
7. Ibid., p. 72.
8. Ibid., pp. 59, 60.
9. Geikie, *Life,* quoted by Miller, pp. 62, 63.
10. Ibid., pp. 74, 75.

4
BIRTH OF THE CHILD

Yea, have ye never read, Out of the mouth of babes and sucklings thou hast perfected praise?
—Matthew 21:16

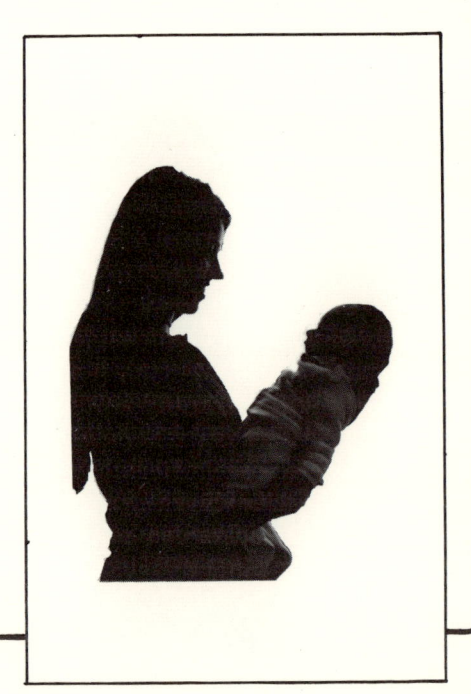

The wonder of birth lingers long before us, long after the doors of the delivery room close behind us, long after the smiling nurse carries the tiny bundle in, so that we can see and touch it, long after we know that we are the parents of our first child, a healthy boy, whom we will name Timothy.

The whole experience of birth has been a miracle of paradoxes. Relentlessly, the glib talk of the delivery room dins in our ears: "He's arrived! Now he's all yours!" All ours? Though he came from our bodies, and though we know that he will have some of our family and character traits, and though in a sense we "made him," is he all ours? We could not give him his life. We really did not make him grow. Much less could we give him his mind and all its capacities, his body with its intricate systems, his soul that will direct his thinking and willing, and his spirit that must place him responsibly before the face of his Maker. All ours? Or all God's, Who just lent him to us for awhile?

"She's having a natural birth," the delivery room talk goes on. If these white-gowned attendants meant that no complications arose, that the process of labor and birth was no longer or more painful than was usual for woman after the curse, then the birth of our son was "natural." To us, the birth was far more than natural. Not only was a new life formed—a soul and body that was no more physically dependent on its mother—but this new life came through the birth canal at precisely the proper moment of its readiness, just exactly the way God had planned it. And this marvelous new creation, feeling out his lungs with screaming cries, has all the properties of the man that he will be. *We* call it a wonder.

"Everything's normal, doctor," the delivery room nurse was saying. If the excitement and bustle of a delivery room is normal, if a happy, tired mother and a squealing infant is normal, then our son had a normal birth. We thank God for a healthy son born under favorable conditions. But we look farther. We thank God for the miracle He performed in the delivery room, the miracle of giving us an unblemished covenant son.

The delivery room nurse was going on again. "We're almost finished checking your new son." Then, "Open your eyes, Mother. Here is your son. Perfect! Just a perfect boy!" Perfect? Or imperfect? Of course, we parents knew that the nurse meant that our son was unblemished and well-formed. We would never be thankful enough for that. But we were covenant parents and confessed that, before the face of our holy God, our son was far from perfect, worse than imperfect—he was dead in trespasses and sins. We believed that he "was called a transgressor from the womb" (Isaiah 48:8). We knew that before long we would teach him the prayer of Psalm 51:3 as his own: "For I acknowledge my transgressions: and my sin is ever before me." But, because we were covenant parents, we could not stop there. We would teach our imperfect child, "Create in me a clean heart, O God," and "Restore unto me the joy of thy salvation," " . . . and my mouth shall show forth thy praise." Until his death, our son would be perfect and imperfect.

Forgetting, for the moment, the delivery room atmosphere, we saw the whole experience of begetting a son as one of psychological and spiritual paradox. As the due date quickly crept

Birth of the Child / 75

closer, we both felt tense. Life would never be quite the same as it had been, not nearly so tranquil; certainly it would never be so easy as it had been, for problems would begin and multiply. Yet, in all this tenseness, we were happy. We did not want life the same as it had been. We wanted progress in our family life and we wanted to grow to mental and spiritual maturity, joyfully, in the handling of all our problems.

Tense and yet happy, eager and yet apprehensive, clinging to our freedom and yet welcoming our responsibilities, we waited for the day when our baby would be born. Apprehensive because of the physical trauma, because of the schedules and care and possible illnesses of the fragile newborn, we clung to the selfishness of a life of limited responsibilities. In the end our eagerness and our welcome of responsibility won out: our eagerness to love our own covenant child and our responsibility to lead him through his whole life in the path of God's Word.

We had one more paradox of feelings. That one will go with us through life. This paradox, with strong spiritual overtones, is one of fear and trust as we begin our lifelong task. Already we have experienced the fear of Psalm 48:6, "Fear took hold upon them there, and pain as of a woman in travail." Both of us had had fears about the ordeal of the birth of our first child. Soon—too soon, probably—we will feel the way Job did; for even though our problems will not approach the magnitude of his, we can look forward to lurking troubles and looming problems; it will be easy for us to understand Job's words: "In thoughts from the visions of the night, when deep sleep falleth upon men, fear came upon me, and trembling which made all my bones to shake." When we look at all the things that *can* happen and most likely *will* happen through a lifetime of bringing up our covenant child—our worries for his physical safety, our warnings about temptations, our caution in making decisions affecting him, and our prayers for his spiritual well-being—we fear.

But, being God's children and living close to Him, we cannot live long with our fears, for as soon as we look up, they cease to haunt us and we can forget them. They are replaced with trust. The last verse of Psalm 73 explains how this all comes about: "But it is good for me to draw near to

God; I have put my trust in the Lord God." Not only will *we* exchange our fears for trust, but soon we will begin teaching our son to take the following Scripture as his own: "The Lord is good, a strong hold in the day of trouble; and he knoweth them that trust in him" (Nahum 1:7). Through all our life with our son, we will fear and trust, but always trust!

* * *

I knew a young married girl, who, after extensive surgery, was told that she could never have children. She was crushed. She wanted children more than anything else in the world, she said as she wept. After she had returned home and was completely well, she still wept because of the children she could not have. I once asked her why she could not accept this as God's will for her life. Her answer was ready and spontaneous, "Why, it will spoil our life with all our other married friends. I can never talk about my pregnancies with my girl friends. We can never compare our children with our friends' children. We'll be the different ones, the childless ones. We'll sit on the sidelines. Our life will be empty. And I always did want to dress a dear little girl," she wailed. "Besides, I did so much want to know just what kind of child I'd have. Of course, I know it's God's will that we won't have any, and we'll accept it in faith," she added pathetically.

Are we sorry for this young girl who longed so much for motherhood and then was deprived of all its joys? I know we are. Can we not imagine the culmination of our dreams, the longings of a lifetime, swept away forever under the surgeon's knife? Can we not almost feel the grief of this childless young lady? Could we not imagine ourselves giving some of these very reasons to explain the emptiness, the grief in our lives?

However, if we look more closely at the motives of this young girl, at the reasons why she *really* wanted a child, we find that they stem from selfishness. Unknowingly, perhaps, our friend and her husband were putting their wishes and goals first. Basically selfish and self-centered is the wish to have children because one's friends have them, and because they furnish good conversation for the social hour. When we stop and seriously consider the motive of having children so that we can be like everyone else, or so that we can compare their achievements with those of our friends' children, our spiritual sensitivity tells us the motives arise only from carnal pride. For there is a real danger, don't you think, for the covenant parent to cultivate a measure of pride in his product? If our child is physically attractive, or has certain striking characteristics, are we not quick to joke that he takes after our side of the family—and half mean it? If he has an even, happy temperament, we reminisce about his grandfather's nature, and mention the calm, unpressured home atmosphere under which we trained him. If he is at the head of the class, we find ourselves bringing the conversation round to school and tests. Without denying all the factors of heredity and environment as they influence our child, and, in fact, using all these circumstances to the utmost of our power for the good of our child, can we ever take the credit for ourselves? What feeling do we have in our hearts over against our child—stinking pride or humble thanks? I use the deprecatory adjective for pride, for in Scripture pride is always spoken of as sinful. When our infant son grows up, let us not, as devout covenant parents, be *proud* of him. We were only God's tools, His servants who did their best, but who now can only murmur, "Thanks, Lord."

There is possibly one more selfish, carnal motive for desiring a child, that of perpetuating a bit of ourselves, our name, our physical characteristics, or our character traits, into the next generation. Or we may want our own flesh and blood to love, and to love us, especially when we grow old. We hear ourselves cite the saying, "Blood is thicker than water." But is it not all right for a Christian to wish natural love from his child? Brillenburg Wurth again has something to say. I will quote a short excerpt from his chapter on the relationship of parents and children.

The family has, even as marriage has, yea in a certain sense still more than the latter, what one could call a physical, biological basis. It comes into existence, thanks to natural descent, through the fact that from a pair, children are born, children who by the wonder of conception are related to their parents physically (*physiek*), in the blood.

That blood-relationship in the family is a factor of very great significance. We should not, as Christians, underestimate the value of it. . . .

Upon that blood relationship rests, among other things, the mutual natural love between parents and children, and no one will dare to deny the importance of this.

That physical bond in the family is something irreplaceable. There can be kinds of circumstances in which children must, instead of in their own family, live and receive their upbringing elsewhere, with step-parents or in institutions. But it has been repeatedly pointed out, correctly, that even if such an upbringing outside of the family technically answers to much better conditions, it can never provide what the child can receive in the way of natural warmth exclusively in his own family and especially by his own mother.

. . . In that physical bond there is something not only purely bodily, a question of external blood relationship, without more. It is not for nothing that the blood in the Bible has such a wonderful, mysterious significance. Here we touch upon the deepest mystery of life. The natural in this sense is not simply natural, but also with respect to love, the basis for all the rest of life and all the other life-relationships.

From this also arises the great emphasis which the demand for natural love receives in Biblical revelation. A mother cannot forget to love her child (Is. 49:15). She would be an unnatural mother, yea, she would no more be a mother if that natural inclination for the child was lacking in her. But she also has the obligation to that motherhood. And it is seen as a terrible degeneration and phenomenon, when in the end of days, natural love disappears (II Tim. 3:3).

That does not take away the fact that the natural bond, the blood relationship, is not the deepest relation in the family. There are, over and above the bonds of blood, also relationships of spiritual and ethical nature in the family, and it is these which deserve our special attention.[1]

At this point we will not explore the spiritual and ethical

Birth of the Child / 79

ties which Dr. Wurth mentions. That will come later. Instead, as we take our tiny son home from the hospital, we will try to begin his life and our life with him in the proper perspective. Though we recognize with each passing day our physical resemblance, that he is our own flesh and blood, we will focus the attention of our lives on our spiritual ties as family. We *know* that we are the covenant parents of a covenant child. How do we, in practice, show it? How is a covenant parent's love for his child different from a non-covenant parent's love? Probably it shows itself first in a selfless devotion to the needs of the child. We determine to love the whole child, failings and all, for himself as a covenant child, to consider his needs and his good rather than our own; all this we will do, not as his slaves, of course, but as responsible parents before God. When we look at him, we see him as a loan from the Lord. We see him as a complex marvel of unity, as a unique person in a beautifully created body intertwined with a soul about which we can fathom little, whose spirit will respond in faith to the call of his Father in heaven. Just as we, merely of ourselves, could not have formed our baby, we feel equally unable to train him. Eagerly we turn to the tools with which the Lord has provided us. We go to the Guide, His Word, to learn how to grow in grace as we train him in its principles. Eagerly we pray *for* and *with* our child, for the help that we unworthy sinners need each day. That is the only way God's people can treat God's loans.

* * *

I once heard an inspiring speech which I cannot forget. The speaker talked of covenant children and laid down somewhat the same principles that we have been discussing so far. He stressed also that a child was born with his character (or personality); and though we may influence it, especially in his first passive years, we can never materially change it. What impressed me, as a covenant parent, was the speaker's distinction between character traits and sinful traits. At the risk of digressing just a bit, let us look at our new son, Timothy, as an example. He may already show, soon after he is home from the hospital, that he has a stubborn insistence to get what he wants, and he may keep on showing that trait as he grows older. How do we handle this character trait? Bend or break his will? Fight his stubbornness? Before we give our almost mechanical affirmative answer, let us look at this trait of stubborn insistence. It is wrong in itself? Think of Martin Luther and all the other stedfast saints, and you will answer that they were not wrong in their stubborn insistence. What, then, is the difference between our son's stubbornness and a saint's stedfastness? The difference, as we have already possibly surmised, is the difference of sin and grace. Stubbornness can be used as the tool of the devil in the service of sin, or as the tool of the Spirit in the fight for the truth. The difference lies in the *use* of the trait.

Perhaps our son begins to show a calm, placid personality. In the service of sin he could become a lazy character. In the service of God his sanctified calm character could make him a deep, quiet thinker.

We could multiply examples about the potential character of our tiny son, but for the present these are enough. What an awesome responsibility it is to watch closely the development of our child's character and then to begin to teach him the sanctified use of his traits. Without God's help we will not be able to guide what we consider weaknesses into potential strength; or, on the contrary, we might not be able to see what we consider a strength to be a potential weakness or source of wicked pride for our son.

To choose the appropriate method and to assume the right attitude takes sanctified Christian judgment; judgment not to say that "what will be will be," and if he is formed with his character traits at birth we should let well enough alone; judgment not to say that we are here to change and mold him as *we* think he should be; but judgment to care for God's gift to us, to accept him as God gave him, to train him as a fit treasure for God's kingdom here on earth as he travels through to life eternal.

That noble and lofty path on which we set our sights is strewn with the mundane inconveniences of life. The routines, irritations, and small problems of each day get in our way and blur the picture of our high objective. Our son is home from the hospital now. Even if we are naturally orderly parents, the new schedule our infant imposes on us will cause tensions, frustrations, interruptions when we would rather not be interrupted, impatient words to son or spouse, and probably even a measure of resentfulness at a greater loss of freedom than we had expected.

In the next chapter we will look at some of these practical aspects in detail, and watch our son as he is encouraged by his covenant parents. We will see the spontaneity of his responses, and learn how to evaluate and interpret those responses, always in the light of Scripture, our Guide, for "out of the mouths of babes and sucklings thou hast perfected praise," Psalm 8:2.

NOTES

1. Wurth, op. cit., pp. 282-284.

5
THE CHILD FROM BIRTH TO NINE MONTHS

To everything there is a season, and a time to every purpose under the heaven.
—Ecclesiastes 3:1

Are you a parent? How do you react to all the details, the ripples and the storms, that fill your life each day? Are you not yet a parent? Have you ever asked yourself what kind of parent you think you would make? A calm parent with a cheerful disposition, with enough rigidity to maintain high standards of family life, but with enough flexibility to adapt to the variables of life, will find that his burdens seem lighter than a tense, outspoken, impatient parent, or a moody, timid, gloomy one. How do you respond to events in the routine of your everyday life? Are you excitable, demanding, ambitious, carefree, conscientious, sullen, stable . . . ? We cannot divorce our personalities and our spontaneous reactions from our new positions as responsible leaders and teachers in the home. For you and I take all of our personality traits into parenthood with us. There is no doubt that to some of us the routines and restrictions of parenthood come easier than to others. For some of us it will mean more effort, more prayers for grace to be a cheerful, loving, covenant parent.

We have for many months conditioned ourselves for the new routine which our son will bring us, only to find out when we take our baby home that there *is* no routine, only utter chaos. Days and nights are reversed, duties are interrupted, sleep is only in snatches, meals are ordeals, father is somewhat bewildered, and mother is never too far from tears.

This is the time, probably in our son's first week at home, to begin to impose very gently the routine that will best fit our life. I use the words "begin" and "very gently," because a well-established routine with a newborn child is a gradual, almost imperceptible program. If our son is too wakeful at night, we take the time to keep him awake and amuse him for increasingly longer periods of time during the day. Take the time! We are training him. If he frets at dinner time and destroys the peace we as parents need, we try to work his schedule so that he will be tired enough for a nap while we enjoy an uninterrupted meal. If he gulps down two ounces and falls asleep, only to awaken half an hour later for another short feeding, we will try harder to keep him awake longer at his feeding and urge him to drink more so that he will have longer naps. We are trying to instill some orderly habits in our young son.

What we are doing, of course, is setting a gradual rule for our son's routine. As we set the pattern for the physical needs of his very early life, we are merely living according to the timeworn adage, "to rule the routine, not to let the routine rule you." With each new experience of bathing our baby, of making his formulas just right, of coping with his fussing and crying or his first case of the sniffles, we are understandably concerned and quite probably more than a little nervous. If, instead of showing uneasiness and uncertainty, we discipline ourselves to create orderliness in a relaxed atmosphere, we and our son will enjoy his training. In this chapter we will discuss the various aspects of this orderliness and examine the relaxed atmosphere. By way of introduction, we should lay down the premise that order is not rigidity, but a controlled flexibility. Our use of order must fit the circumstances we meet and the problems we find or make for ourselves. Solomon, in his knowledge of reality, recognized that there is "a **time to weep**, and a time to laugh; . . . a time to embrace, and a time to refrain from embracing; a time to get, and a time to lose; . . . a time to keep silence, and a time to speak. . . . " Ecclesiastes 3:4-7. We will try to do what Solomon tells us—to make our activity fit the reality of the situation, with enough flexibility in our lives to see the need and proceed in an orderly way to meet it.

In order for us to know when it is "a time to," we will need the proper perspective in our lives with our son. He is important. He is helpless. He is demanding. He is also a priceless treasure to guard, to nourish, to polish, and to refine. Therefore, we drop our other work, our own entertainment and enjoyment, and care for him first, with patience and with gladness. But in all our joy and self-sacrificing, and in all our eagerness to fill his needs, we cannot let him occupy our whole life. He may be "baby first," but not "baby all." Our relationships to our spouse, our family, friends, church life, and to our God are the same as they were, and we make room for their demands on our time. If we *do* impose a gentle routine and good habits early, we will have ample room in our lives for comradely husband-wife talks, for socializing, reading, studying the Scriptures, and above all, devotions.

First, then, we set out to become acquainted with Timothy. And the best way to get to know someone is to communicate. We as parents will take the initiative in letting our son know how we feel about him, and we will do this first by our touch. We are timid and uncertain when we first bathe and feed him. But we will discipline ourselves to conquer our feelings of hesitancy or even fright, and grasp our son with the firmness and confidence we soon hope to feel in our quaking arms. If we forget to be calm, or if we panic when he screams, he will respond to our jerky movements and harried attitude with louder cries of fright. But if we meet the minor crises by picking him up with a reassuring grip and a low, calm voice which we hope will be convincing, he will sense that we are master of the situation and may begin to quiet down.

When we think into the helplessness and loneliness of our Timothy as he begins life in his large world of strange surroundings, we will better understand what our gentle touch can do for him. He cannot control the erratic thrashings of his tiny arms and legs and cannot guess what sensations will flood upon him next in this unpredictable world. Worse, we are told that he cannot see, or at least see in meaningful focus, the objects and movements around him. Many psychologists insist that at this stage of his life he is as yet a bundle of reflexes. "In the newborn child there is indeed a wealth of highly adaptive reflex activity of the organism,"[1] writes Curti. And in the next paragraph she says, "But much of this generality (mass activity) seems actually to consist of responses which are essentially reflex in character." Although we will not dispute the fact that many of our son's actions are spontaneous reflexes, as are our own, we may take exception to the statement that his responses are "essentially reflex in character." How do we know that there is no thought in the mind of our week-old child? The potential is there. When we as mothers grasp our infant confidently, to let him know he is safe in our arms, does our infant experience safety by reflex response, or does he *know* he is safe? If we cuddle him, comfort him, pat his tiny cheek, feed and clothe him when he needs it, is he content because he is comfortable or does he know that we love him?

In view of the fact that in this chapter I hope to show that he can be trained at a much earlier age than is usually thought possible, I tend not to sell our son short. I believe he knows more at a very early age than we generally think he does. There is another reason, too, that we as covenant parents should consider. Unlike the behaviorists, who depend on a chain of stimulus-reaction techniques, we look upon our son from the moment he is born as a regenerated child of God, with the full potential for both his natural and spiritual life. If God has already put His Spirit into that tiny heart, who are we to say that our son's actions at this stage are merely motor-neural responses? Could he not be beginning, in a small measure, to use his faculties of body and soul, particularly of his intellect, as it takes in the outside world? Surely our son's potential has only just begun to develop, and will develop in the orderly fashion that God has planned for him. Surely, too, there is much room for speculation in this area, because we cannot communicate verbally, and we will never have certain and factual answers. But I repeat: as covenant parents, do not give him too little credit.

I would like to discuss one example which clearly shows that at a very early age our son is using the faculties with which he is gifted. Have you ever seen an infant of Timothy's age—under two weeks—have a temper tantrum? He awakes from a longer-than-usual, sound, healthful sleep and is ravenously hungry, but also soaking wet through several layers of clothes. As mothers, we choose to give him dry clothes before we feed him. But our son wants food, not only before we change his clothes, but before we have time to prepare it. His crying is not the whimpering sobs of discomfort, but the red-faced, breath-holding, fist-clenching screams of anger. Then, if we remember that our son's emotions are an act of his will reacting on what his intellect perceives, we will know that he wills to have a tantrum, to be impatient and self-willed, to sin. Now certainly we will all agree that he does not yet know sin as sin. Yet his depraved nature is coming to expression, and if we are covenant parents, our firm touch and disapproving tone may bring him up short. We are rebuking our son for doing wrong. When we see incidents such as this in his early life, we as covenant parents should be alert to recognize his behavior as showing his intellect and will in action, and we should never forget that our small child also stands before the just Judge of heaven and earth, responsible for his sin with which he is born. Not only our methods of handling our child but also our insights into his reactions belong to our duties as parental guides. Because we know ourselves so well as miserable sinners before God, inclined to the same rotten behavior as he is, we can so well understand our son's rebellious sins, and in sorrow for the sins of us both, fight our lifelong struggle together.

The use of our voice is another effective means of communicating with our son. A calm, low-pitched voice saying, "Now, now:—no reason to be so upset," may not stop his crying, but will let him know that we, his guardians, are not too perturbed. But what if he continues his fussing without apparent reason, and our calm voice and tender touch bring no quieting results? Instead of giving way to our own insecurities and fears about our son, we might try using our voices to sing to him. Lullabies, quiet psalms and hymns often bring the peace and reassurance our son seeks.

Soon our son will be responding to another avenue of communication, that of our facial expression. When we smile down at him to show him our love and care for him, are we not thrilled at the first erratic movements of his hands as they try to reach for that smile? As the weeks pass, we use these three media—touch, voice, and facial expression—in the task of training our son.

* * *

Before we discuss the practical side of the training of our son, the training that at this stage of his life is mostly physical, we will look once more at ourselves, and reinforce our grasp of the principles underlying our attitudes toward this task. Our son will be largely passive; his responses will be mostly those that we evoke. In a certain sense *any* parent, regenerated or not, could train his child using the methods we will present in this chapter. Outwardly the procedure and results would seem the same. The reason is that an observer cannot see or measure the principles, attitudes, and dedication behind the actions of the covenant parent.

As long as our child is under a year old, we are the ones who take the initiative and he either responds or fails to respond. Both parents, but especially the mothers, on whom most of the responsibility for his care falls in this first year, will be trying conscientiously to establish healthy spiritual attitudes in themselves and in their son. We as parents will not only work diligently and consistently, but will also do our tasks cheerfully. We will not be afraid of hard work, nor of exercising a large measure of self-control. And, although the covenant parent's approach to his child is always a spiritual one, this does not preclude the fact that in the practical, physical matters to be discussed in this chapter he must use his down-to-earth common sense which the Lord has given him. There are those areas in a child's life, such as putting spoonfuls of food into his mouth, that fall into a category that we may call "functional," for want of a better term. However, even in these "functional" chores, the covenant parent maintains his basic spiritual outlook. Summarized, the heart of the training of our child lies in our *approach*.

The question may arise in our minds: is his training then completely one-sided? What about our child's responses to our training? As we shall see, many of our baby's reactions at first are almost completely physical; but in some areas, in verbal communication and in the beginning of spiritual training, we will detect the glimmerings of the obedient responses of a covenant child. But let us go on to his care and training, and many of these principles will become clear by way of example.

That the training of our children begins at birth is universally recognized. Jersild says:

> Almost from the moment of birth, infants seem to exhibit differences in personality. Some are decidedly more mobile, active, and on the go than others. During ensuing hours and days, some babies tend to be more or less restless, irritable, fussy, whereas others are more placid and serene.

A little farther on he says:

> The interaction of hereditary and environmental factors in a child's development is so complex that it would be difficult to isolate either in pure form. Apart from the question of whether, to what extent, early differences in personality are inborn, it is obvious that differences in behavior can also be traced to conditions in the environment. Crying in infants exemplifies this. The infant is likely to cry more if the adult is preoccupied with other things or if . . . he is used to a fixed schedule of feeding and is not fed when hungry. The very fact that there are vast individual differences among adults who are caring for infants means differences in the environments to which the infants are exposed. The personality of the adult is bound to influence his general attitude toward the child.[2]

What this author says is true from a formal viewpoint. That there is a vast interplay between hereditary and environmental elements in his life is obvious. But it is a cold statement of fact. There is more than a cold relationship of personalities in a given set of surroundings. There is an attitude, an atmosphere, a direction on the part of both child and parents, an ethical, spiritual relationship which is of prime importance, and of which Jersild knows nothing.

Jersild goes on to the subject of learning during the first weeks of life, and details elaborate experiments of conditioned responses, mostly in the area of feeding times. After showing charts and pages of results of these experiments to "condition" the child what to expect, he says: "Thus during the first days of life does a child reveal a resiliency, a capacity to adapt to what the environment demands or affords. As time goes on he will continue to show this capacity as he adapts to countless demands."[3]

Again, the same criticism is valid. Jersild treats the child as a behavioral instrument who learns through mechanical devices. The author has showed us his humanistic evaluation of the tiny baby in its concrete, tangible surroundings. That is as far as he can go. Of the inner life of the soul and spirit he has nothing to say.

Let us see what another author has to say on this subject. In the Foreword of her book Gera Kraan says that the material she writes about is as old as mankind itself, but it is the concern of each new generation. She writes the life story of a hypothetical little girl:

> The training of the child begins at its first meal. The dozing little one is taken from the crib on time and during the feeding is kept awake, if need be by a couple drops of cold water on his little face, or a pinch on the cheek. Do not dally or stop repeatedly, but keep going; you let your time go past, you get no more . . . those are the first rules with which a child comes into contact. And almost simultaneously he must learn to adjust to regularity. It doesn't get its way when it cries, but has to learn to wait until it is time. And it is noteworthy how in the first fourteen days it already becomes evident who will later be the loiterers and the poor eaters, the quiet punctual people and the indus-

trious workers, the healthy sleepers and the restless night-disturbers.[4]

We may like this author's approach better. In her book she takes the Christian parent's approach to the child, and the point of view that early training of covenant children is essential.

Hereditary traits and characteristics and peculiarities of the nature of the child appear very soon. If we are ready to note them, we will probably be better equipped to deal with them; for by our actions and reactions we are training. This training, as does all training, has its negative and its positive aspects. And though we as Christian parents should and do stress the *positive* in our lives and in the lives of our children, though we should and do show him the *right* way to go and the right things to do by word and example; yet we know that is not the end of our calling. We should and do point out the *wrong,* and chastise our child if he does the wrong or will not listen to the right.

Even with a child as tiny as our son is, the negative aspect of his training occupies a large place in our lives. Never can we go along with the godless philosophy that our child is innocent, that he does not know what he is doing, that he is not responsible. Never may we forget that our son by nature is totally depraved; and by nature, apart from God's grace, he loves to show that depravity. For us, it is important how we view that negative aspect of the discipline we are about to begin with our son. In our relationship with our son our negative discipline must show not anger, but sorrow over his and our sins. We will be firm and decisive in enforcing our "no," even though our child does not understand our reasons. The negative part of the training of our child is often misunderstood by those whose motives are good. Many parents, also many covenant parents, equate a heavy hand and a loud voice in training their children with complete control and absolute authority. After a well-meaning but mistaken father one day had slapped his tiny daughter's hand with a resounding thwack, pushed her roughly away from the forbidden candy dish, and thundered, "Now you stay away! You hear?", he turned in a quiet aside to me and said, "I have to let her know I mean it, you know." This father had not yet learned that a raised eyebrow or a firm "no" in a quiet voice would produce better results. If the child were trained in a godly atmosphere for prompt obedience to a mild tone of voice or a mild reprimand, the occasions for the loud voice and the physical force would be far less frequent. This atmosphere in a covenant home does not come ready-made. It is an atmosphere we have to create and foster through a constant study of the principles shown in God's Word and a putting of those principles patiently into practice.

Using some of these principles of positive and negative discipline, let us follow our Timmy through part of a typical day in early babyhood. He has had a wakeful evening. His first smiles and happy noises have delighted both Timmy and his parents. But he is yawning and beginning to fret—the signal for mother to prepare him for bed. After a change of clothes and a bedtime feeding, she tucks him into his crib and leaves. Timmy cries. If, on checking, she finds nothing wrong, if his cries are not screams of pain or whines of discomfort, but cries of dissatisfaction, mother leaves. He wants to have some more fun, but mother says it is time for him to sleep. His cries will quite likely increase in volume and intensity. No parent of a young baby enjoys hearing those lusty, breath-holding squalls, and either father or mother may suggest to pick him up and hold him for a while, and probably rock him to sleep. If, however, they are wise, and willing to train their young son not to rebel with squalls of anger when it is bedtime, they will resist this impulse. Instead, mother will go into the bedroom, and with exaggerated calm, examine Timmy for any possible discomfort. If he is all right—and he usually is—she will immediately lay him down again and tell him in a firm, quiet voice to settle down and go to sleep. Most likely he will not. After another quarter hour of enduring his crying, mother may want to re-examine him, picking him up silently, and once again laying him down immediately.

Why do it this way? Why not let him cry himself to sleep without interference? One reason is that by picking him up we let him know that we are still right there caring for him. Another is that, by putting him down repeatedly, we are reminding him that, though our care is near, we are teaching him to go to sleep quietly when it is his bedtime. It may take Timmy several firm "settling downs" on several successive evenings before he learns to go to sleep quietly, obediently, without crying. The whole experience is more than a training session for Timmy. It has been an experience of self-discipline for us as parents. The apparently easy way would be to hold him, to rock him to sleep, to give in because he is so little. The method with foresight, with the true love and future well-being of our son in view, is the one that trains him, while he is very young, in habits of order and obedience. Soon he will go to sleep promptly and happily. He has learned a lesson in obedience, and that without a raised voice on the part of the parent. For us, the experience of firm bedtime training has given an insight into the struggle with the disobedient sinful nature which we will encounter in all our life with Timmy; and it has also given the positive fruits of an easy, no-nonsense bedtime routine for us all.

When Timmy is old enough to begin to roll over by himself and to help with the dressing process by holding out an arm or a leg, we observe that he is usually happy, exuberant, and full of bounce. As we bathe and dress him, his irrepressible good humor or his impatience impel him to wiggle and turn over just as we are ready to diaper him. We turn him right side up, only to have him upside down again before we can reach for a safety pin. We have three choices: we can tell ourselves that he is so small that he doesn't know what he is doing, so we will cope with the wiggler and get him dressed as best we can in whatever position he chooses; we can also flare up a little inside and with a rough hand and harsh voice turn him over and slam him down, right side up; or we can train him firmly and quietly always to lie still in the proper position until the diapering is finished. How? First, with firm hand and gentle pressure, turn Timmy over and say a decisive "No!" without raising the voice, and then proceed with the diapering. For some children this may be enough, but it is not enough for Timmy. He will turn right over again and try to squirm out of our grasp. The next step is turning him over again with the same firm grasp, and adding a sharp "stinger" with the fingers, to the offending area. The "stinger" we will do well to warn ourselves, is merely a finger-tip slap, not intended to hurt or harm our son, but meant to convey, by touch, our message. If anger or frustration does not well up in us, the "stinger" will never be more than that. Our message of disapproval will bring him only discomfort and an awareness of our disapproval.

If, however, we feel hot anger flushing our face or if we feel like stamping our foot, we would do better to omit the slap. We would merely be venting our own anger on our son.

Our controlled finger-slap will bring tears from Timmy, but we will continue in silence to dress him. Our silence will not be the sullenness of a parent whose will has been crossed. It is a short, purposeful silence, a letting our son know that he did wrong and we are displeased. We could scold, but he will not understand our words; we could commiserate with him and murmur how sorry we are that we ever had to do such a thing to him, but that would truly confuse him. Therefore we choose a short silence to let the impact of our action sink in upon his consciousness. Make the silence short, and then go on, without recriminations, with the rest of Timmy's care.

But parents, covenant parents, do not be so optimistic that you believe this problem is over now. Not with our Timmy. He will try to turn over again and again. Sometimes it may take more than one or two "stingers" before he settles down to obey. But if we say, with our voice and our attitude and our actions, "I'm trying to train you, Timmy," he will learn, and he will know that he *must* lie still because we expect it and expect it consistently. Do not overlook the benefit of this struggle for ourselves: we have attained an effortless, orderly routine—at a price, no doubt—but well worth that price.

After the difficulties of adjusting the formula and size of nipples, Timmy takes his bottle eagerly, without fuss. But, after a few weeks, when his body needs solid foods, he may try to turn feeding time into a frenzy, or a battle of wills. He need do neither, if, as parents, we prepare for the next step in his feeding routine—prepare with understanding as well as with food. When a cold hard spoon with some undefinable sticky mush hits his soft warm lips and bare gums, we can understand that Timmy may have a mild or not so mild disapproval at first. And if he does get some into his mouth, what does he do with the lumpy mess? His tongue and lips have not yet learned to coordinate with his swallowing, and most of his cereal may end outside his mouth. Again there are three things we may do. We may be determined that *this* Timmy will eat. We force it down; we end the battle with tears, choking, and a mess. But we resolve to do better battle next time. Or we may give up, at least for a time. Timmy is probably not yet ready for solid food. Maybe we even believe a little bit in the "self-demand" principle of child feeding, in which a child will instinctively choose what is best for himself at a given time.[5]

But if we examine these two approaches, we see that neither teaches the child anything. The first stems from the philosophy that "I'm boss," and the second, that "he's boss." Instead, let us be consistent with the basic Christian principles of guidance which we are following, and even in this seemingly small matter of feeding him, train him in the proper responsive, obedient habits of eating. We know that Timmy may pull away from the hard spoon. He does. He shivers and resists the stuff. After a few mouthfuls we stop and throw the rest of the cereal away. We hadn't made much, anyway. That is not all, however. Timmy will be watching for our reaction. Calmly, as we push the familiar bottle into his mouth, or better still, as we hold him close and breast feed him, we say, "It wasn't too bad, Timmy. Next time it will go better." He senses that the experience was not an ordeal for us. Why should it be for him? Next time we may want to talk in an encouraging voice. This time we will set as our goal two or three more tries with the spoon. Knowing Timmy by now, it will not go too much better. But he hears the same reaction: encouraging without being anxious. A confident parent is taking this aspect of his training in stride, too. With Timmy, we may need several feedings, each a little longer than the preceding one, to accustom him to his cereal. We also need patience, perseverance, and consistency. Even a dedicated Christian parent is tempted to fling away the spoon and say in impatience, "Forget it!" But if she remembers her calling before God to train her son in all his life, she will ask God daily for the priceless gifts of grace and patience she needs for his training.

Timmy will soon be introduced to a wide variety of foods. If he is normal—and most of our Timmys are—he will enjoy the new foods. How about one certain food—the proverbial spinach—which he consistently rejects? Shall we camouflage it, sneak it, force it? Why should we? If we are understanding parents, we will know that Timmy is an individual with different likes and dislikes from ours. He doesn't like spinach: we cannot tolerate carrots. However, if he tolerates only one or two foods and rejects the rest, let us look at ourselves. Have we failed, with patience and consistency, to teach him to accept these foods?

After his first few weeks of life, Timmy is awake more often at mealtime. Early babyhood, as early as four or five months, is a good time to begin to train him in proper conduct during mealtime. At times Timmy will not feel as contented and happy as at other times. Neither do we. If he is not satisfied with a cracker or hard biscuit or a piece of an orange, and throws it down repeatedly, we may try bringing him to another room with his toys. Or better, if he is tired and bored, he may welcome the diversion of mother's lap. Especially at the time of mealtime devotions it is the ideal that our baby be made to feel as one of the family unit. When father or mother reaches for the Bible, the firm pressure and the tone of the whisper, "We're quiet now," and the atmosphere of reverence for God's Word will make its impression on Timmy. We will not always see that it impresses him. For if his cantankerous mood persists, he will bang with a spoon or howl in frustration because he does not want to sit still. And I think one of the saddest sights we can see is that of a child being restrained by sheer physical force, by the domineering anger of a parent who says, "You *will* sit still."

A wise parent will know that although Timmy can sense the mood, he cannot know the reason for sitting still, and he cannot understand the reading of God's Word. This kind of training is not accomplished overnight. It is a gentle process, a slow progress, a continual training in the love and reverence of God's Word.

Exactly what can we say or do to awaken the spiritual consciousness of our son? When it is time for Scripture reading, or at any other time that we mention the name of our God in the presence of our son, we will use His name with utmost reverence. We can point toward the sky and tell him of our Father's home there. A tiny child needs to be taught concretely. You and I have no way of knowing how much of this he can understand. But if he is one of God's own children—and we recognize the painful fact that not everyone of *our* children is one of *God's* children—he will understand more than we think he does. If, in our family, father is the one who usually reads the Bible at the table, have him take Timmy on his lap. The sight of the open Bible, the security of being in father's arms in a quiet atmosphere, and the rhythmic breathing and vibrations of speaking will combine to show Timmy that this is a "listening time." If he does sit quietly, we will show him with our praise that *this* is the kind of behavior for which we are training him.

Instead of letting our son play, or putting him to bed during devotions, we can try to have him present. We will show him how we bow our heads and close our eyes during prayer; if he does not resist, we will gently fold his hands and shade his eyes. Training him in the spiritual sphere is much more difficult than any other area of his training. There is no way of measuring tangible results, because there are none. For that reason, we will try harder, with more patience and more prayer, that God will give His rich grace to both us and our child. Difficult and intangible though it is, this training will not take as long as you may think it will. Have you tried it?

I would like to discuss one more area of babyhood training, that of bowel and bladder control. Neither parents nor authorities agree on just how and when to go about this training. Most begin far too late in babyhood, with dubious degrees of success and many emotional battles. Jersild, an author with a flair for detail, says:

> Children and parents alike would be spared much trouble if infants were housebroken at birth. As it is, tl development of bladder and bowel control is a relativeiy slow, often laborious process, entailing much labor on

the parent's part and frequently a good deal of emotional complication as far as the child is concerned. Control of elimination requires the ability to inhibit processes that are completely involuntary at the start and it involves the control of muscle groups that are obscure and unseen. As in other aspects of the child's development, it is important to scale the child's training to his growth. At the start, the child lacks the nervous mechanism for voluntary control and would be unable to control his elimination even if, by some freak of nature, he had a desire to do so.[6]

After expanding on this thought for a few paragraphs, Jersild says, "For a considerable time, the infant's 'bladder control' is largely a control exercised by the vigilant parent who anticipates voidance of the bladder before it occurs."[7]

The author does not say whether or not he encourages this type of training. He does give examples of experiments of children who received "training" in voidance at an early age and those who did not. The results for each child were about the same. The "trained" child did not have much more control than the one who was not "trained." He concludes with:

Definitive statements as to when the child may be expected to assume full responsibility in these matters cannot be made because of individual differences in children and because of differences in the circumstances in which the training occurs. In an investigation by Scoe it was found that most of the children who were studied had established control by the time they reached their second birthday, but that many children who turn out to be fine citizens do not achieve control as a regular habit until the age of three or even four or five.[8]

Do we agree with what this author says? We are realistic parents, and we know that our baby's nervous system must develop for many years before reaching maturity and full capacity for use. We also know that toilet training a child takes work. Surely, too, bladder control is a matter of vigilance for a parent. Why not? And we love our infant. We will not do anything rash or precipitate that will endanger our child or frustrate us as parents.

However, in my observations of many parents, I find that we always tend to underestimate our baby, that our tendency (influenced by the textbooks and articles we read) is to start training, in all areas, too late rather than too soon. When finally we do work at his toilet training, often it is the wrong kind of work; it may be sporadic, harsh at one time and lax the next, or it may be a crash plan, bewildering to the child and unsuccessful to us. The wise Preacher has said that there is a time for everything. Let us see if we can find that time in this area of his training.

With my own children and several others who were placed temporarily in my care, I have found an early, happy, successful method. Using Timmy as an example, let us follow this method from start to finish. All that we as parents will need are the following tools: a dedication to work hard and consistently—*consistently*—to achieve our goal; an attitude of calm cheerfulness and encouragement in successes and failures; and a relaxed atmosphere, free from tensions, but not free from firm guidance.

Timmy is three and a half months old and is beginning to enjoy sitting up for short periods of time. As observant mothers, we have been watching the pattern of Timmy's life. He has been setting for himself a more regular time for a bowel movement. Is it just before bedtime? Immediately before his morning bath? If his usual habit is in the morning, we tie him, with something soft or woolly, onto his training seat and give him a large cuddly toy. If he panics or cries, we take him off and go on with the bath. Next morning, with soft voice and firm grasp, we try again. If he cries, we may want to wait a week. By the time he is four months, if we try again when we know he is ready for his bowel movement, and stay with him with caresses and encouraging tones, we will quite likely have success. We may praise him quietly as if that is, after all, what we expected, even though we doubt that he knows as yet what this strange procedure is all about. The next day the routine should be easier. We will always stay with him, giving him his toy and security and encouragement; and if we are not inhibited parents, motivation by a grunt or two.

Not always will we succeed. Timmy may not feel so well,

be off schedule, or be plain contrary. If he has no success after five minutes, or ten at the most, or if he fidgets, we take him off with the same cheerfulness that says that life is not all successes. Before many weeks pass, Timmy, being an average baby, will alert us by a spontaneous wide-eyed grunt when he feels the pressure of a bowel movement. Usually he waits until he is comfortably seated. He is also exercising muscular control. From now on Timmy will alert us at bath time, but also at other times of the day. His record at this age will be far from perfect, but by now we can easily say, "Whoops, an accident!" in the same voice as we say, "Dandy boy!" Why then does Timmy alert us and have mostly successes? Is he trying to please us, his parents? That may be part of the answer, for an obedient child does want to please his parents. But he is quite young for highly conscious obedience. Psychologists would say that he is "conditioned" by association to respond with his bowel habits in this way. I do not like that word "conditioned," for it has no place in Biblical thought. I prefer the Biblical term "training," for training implies so much more than a cold, mechanical conditioning. Training, Christian training, implies love and tender care as long as the path in which our son should go. At this point, *we* are the ones who set the atmosphere and the pace in his training, and he responds *because* we not only work diligently, but because we are going about in the proper systematic, relaxed way.

Back to Timmy's toilet training. Between the ages of six and nine months, depending on the nature of the child, we will want to begin training for bladder control. An alert baby, precocious according to normal standards, who gives promise of being a quick learner, may be ready at half a year for training in which "the vigilant parent anticipates voidance of the bladder before it occurs." Other babies, slow, sluggish, frail, and probably ornery and contrary by nature, will wait until nine or ten months.

Since Timmy falls in neither category, but somewhere between, we will begin his training between seven and eight months. Before we start this area of his training, we will remind ourselves that not only the duty we have to perform, but *how* we perform that duty is of prime importance for our son's future well-being. If we approach his training with distaste and view it as a disagreeable chore, we will not succeed. We may be inclined to ask the question here, "Is it worth it?" Is the diligence, vigilance, consistence, and self-denial worth the goal we have set—in this case, the complete toilet training of our son? If we are Christian parents not only in name, but spiritually devout as well, we will sense that we asked the wrong question. The question is parent- (or self-) centered. We are merely counting the cost to ourselves. If we truly love our son with the love which God has put in our hearts, we will not look at the magnitude of the task nor the hardship for us, but rather at the *worth* of the goal for our son. Strictly speaking, that is the only way we may look at it, because it is our calling before God. We will be prepared for hard work, with cheerful enthusiasm, in a spirit of patient selflessness, all for Timmy. This outlook will soon become a part of us, a way of life, a life that will never be a life of ease, but will take less conscious efforts as this approach to our child becomes part of our whole being.

First, then, we must get Timmy to *want* to work with us. But he does not even know what we want him to do, and he is too young to understand a verbal explanation. So we begin training him with our hands and our heart. If he is still dry about an hour after diapering him some afternoon, we will put him on his training seat, give him a drink of water, and probably run the water in the tap. If he urinates, we will hug and encourage him. If he does not, we take him off and still hug and encourage him. After another sixty or ninety minutes, if his diaper is still dry, we repeat the performance. We do not let him sit—not more than five minutes—and never alone. During Timmy's waking daytime hours this is not hard to do, and Timmy will learn to expect the routine. After several days, by his excited actions, flailing of arms and legs when he has urinated, *we* will know that he knows why *he* has been put on his training seat.

Often at this age a baby sleeps dry through his daytime naps, but soaks himself as he lies cooing and playing after he awakes. That will be the next phase of our training. As mothers, we always hear the first quiet "uh" that tells us Timmy is awake.

It might be easier for us to let him lie and coo for fifteen minutes and finish the chore with which we are busy; but if we truly want to train him, we will pick him up and have instant success this time! But, someone may protest, Timmy may want that fifteen minutes of quiet cooing and talking to his crib pets. Well, then, put him back. If he is content, we can still finish our chore while he plays. And we have taught Timmy something.

By this time some weeks have passed. No part of the training so far has been unpleasant for either Timmy or us. We have had our good and bad days, but we did not give up, nor lose our cheerful good humor. Timmy is being trained to the feeling of a dry diaper and by now he can hardly tolerate the feeling of a cold, wet one. And, contrary to what many psychologists say, Timmy can give a moment's notice and wait until he has been put on his training seat. For that is what he is doing now: giving a little urgent "uh" and at the same time reaching for his cuddly "bathroom toy."

Through these weeks—or months—we have trained Timmy to want to be dry, to know what feeling to associate with the training seat, and to tell us when he has that feeling. Although we do not have the failures we had at first, we still have them along with our successes. Timmy is too absorbed in his play, or mother is busy with a telephone conversation, and we don't make it in time. But for the most part, after about three months' effort, Timmy is dry during the day, and our laundry loads have appreciably decreased. He does not do what many children who are trained at a much later age do—secret themselves in a corner instead of telling their parents to hurry them to the bathroom. He was trained too early to try this, and by the time he is old enough to think of that trick, his habits and training are too firmly formed for him to consider it.

Timmy will be close to a year at this stage of his training and beginning to walk and wear training pants instead of diapers during the day. (Some children may be a little older before they reach this stage; we cannot lay down set patterns to fit the complexities of our children's natures.) Now it is time to think about nighttime training. The earlier it is started, the easier it is for our child and for us. A younger child has a greater resiliency and adaptability than he does when he grows older. If we somewhat limit Timmy's liquid intake before bedtime at night and pick him up when we go to bed, he will, quite likely (but not always, of course) be dry. Isn't a year quite young to pick a slumbering baby from his nice warm crib? Doesn't he resist and rebel? I have found that he does not mind it at all. He knows by now why he is being put on his training seat, and he usually gives a sleepy-eyed grin. I think he enjoys the middle-of-the-night whispers and hugs and kisses, with both father and mother hovering comfortably over him; he likes being tucked in, dry and warm, a second time for the night. In the morning, of course, we must discipline ourselves to forego the extra winks for the sake of training our son as we hear he is awake, or snatch those winks after the bathroom routine.

On most days from now on Timmy will be dry for all of the twenty-four hours. There have been no scoldings, no scenes, little stubbornness; there have been effort, consistency, and the rewards of success that are taken happily for granted by both parents and child.

I have found that there is less backsliding in a baby who was trained early. That training is as habitual and instinctive as blinking an eye. Mothers reap the reward of being able to take younger children on outings and trips with much less work and much more confidence. Even from the point of view of work, the laundry and bed-changing load has now dwindled considerably.

I would like to end this discussion with a true story of a child who responded especially well to toilet training. At ten and a half months she wore training pants during the day and her mother had stopped worrying about accidents. The baby always gave an urgent little "uh." During a trip of about three and a half hours at that time, her mother diapered her and decided to forego a restroom stop for her until they reached their destination. About halfway the family stopped at a gas station and father announced a bathroom stop for the older children in the family. The baby girl became excited, begged to get out, and finally cried. "I can't take a *baby* into a restroom here," the mother protested. But father was already getting the training seat from the trunk. "She's telling you she needs a bathroom. If you have done your training so well up till now, we won't let her down on a trip," he said. Mother and babe came out shortly, beaming and successful.

Try the method, parents.

Before we move on to Timmy's further training, we will want to evaluate the results of our training so far. Remember that he is a unique individual with the character strengths and weaknesses that the Lord has given him. We know that both the strengths and weaknesses *can* be used in the service of sin, and often are. It has been our duty, in the first nine months of his life, to show him a sanctified method of training. We have taught him, by our example, reverence, order, dedication, love, cheerfulness, consistency, and a host of other virtues which covenant parents, by the grace of God, possess. We have taught him, by word and action, the beginnings of the meaning of obedience. We have not feared to say "no," the quiet, firm "no" with enforcement behind it, without any exceptions. We have given him encouragement that covenant children need when they do the right. And I think we have begun to give him the knowledge of things spiritual. Although we can never truly know how much he grasps at this age, I repeat that we usually give him too little credit. Our Father is his Father, too. He has regenerated our son, and put His Spirit into his little heart. We believe that the Spirit works, don't we, also in the heart of a young child? Let us teach him early what prayer is, who God is, and how we listen to His Word. Above all, let us surround him with the songs of Zion. Sing while we are working, and he will sing along in his heart. Let us take a lesson from Moses' mother. Why did she instruct Miriam to suggest to Pharaoh's daughter that the child's own mother be a wet-nurse for Moses? Because she craved the physical care of her son? Any mother would. But, far more, she wanted him, from early infancy, under her covenantal care and spiritual guidance, from early babyhood until she had to relinquish him to the palace. She knew how important the training of his babyhood years was. From Hebrews 11 we know that she saw he was a "proper child," and we can be sure that she used all her time to instruct that child. Have we done the same for our covenant child?

There have been many rewards for *us,* too, in these nine months of his life. From a formal viewpoint, we have the ease and order in our household resulting from a systematic handling of our baby and his problems. Often we have a calm, relaxed child—not necessarily, though. There are the exceptions, the children with physical malfunctions, or those more gloomy, cantankerous, or self-willed than the average child. These children take more time, more patience, and more prayer. For ourselves, we have seen a growth in personal discipline. Our selfish little wishes, our petty wants have disappeared before our richer goal of training covenant seed. The awareness of our sins and those of our child, of our complete incapability of being a devout Christian parent without God's ever-present grace, becomes a more stark reality in our lives. We fight harder, for our sakes and for his, to leave our sinful impulses and do the right. Possibly the greatest awareness is that of the great responsibility we now have, and will have for years to come. In the text quoted at the head of this chapter, Solomon says, "To everything there is a season, and a time to every purpose under the sun." This is our time of responsibility before God.

NOTES

1. Curti, op. cit., p. 62.
2. A. T. Jersild, *Child Psychology* (New York: Prentice-Hall, Inc., 1948), pp. 25-27.
3. Ibid., pp. 27-33.
4. Gera Kraan - Van den Burg, *Moeder, Zeg Me Eens* (Kampen: J. H. Kok, 1952), translated from the Dutch, p. 15.
5. Jersild, op. cit., pp. 66-72.
6. Op. cit. p. 88.
7. Ibid., p. 89.
8. Ibid., p. 91.

6

THE CHILD FROM NINE MONTHS TO TWO YEARS

But Jesus said, Suffer little children, and forbid them not, to come unto me: for of such is the kingdom of heaven.
—Matthew 19:14

IN OUR DISCUSSION OF THE CHILD FROM BIRTH TO NINE months we have seen many signs of his physical development. His larger muscles have begun to coordinate so that he can reach for and grasp his toys. He has made attempts to feed himself and to get up by himself—his first steps toward independence. He has begun to understand what it means to obey, and is responding to training in all the areas of his life. From the age of nine to twenty-four months Timmy will begin to walk alone (at about a year), say individual words, phrases, and even a few sentences, start to eat by himself, and help us with the dressing process.

This period is the beginning of the outward signs of his emergence as a distinctive individual, distinct in his personality from you and me, distinct in his actions and reactions from anyone else. In many areas of his life, Timmy is still a passive baby: *we* make the decisions for him about his food, clothes, and schedules; *we* make the rules for his conduct; *we* guide and he follows. At this age Timmy is still self-centered, selfish, and often unresponsive. Engle gives an interesting word picture of the child of Timmy's age: he "seems to be concerned primarily with his own body comfort. He wants food, toys, and attention regardless of the inconvenience caused others. He is likely to be rather uncooperative. His greatest need is for security, and he learns to recognize those who provide security for him. As he experiences many acts of kindness and receives more and more love from his parents and others in the family, he learns to love them more and more. . . . He develops a desire to give of himself to others rather than always take from others."[1]

Having lived with Timmy for nine months, we agree from experience with much of what Engle says. When our baby was hungry, he wanted food immediately. If it was not there, he demanded it with crying or screaming, whether it was convenient for us or not to give him food at that minute. If we were tired or ill but he wanted to be amused, he had no thoughts of kindness or sympathy for our feelings. He was very often uncooperative while being dressed, fighting our efforts when we put on his warm coat and cap. But so far we have not minded his selfish interests. We know that it is in the nature of the small baby to be concerned only with his own well-being and to expect us to supply his demands. During the next period of Timmy's life, this self-centeredness will gradually begin to change, even as Engle says that it will. Timmy will begin to learn to show love to others, to be kind and considerate, to give. He will not learn love merely because he receives love from us as Engle suggests. He will not learn love, love for God's sake, if we do not teach him. This process of teaching him the love of God and the love of the neighbor will only *begin* in the next fifteen months. But we will not wait! We will start!

From this passive, self-centered baby we will begin to see a more active, even aggressive child begin to assert himself. In the descriptions of our child and the suggestions for his training in this chapter we will remember that in all his character traits, his likes and dislikes, his moods and his questions, we are not merely dealing with a boy of character: we are training a boy whose character reflects sin and grace. Sin will appeal to his corrupt nature, just as it does to ours. Let us not, as parents, treat sin with sin, anger with anger, rebellion with beatings. Let us not ignore his wicked nature, either, or postpone chastisement "until he is older." Let us show him the love of God shining through our training: love that often takes a firm hand to chasten the wrongdoer, love that cheerfully shows and encourages the right. If he has the grace of God in his heart, he will respond with repentance.

Timmy's likes and dislikes are starting to show. Even in his play, he lets us know what he likes: riding fast through the house in his taylor-tot rather than sitting still and building a house with blocks, banging fiercely on the bottoms of old pans rather than hugging a cuddly toy. He has strong likes and dislikes for food, for certain clothes, for people. In the area of *deeds,* however, his wilful nature comes out the most. Especially trying for parents can be the six-month period from nine to fifteen months. Our child can obey "yes" and "no," but he is not old enough for us to sit down and explain and reason with him, to tell him *why* we say no, or *why* we insist. Our word of authority at this age must be enough for him. We know from experience that often it is not. Our "no" evokes a stamped foot and a defiant "yes." Though we know it is hard for him to obey what he cannot understand, we also realize it is sinful rebellion not to obey; and as covenant parents we will have to begin to use the rod to teach him the response of the covenant child.

Dr. Wurth explains our authority over our child in this way:

> We should also discuss the weighty authority problem that is so important for the life of the family. Though the authority crisis today in itself is regrettable, it is a happy consequence in our modern social life that people are more and more deeply impressed with the necessity of the questions which have to do with authority. . . .
>
> The word "authority" (*gezag*) is derived from the verb "to say" (*zeggen*). Someone has authority (*gezag*) who possesses "say-so" (*zeggenschap*) over another, who with a view to his fellow men has "something to say."
>
> Here we see afresh the significance of "the word." The word is not merely an empty sound. The word does something. It exercises power. From it goes influence, influence

which is greater according as the person who stands behind it is greater, more influential.

But not only does it exercise power; it is also the bearer of authority. Authority is after all something more than might. Authority is something to which conscious, voluntary subjection is owed. Reverence (*ontzag*) corresponds to authority (*gezag*), the readiness to listen, to obey, to let yourself be told.

This also holds for the parents over against their children. They are bearers of authority to those children. They have "say-so" over them; and their children are to be "able to be told," obedient.

A further distinction is still necessary. One can have authority over another in a two-fold sense. His authority can rest either upon his qualities or his position.

We human beings are in various respects distinct from each other. One is greater and the other is smaller; one is stronger and the other is weaker; one has more intelligence or moral capacities and the other has less. And the result is that one man in life has more authority than the other.

Nevertheless, that is not the real authority, at least not the authority which is emphatically intended by God in the fifth commandment. There the authority rests not upon certain qualities which people as parents possess and by which they are greater than their children. The authority rests upon the particular position in which one is placed by God; one could also say, upon the particular office with which one is clothed by God as parent in the family.

Although we may differ in various respects, also with respect to our gifts and abilities and qualities, we are not to be distinguished from one another in rank. Not a single man has of himself the right to place himself above one of his fellow men, whoever he may be, to command him and impose his will upon him. According to the Bible, only One possesses authority in that real sense of the word; that is, the right, the power to command and to require obedience of another, namely God. His Word alone is, in that absolute sense, law. Only when He speaks must all that lives, men, high or low—that makes no difference—listen and bow and allow themselves to be told.

But now it has pleased Him in His majesty to delegate something of His divine authority to us, to clothe us in definite positions with authority. That is, therefore, no original authority, but a derived one; no authority that rests in ourselves, but one which we derive from Him, a bestowed authority, an authority only by His grace.[2]

No, our little one will not understand all this. He only knows by now that he must obey our "say-so," but he cannot begin to know why *he* must listen to *us*. Even *we* must be reminded continually of the true meaning of authority and the depths of its spiritual implications for our lives as parents. We do well to heed Dr. Wurth's explanation of that authority. However, we may take exception to the last phrase of this quotation from Dr. Wurth. God's authority is not delegated to men only by grace; then the ungodly could never be in authority. However, we know that God gives it to whom He will on this earth, even though they do not properly use it. Think of Pharaoh, Cyrus, Caesar. . . .

Aside from that, I think we can accept the author's statements as being Scripture's presentation of the nature of authority, and use this approach during some of the most difficult childhood days of our son.

These months of Timmy's life are marked by his strong curiosity. He is curious to see, taste, feel, and know the unknown, but above all, to *taste*. He knows so little about his vast surroundings and, to make matters worse, he is far too small to see most of it. No wonder he pulls himself up by a table leg and tries to reach some of the hidden mysteries on top. He is ready to grasp anything in his reach, oblivious to dangers of being burned, cut, or poisoned; more serious, if he can handle it, he is impelled to give it the taste test.

As yet, we cannot tell him about the dangers involved in pulling a corner of the tablecloth when a hot meal is on the table, of playing with electric outlets, of sampling the bleach in the cupboard under the sink, of climbing onto a chair, then the table or stove. All that we can do is make Timmy's surroundings as safe as possible, watch him, and teach him constantly what is forbidden.

Never can he be left in a room, free to roam, without watching—not for five minutes. If we must leave him alone, we will put him in a place free from potential danger. He may sputter and cry when mother puts him into his playpen or high chair when a small household emergency arises, but it is better than risking an accident, is it not? So much of our care of Timmy lies in the area of prevention. We are watchful and we plan ahead so that his insatiable curiosity will not get him (and us) hurt. Watching him diligently and teaching him all the while during his waking hours is not so easy. The rewards will be a growing awareness on the part of Timmy that many things are "off limits" for him. In our watchfulness we will not only keep him from danger; we will educate him. He is old enough now to understand "ouch" and "hot" and "it will make you sick!"

Perhaps, before we go on, we should qualify that watchfulness: it will be an unobtrusive alertness rather than a harried, nervous fluttering over him. Remember, we are working hard to create a relaxed atmosphere, so that our baby will respond calmly to our calm words. We don't want to be jittery parents hovering over a jumpy child.

Timmy's curiosity will not always end in danger. Sometimes it only gets him into trouble. He just *must* know what happens when he gives a quick tug on the wastepaper basket so that it tips over; the leaves dangling in front of the planter are the greatest things to pull, before the planter comes crashing down; climbing higher and to more challenging places is exciting, until it ends in a tumble. What about this curiosity? Must it not be satisfied? There are those who answer that the child cannot learn to satisfy his curiosity except by discovering for himself. He does not know. He wants to know. He gets busy to find out. In a certain sense this is true, if we add that his curiosity must be satisfied *in the right way*. But our philosophy is not child-centered in the sense that he must discover his world by himself, but instead that he must learn it by being taught. We will not let Timmy pull over the wastebasket. He can learn now not to make a mess even though he enjoys satisfying his curiosity this way. The art of climbing is fine, in its time and place. When Timmy is older and has mastered the jungle gym, he may climb. But neither Timmy at twelve months nor our furniture and appliances are suited to climbing. Besides, a climbing child, left undiscouraged or discouraged too little, will go to new heights of trouble and danger.

How then shall we handle our curious Timmy? First, and I have found repeated success with this method, we take the time, in the proper way, to satisfy all his curiosities. Lift him often. As we mothers set the table, pick him up and say, "See, Timmy?" Tell him the names of the articles on the table. Let him play with something we have put there, if possible. We will show him the planter; with his hands in ours, we will guide him to touch it and examine it, and then add, in expressive, quiet tones, "It is pretty, but we don't *play* with it." He understands. If we daily anticipate his curiosity and look for his signs of wanting to know, much of his curiosity will already be satisfied. We know, however, that curiosity in Timmy is not an isolated facet in his learning process. Because he is a sinner by nature, he will often use his curiosity in the service of sin. Then we will use our God-given authority, not to divert his attention but to tell him "no." If he listens, well; if not, he needs the kind of stinger we described in the last chapter. By the time he is about one year, Timmy knows and watches for our facial expressions, which reflect our feelings. If we accompany our stinger with a solemn, "That's too bad, Timmy. That was wrong to do," instead of a sharp, "Hey, cut that out!" we will impress Timmy much more. Do we not see that this is the way to teach him the difference between a right and a wrong sense of curiosity?

Soon he will stand near forbidden areas murmuring, "no, no," to himself. If he obeys and leaves the forbidden alone, we encourage and praise him. He needs it. If he disobeys, we let him feel physical pain—in love. He needs that, too.

With some variations, according to the personality and intellectual acumen of our child, he will assert a degree of independence during this age period from nine months to two years. In other words, he is showing that he wants to learn to know and do things for himself. His will to be independent is the direct result of our teaching. He is learning. Learning has been variously defined as a "change of behavior resulting from experience," or "the activity of a person as he focuses his attention upon an object for understanding and acceptance of it in its true nature."[3] Rather than use these behavioristic definitions we might use as a working definition, "the receiving of and the training in knowledge in the fear of the Lord, so that the man of God may be perfect, thoroughly furnished unto all good works." This definition leads us, of course, to our final goal for Timmy. The small, seemingly insignificant details of the dispensing and receiving of knowledge all have their individual places in the whole of the training in the fear of the Lord.

It is not necessary, I believe, to discuss the kinds of learning involved in our tiny child's life. It would lead into too faraway technical fields. Let it suffice in this non-technical discussion of Timmy, to say that his curiosity and exploration lead him into doing things for himself. Before he is fifteen months old he will grasp the shoe that we are ready to put on his foot and with a gleam of defiance, shout, "No!" or if he is a very early talker, "Timmy do it!" Backwards and upside-down, with perspiration and exasperation, he will try to put on his own shoe. He does not easily give up. He wants to succeed. He wants to begin to be independent.

Gradually he will want to assert his independence in other areas. How will we treat this newly emerging trait? Timmy may want to try too many things too soon, or he may be sluggish and need encouragement to strike out on his own. It is up to us, as the guides for his life, to use moderation here, too. Timmy does not yet know what is good for him. "Foolishness is bound in the heart of the child," Proverbs 22:15. If we are serious, devoted covenant parents, we *do* know what is good for Timmy.

Timmy knows, for example, that an implement called a spoon may be used to shovel an amount of pudding from a dish, brought to the mouth, and, if the mouth is opened at the right moment, just the proper mouthful of pudding will be inserted. It tastes good, and he swallows it. Such a smooth operation, with father or mother wielding the spoon, cannot go unchallenged. Timmy must see if he can do it for himself: his spoonfuls will be bigger, sloppier, and in far more rapid sequence than those of his parents. Is this good? Parents often say, "He insists on doing it himself, but he makes such a mess of himself and his surroundings. What should I do?"

I would answer that if Timmy is making a big mess, unintentionally or intentionally, he is not ready to do it alone. He needs more guidance. The two extremes of options are, obviously, to let him strictly alone and clean up a mess, or not to let him feed himself at all. I believe that the position of wise parents lies somewhere in the middle. (This is a good rule, not only for his eating habits, but for most of his training.) If we feed him continually, how will his little hands learn to manipulate a spoon? If he does it his trial and error way or his wilful way, how will he learn the correct way? With Timmy, we will err on the side of guidance, and fill the spoon for him, and let him bring spoonfuls to his mouth. If the pudding spills, our "oops" will draw his attention to it, and we can guide him to pick it up. Does he get impatient about it? Let us not be impatient with him. He will learn to be patient by our matter-of-fact serenity in insisting on neat eating habits. And he knows when he makes a mess. Draw his attention to it, and talk to him, train him every day in the proper methods. Again, it is easier to leave him to himself, to let him poke his fingers into his food, smear his face and hair with the bowl or contents, or both. But is it proper training?

If his eating coincides with our family meal, and by this age it normally should, Timmy will finish his food before we finish ours. Then we will hear him use another word in his new-found vocabulary: "Out!" Shall we think, "He is too little to sit any longer. We cannot forcefully restrain him and keep peace"? Or shall we think, "He *will* stay there until we've finished"? Or shall we think neither? We know that he should stay in his high chair and listen, or at least be quiet during family devotions. But if he cries and we shout, we are not training him. Sometimes a cracker or a toy, accompanied by a "Not yet, Timmy" helps him to be quiet. But if Timmy is visibly impatient, or if he cries, we gain nothing for Timmy nor ourselves. Perhaps at this time he will be happy to sit on a parent's lap during devotions. If we are not yet finished with our last cup of coffee, we may let him stretch his restless legs by walking around the table. At devotions time shall we let him play—in the kitchen or in another room? Are we being consistent? If we have been diligent Christian parents, Timmy will expect us to take him onto a lap and to tell him to "sit still now." Even though he expects it, he will not always do what *we* expect of him. We expect it nonetheless. We will tell him quietly, "You must sit still." If scoldings and frowns don't help, a stinger may. But we will insist that he learn to sit quietly for these few moments.

Being a rather restless child, Timmy may use this occasion to build himself up to another mealtime scene of rebellion. It is natural for us to respond by building up tension; and the result *could* be a traumatic battle of wills. To avoid this, we can talk to Timmy—very simply—during the day; we will tell him with a solemn face that we are *always* quiet when daddy reads the Bible, that Timmy must be good at the table, etc. . . . This preparation shows Timmy that we have not forgotten, that we have not lowered our standards because of his misdeeds. If he does not understand our words, he will understand our manner. But again, do not underestimate!

This preparation may prevent Timmy's rebellion the next time. Or it may not. He may still resist and rebel. If he does, we will be careful how we view his resistance. We are surrounded with so much so-called psychology today, that in spite of ourselves, we may assimilate some of its philosophies. For example, Jersild says:

Actually, much of a child's resistance is a feature of his effort to achieve self-help and independence and is only incidentally a form of oposition to others. . . . In the young child, resistance frequently takes the form of failure to comply with apparently understood requests, of apparent stubbornness in matters of eating and the daily routine, and of countless little acts of self-assertion. . . . The fact that children show resistance is, of course, not remarkable when one considers how much they are pushed around, even by parents who are patient and wise. The parents themselves are subject to many rules and restraints which they take for

granted. The culture into which the child is being reared is full of countless regulations. . . .
Older children . . . were less resistant than younger, although there were many exceptions to the rule. The decline in resistance with age takes place partly because the older child understands better what is expected of him, is better able to comply, and has learned that he will be more comfortable if he complies with the wishes of others, and also because he has learned to express himself better by means of words and has acquired other more subtle means of asserting his independence. A decline in resistance may also be due to the fact that a child's elders have been learning how to handle issues that are likely to provoke resistance.[4]

I doubt that the author refers, in "learning how to handle issues" to the rod of correction in Proverbs 22:15. How different in tone and method from our covenantal outlook. How foreign to our concept of sin and grace! For, going back to Timmy now, we know that his resistance is sinful. In firmness and love, we will teach him repeatedly—as often as necessary—until he is obedient.

Admittedly, this was a long discussion about Timmy at mealtime; however, these principles will carry through in all the facets of his life, the details differing with the circumstances. In his bathing and dressing time, his playtime, in his likes and dislikes, if we cannot quite judge the wise way to handle a situation, the safe rule is to use the firm rather than the lax method. Firm, remember—not harsh. Firm . . . and kindly. Firm . . . and insistent.

The rest of this chapter we will devote to some practical suggestions, both negative and positive, in caring for and occupying the time of our nine- to twenty-four-month-old son. It is one of the more difficult periods of time to plan, for he is at a restless age, an age in which he is active but often aimless, an age in which he has not yet developed the power of concentration.

* * *

We love our child dearly. We want him to be happy. And *we*

want to be happy. If we are busy with him during all of his waking moments, in the sense that we are "on top of" each other, both of us will chafe and become irritated merely by the fact that we cannot get away from each other. Each in his own way needs a period of solitude and peace.

So, at the age of nine months, or before, we will teach Timmy how to play. Any parent who has lived through these months with his child will know that the cardinal rule is to keep his periods of play in one area very short. He constantly has need of something different to see and handle, somewhere else to be. I have found that he will stay in an enclosed place (playpen, barricade of furniture, etc.) if he has only a few toys which are exchanged often for a few different ones. Watch a child of about a year, surrounded by a dozen or more toys. Because as yet he cannot concentrate on a definite purpose, he sees a maze of toys, and is unable to fix his attention on just one of his choice. He is like us—we cannot choose when we have too many choices. Watch him wade through them all, disregarding the whole lot, and probably throw up his arms in frustration.

Instead we pick up two or three of the larger toys. We present him with one of them and put the other two nearby. If nothing else is bothering him, he will accept the one toy, and play with it briefly. What does he like? Certain toys he will always want within sight of reach, usually the "security" kind: the furry pink lamb, the yellow rabbit with only one ear, or the rag doll with only half its stuffing. But after the initial pleasure has worn off, he will impatiently reject many of his other toys. We will put them away awhile so he can forget them, and substitute . . . what? Newspapers? If Timmy can be trusted—for the most part, with a minimum of supervision—to skip the taste test, he will enjoy ripping and scattering old newspapers. If we as parents can tolerate a temporary mess and later pick up the pieces, Timmy will have a great time. Tearing newspapers, rolling pieces into balls, and wading through the disorder is good for his large muscles. While he is amusing himself, he is learning some large muscle control.

Although he is often content to play with his own toys, Timmy is intrigued with the objects of the adult world, especially the adult world of pots and pans. He will find or make the opportunity to investigate the cupboard and relieve it of its contents. Someone will surely ask, "Why shouldn't he?" We could counter, "Why should he? Apart from the element of danger to Timmy, we risk damage to our utensils and confusion to our kitchen. Besides," we will argue, "Timmy is never too young to learn that he has his sphere and we have ours. His boundaries as yet are very limited, and he will have to learn to stay within them. All our life we meet limits, boundaries, and barriers, and are forbidden to encroach on the spheres of others. Timmy must learn this reality, too."

But Timmy does not know all about these restrictions. And we will not offer our baby a swift ultimatum and rush him out of the kitchen. No, that is not our way with Timmy. Besides, pots and pans *do* make good toys. Why not give Timmy an old one, or buy an inexpensive one? With a large tin spoon for banging, he has a drum.

For my own children, the best and most inexpensive toy I ever bought was a small coffee pot, percolator style. They spent hours taking it apart, putting it together, filling it with blocks or other toys, and when they were a little older, with sand from the sandbox and water from the wading pool.

If Timmy has his own coffee pot, pan, spoon, and a plastic cup or two, he will soon be trying to store them in one of mother's cupboards. Self-assertive Timmy will be insisting on it. Why not, so long as he obeys us and leaves mother's pots and pans alone?

Timmy is happier when we *anticipate* his boredom. Before he whimpers, and long before he howls in frustration, we know by observation that he is ready for a change. If we let him cry for a while in unhappiness (even though *we* can see no reason for his unhappiness), then pick him up, with a bit too much impatience showing, put him in his high chair and give him a cracker, he will promptly shove it off. We will be tempted to slap his hand and say, "Naughty!" when we truly *should* say it to ourselves. If, instead, we do not allow unhappiness to arise —and that is often, if not usually, possible—we have no hurts to heal.

Before he is finished enjoying his coffee pot, we will prepare a little snack for him. Plain old crackers are just as tiring for him as they are for us. How about a party instead? Tiny tots enjoy parties as much as we do. Timmy's party, made in his favorite blue plastic cup, will be raisins, Cheerios, pretzels, probably with a surprise on top. Each time the surprise is different: a candy corn, chocolate chip, miniature marshmallow, etc. Now watch Timmy's smaller muscles work. After he eats the surprise first—always—watch him dump the party on the high chair tray and separate the Cheerios from the raisins, and then carefully pick them up, one by one. And he won't have to be very much older to know that Cheerios can be strung on pretzels and eaten off one at a time.

We will keep his snacks small, so that he learns to eat regular meals at mealtimes. What, then, if he clamors for more party? Our answer is a calm, "No more now." Timmy insists. "No, Timmy. That's the way it is. No more." Perhaps the finality of our tone will convey more than our words. Timmy knows from previous experience with our consistent handling of him that we will not relent. But we do not want to have Timmy begging and crying for more every time we give him a snack. We must teach him one more thing—not to ask for more. He may have to be told several times at first, with finality and even sharpness; but he must learn to obey also these bounds which we set for him. Soon he will be asking, "That's all?" and we will be saying, "That's all." And then he won't ask at all.

In our lives as adults we want a basic routine and a basic order. Our God is a God of order. Night follows day, summer follows spring, the fruit follows the bud. We as creatures have a basic increated order: work and rest, wake and sleep, six days of work and one of rest. But our God did not create us mechanical robots subject to unchanging routine. We enjoy variety, anticipation, surprise. These truths apply to our child as well. He needs a basic routine to find his stride, his pace in life. But neither he nor we are servants to that routine. Keeping it basically stable, we will vary it with the unexpected: new things to do, new places to go, new foods to eat—or just a nice surprise!

This kind of life with Timmy does not just happen by itself. In the evening, after Timmy has been put to bed, we will try to prepare for the life of a new day tomorrow. Though we know that we view the unknown future of tomorrows only by faith, we also know that the Lord has made us responsible stewards of all that He gave us; and as faithful stewards we will plan ahead in the fear of the Lord. Our child will notice our diligence combined with our cheerfulness without our ever telling him about it. He will sense it as an attitude of love and an atmosphere of Christian contentment in a home where God's love prevails.

* * *

So far in this chapter we have pictured only a few hypothetical situations which will arise in our lives while Timmy is under two years old, and we have already suggested that most of the guidelines we used would fit other concrete incidents in his life. Before we take Timmy farther, we want to summarize the "do's and don't's" for covenant parents, and possibly add a few more that we have not mentioned. Some we have examined so closely that we need only to list them. Others we may want to discuss in more detail.

First, then, the "don't's."

To teach and train our son in the fear of the Lord, we will never, in our thoughts or in our actions, set ourselves up as boss for the sake of being boss, for the sake of the feeling of power it gives us. Nor will we ever put ourselves and our authority over against his necessary submission as one camp of the enemy over against the other camp. With that philosophy, life becomes a series of strategics, if not a battlefield, and the best man wins. No, but we will let God's Word teach us and we will teach our child that his obedience and our authority are both for God's sake, that each in his sphere is working towards the same goal.

Not even before our own consciousness, much less in communication with our child, will we equate firmness with meanness, or firmness with crossness. If we say, "I'll really be angry if you dare to touch it," or, worse yet, "You don't want me to be mean to you, do you? Then do as I say," we are speaking the language of human philosophy, and bad human philosophy at that. Do we truly want Timmy to obey so that *we* won't be angry about it? And imagine Timmy growing up believing that discipline and correction in God's fear are the same as our meanness.

When it is necessary that we give a decisive "no" to Timmy, we will give even that "no" as Christian parents. First, we will speak it, not shout it. If he knows that we mean it (and he should by now) and we know that we mean it (God gave us the authority) why should we shout it? Is a shouted "no" more effective than a soft-spoken one . . . with finality in its tone? If we do become "no" shouters, our child (he is *very* alert in these areas) will identify the loudest shouts with the most authority; and, being a sinner, he may shout back. If we always speak our "no's" quietly, our child will learn that these quiet "no's" are the verdict, the end of the matter.

He *knows* that is the end of the matter, but he is not always obedient to that quiet "no." He may cry. Or stamp. Or shout. We look at him and realize that he must obey so many "no's" which he cannot really understand, and we wonder if it is of great importance that we enforce this "no"—it was only a minor infraction. We look at him again, and realize that our "no" was a wise and good one, that in even minor matters he must be subject to us without question and without argument, and we know that he is being sinfully disobedient. We scold him, tell him to stop, and insist on his obedience.

Now that there has been unhappiness about this small infraction, Timmy, sinful Timmy, may soon try the same infraction. He knows we do not like a "scene" of his rebellion and our insistence, of his tears and our anguish. Timmy wants to know if we will risk more disobedience to our discipline, or if we will look the other way and ignore the disobedience this time. It would be easier for us to look the other way. But because we are devoted, consistent parents, he should know that we will not say "no" one time and "yes" the next, thereby undermining our consistent good discipline for the sake of peace, which really is no peace at all.

If our child is tired or out of sorts we may want to soften our "no" to him by drawing his attention from the forbidden to the permissible. Or we may soften the "no" by a little game of "That's no, that's yes, that's you, that's me." Sometimes it will be the part of wisdom and tact to draw away the attention, to change the subject, to be nonchalant about the "no-no." But not always, and not as a general rule. If we always soften our "no" by a gimmick or a laugh, our child will get the impression (and rightly so) that we are somehow ashamed of our "no," and apologetic. Usually we will make our "no's" short, simple, and final.

One more type of behavior for which we should be alert is whining when he is forbidden something but still wants it. Take, for example, snack time. Timmy may want another party on his high chair tray, but we say, "No more now." We have all seen Timmys point to the cupboard and whine and groan for more. Whining is not a pleasant sound to hear. To stop it, merely to stop the whining, we *could* get Timmy another party. But to stop it in the right way we insist on our "No more now," and we insist that he stop his whining. If he does not obey our reprimand, we will have to spank him—not banish him where he can whine in private. For we know that if we tolerate whining we tolerate disobedience. And *that* we are not allowed to do. Besides, whining, left unchecked, becomes a habit—a wrong one—on the part of the child; and the habit is harder to correct the longer the child has it. Therefore, we will not let him acquire it.

Now what are some of the positive summarizations for Timmy?

As much as we are able, we will be calm and matter-of-fact in the everyday happenings of life and in our relationship to Timmy. No one, I think, is on a placid, even keel all the time; no one is even outwardly calm all the time. But we can try to be; we can discipline ourselves to be. Our child will generally respond by being more calm and peaceful, too.

The second positive principle is probably one of the more important ones. We have heard it often. Psychologists stress it. Be consistent. We have already discovered that we are never harshly nor arbitrarily consistent; but our consistence follows our proper psychological and spiritual approach. We will train our child—and he will learn—to expect it. Not only is the consistent way easier for the parent, but it will make our child happier, and secure because he knows what to expect, and accepts it.

When his behavior is negative, or more correctly, when it is sinful, we can still chasten him positively. If, for example, he gets carried away with fun and violent splashing in the bathtub so that he is beginning to soak both parent and bathroom, we will tell him not to splash so hard. But Timmy, who likes to do things with vehemence, *wants* to splash wildly. When we take his arm and frown, he cries. We tell him, "That's enough. Stop crying and stop splashing." Timmy cries loudly. Quietly, without anger, we will spank him, or dry him and banish him to a safe place where he can sit alone. That is not all. Perhaps the most important part (the positive part) is to talk to him after he is calm. You doubt he will understand? Don't doubt it. He knew how to be naughty, didn't he? He understands when we talk quietly to him and tell him that such a thing may *never* happen again, that it was very naughty, etc. Most likely our calm, serious talk will impress him as much as our stinger on his bottom. Of course, we cannot enter into lengthy explanations and expect Timmy, under two, to know their meanings. We will keep it short and simple.

Timmy, our Timmy of ofttimes vehement nature, will not always calm down if we spank or banish him. He may, instead of being docile and obedient when we put him by himself, cry more loudly, scream, shout, stamp, pound, hold his breath—in other words, work himself into a tantrum. If we go to him, he will stop and probably say pitifully, "Tub!" Secretly, because the experience is new to us, we are afraid of this tantrum, afraid for his safety and afraid to have him hold his breath. This fear may at first be stronger than a far worse fear—that he is vehemently saying "no" to our authority and God's. Now we know that our child is not saying this articulately before his consciousness. He is not nearly understanding enough. But *we* know it, and if we do not train him in obedience to us and to God, he *will* soon be saying it.

What shall we do to this writhing child, flailing arms and legs in all directions? We will pick him up quickly and firmly, but not angrily. The suddenness of it, and that certain warning in our eyes may stop him. If, however, his tantrum rages unabated, we may take him, small as he is, to a rug in the bathroom, set him on it, and pour a glass of cold water over his head—two glasses, if necessary. He will gasp and quiet down, and sit there dripping while we both contemplate what has happened.

Then, after he is finished dripping, and is calm and ashamed, we can have our quiet talk with him. Does the treatment seem drastic for such a small child? Consider the alternative: more open rebellion (for that is what a tantrum is), increasing in frequency and force as our child grows older and stronger. Consider, too, that we neglect our duties as covenant parents if we do not correct him when he rebels.

We should mention one thing more while we are talking about our son's misdeeds. As we use Scriptural concepts, we also should use Scriptural terms. And the term *punishment* in Scripture, when viewed as the Lord doing the punishing, is used for the ungodly, the unregenerate. For example, we read in II Peter 2:9, "The Lord knoweth how to deliver the godly out of temptation, and to reserve the unjust unto the day of judgment to be punished." Isaiah 13:11 says, "And I will punish the world for their evil, and the wicked for their iniquity." Scriptural examples abound, but these two examples are enough for now.

However, Scripture uses the word *chasten* when the Lord speaks of or to His own people. For example, " . . . as a man chasteneth his son, so the Lord thy God chasteneth thee," Deuteronomy 8:5; and "For whom the Lord loveth he chasteneth . . . " Hebrews 12:6; and " . . . therefore despise not thou the chastening of the Almighty," Job 5:17.

Another Scriptural term is *correct*. "Behold, happy is the man whom God correcteth," Job 5:17; and "For whom the Lord loveth he correcteth," Proverbs 3:12.

We would do well to adopt this Scripturally sound vocabulary as our own, and instead of speaking of *punishment,* use the words of Proverbs 19:18: *"Chasten* thy son while there is hope, and let not thy soul spare for his crying," and the words of Proverbs 29:17: *"Correct* thy son and he shall give thee rest."

By now we will agree that training a child is a serious business. But that does not mean that we walk with a staid, solemn face day after day. A sense of humor is a vital asset to the Christian parent.

On the days when things just won't go right, when Timmy is cross and we are irritable, and when, finally, in frustration, he flings a toy across the room with a vengeance, we would do better to laugh than to scold. It will break the tension for both of us and help us to see that the ripples in life are not worth being cross about. If we are ready to laugh with our son, or even *at* his mild problems in a kindly way, he will see the funny side, too, and laugh with us.

Funny games, silly baby games, are the frosting of childhood. Games make pleasures out of humdrum activities such as dressing, waiting, or picking up toys. Laughing and inventing games with our child while waiting in a doctor's office not only changes tedium into pleasure, but it helps us to get to know each other better. A sense of humor helps us as parents to keep our psychological balance in life. It helps us to see things in perspective and sort out the important from the unimportant. If, for instance, our son has developed the habit of thumb-sucking, how important do we consider it? We would rather he didn't suck his thumb. Are we going on an all-out campaign to break his habit? Or will we laugh a little with him about it, or at least shrug it off as we gently discourage him, and wait until he is older, when he will stop voluntarily? Most children do. Laughing at a little accident—a tipped glass of milk by our son, or a broken dish that just would not stay in *our* hands—is better for the general atmosphere than scolding. We cannot put the milk back or make the dish whole anyway, and there really *is* something funny about the suddenness and clumsiness of accidents. A wholesome light-heartedness about the trivia of life helps us to see our lives in perspective, to sort out the important from the minor, and to react accordingly.

A good rule for all of us, one which I learned from a wise grandmother, is that we take our lives and our position of responsibility as parents very seriously before the face of God, but that we do not take *ourselves* seriously. We will not think first of our own pleasures or pain, we will not be overly sensitive and too easily hurt by real or imagined grievances, and we will be slow to take our neighbor's (and our children's) remarks ill. We will be able to belittle our own discomfort, to laugh at petty annoyances, and to be concerned for the feelings and comfort of others.

Now our son is almost two years old. He has learned much. We have, too. Learning the discipline and grace of patience has perhaps been our biggest lesson: patience to train him early in his life in the habits of good grooming, behavior, and responsibility—in other words, in the beginnings of Christian stewardship.

That is not all. Almost any parent who sets that goal can educate his child in the rudiments of a "good, clean, moral life." Remember, in many aspects, the outward appearances will be the same. Remember, too, it is the intangibles, the foundation of faith and trust in our God, the firm belief in His Word, the spiritual approach to our child, and a life of sanctification that make the difference.

The "intangibles" are not far away from us, divorced from reality, or way out in space somewhere. In fact, in a certain sense, these intangibles are very tangible. These foundations of faith, of a struggle against evil, and of a prayer for grace are the bases for our home atmosphere, the total surroundings of our two-year-old.

He notices it, too, and drinks it all in. Watch his little face if mother snaps at father, or if father slams down his book in disgust. Watch it again when father embraces mother just because he loves her; he immediately begs, "Me, too! Me, too!" But Timmy notices much more than just actions. He sees the deep undercurrent of selfless love which devoted parents have for one another, the wish for each parent to be helps meet for the other, the unselfish desire to please the other, the basic spiritual unity and agreement between them. He sees how much we love *him* by the way we look at him, pat his hand, and listen to him. These are precepts which we cannot as yet discuss with our two-year-old. Yet he sees them all, he learns them, unconsciously perhaps; but he knows what kind of atmosphere our home possesses. It is almost as if he learns it by passive assimilation. And it is this kind of teaching, usually unnoticed by us parents, that is tremendously important for Timmy, from this early age of two years until his maturity.

For in all that we do for our son, we are teaching him the joy of his salvation. In the past two years we have tried (and failed and succeeded) to work out all the many details in our lives with spiritual motives and goals in view. Just as we believed with all our hearts that we received our child as a gift from God, we have also tried (and failed and succeeded) to view his training as our task given to us by God. We have tried (and failed and succeeded) to be an example as a Christian parent and to lead a prayerful, sanctified life before our child and all God's people.

Our son will notice that we love the Lord, that we try to do the right, that we teach him according to the Word of God. We never underestimate him! He begins to see what is right and wrong, and is even starting to ask *why* it is right or wrong. Concretely, what do we do and say to so small a child so that he, too, may know the joy of his salvation? If we are mothers, we can begin by chanting a simple prayer to him. As long as he has been able to say the little word "Amen," he has been taught to say it after his daddy's "Amen" at mealtime prayers. Now if he can say the words of a mealtime or bedtime prayer, we teach him to say the words *with* us, then *after* us, and then *alone,* as far as he can.

At mealtime, we insist, if he is able to say words in sequence at this age (and most children can), that he repeat his "Lord bless this food . . ." after us. Also at night, if we choose the familiar "Now I lay me down to sleep," we train him to repeat the words after us, until he can say them independently. These are Timmy's first steps in learning what prayer is. He learns that prayer is formal, serious, reverent (hands always folded, eyes always closed) and that prayers, for him, are memorized.

We also want to teach Timmy some short, simple, beautiful Scripture passages. We need not necessarily make *this* a formal situation. Do it while we iron or as our toddler trails us when we dust. Say "The Lord is my Shepherd," and show him a picture of a shepherd and sheep. If we are fathers, we put aside our newspaper and hoist him to our shoulders and say, "Suffer little children and forbid them not, to come unto me. . . ."

But above all, we sing the songs of salvation to him. Sing many, and sing often. I have said before that we tend to underestimate the effect on a very small child of being surrounded with spirituality. Surely, he will not understand it all. He need not, either. But as he begins to talk, he will repeat our favorite texts and songs and recite and sing them with us.

Scripture has no room for the philosophy that a child must first thoroughly understand before he can learn. For example, when we teach Timmy, "The Lord is my Shepherd," he understands some elements of what we are saying. That is good, for understanding, even a measure of understanding, aids in learning. Complete understanding is considered by many educators to be a prerequisite in learning. But this is not necessarily so, especially not in young children of the Lord. Now let us go back to the figure of the shepherd. Timmy knows that his *Lord* is in heaven. He knows what a *shepherd* is and what he does, and how his *sheep* depend on him. But it will take years before he understands just how God's Word is *his* green pasture, or how goodness and mercy shall follow him all the days of his life. Right now he cannot comprehend the depths and the beauties of Psalm 23. Why, then, teach Timmy these truths *now?*

For a covenant child it is not mandatory that he have a *full* understanding when we begin to teach him. For those truths which he must learn, those ideas which he must assimilate, and those texts which he must memorize are the foundation for his whole life—the spiritual foundation. And it is the rule, in foundation-laying, that it is laid *first*. In a child, it is laid very early in life. He will use this foundation all the rest of his life; for Christ said, "Whosoever cometh to me, and heareth my sayings, and doeth them, I will show you to whom he is like: he is like a man which built an house, and digged deep, and laid the foundation on a rock," Luke 6:46, 47. We are doing this to Timmy, building his foundation on the spiritual rock of God's promises. This early learning stays with him all his life, and he uses it to build on, step by step, for the rest of his life. Understanding this principle, we will not be afraid to teach our child the profound truths of God's Word, even though at the beginning he cannot comprehend it all.

Therefore we will teach our babes, and they will learn the things of Zion and gradually understand more and more of the beauties of their salvation. For Jesus said, "Suffer little children, and forbid them not, to come unto me: for of such is the kingdom of heaven," Matthew 19:14.

NOTES

1. T. L. Engle, *Psychology, Its Principles and Applications* (New York: Harcourt, Brace and World, Inc., 1964), p. 489.
2. Wurth, op. cit., pp. 285, 286.
3. Jaarsma, op. cit., pp. 169, 170.
4. Jersild, op. cit., pp. 141-145.

7

THE CHILD FROM TWO TO FIVE YEARS

Train up a child in the way he should go; and when he is old, he will not depart from it.
—Proverbs 22:6

THE THREE YEARS IN THE LIFE OF OUR CHILD FROM THE age of two years until five will be some of his most precious years to us. In the next two chapters we will live through these three years with him. In this chapter we will look at the characteristics of our child at this age and make practical suggestions for his activities, his responsibilities, and his expanding social life. The methods of handling our child at this age, the tone of our teaching, and the instilling of a Christian outlook on his life will be discussed in the next chapter.

First, then, our son's characteristics. Timmy is not a baby any longer. Although he does not know what a year is, if we ask him how old he is, he will carefully hold up two chubby fingers. But blond, blue-eyed, fair-skinned Timmy does know *who* he is. He will enjoy telling people his name, even though by this time he has dropped his name when he refers to himself. "Timmy will do it" has now become "I will do it." He has come to *self*-consciousness, the consciousness of himself as a person, as an "I," as we described in Chapter II. He has had a mind and will for two years, but now he begins to realize that he is a distinct individual who exercises control over that mind and will. As a unique person in his own right, he enjoys emphasizing the "I."

Alongside of his new awareness of himself as a person comes the physical ability to assert his individuality. When he says, "I do it my own way, dad," very likely he has the ability to do it his own way; for during these years many of his smaller muscles are developing a coordination and power he did not know he had. He enjoys the control he can exercise over his fingers, and perseveres in practicing to use them well. This is the age when we tire long before he does of making shadow figures on the wall, of manipulating each joint and knuckle just right, to form a rabbit, a duck, or a bear. At dinner time, if we glance across the table at him and see both elbows on the table, chin in his hands, and a serious frown on his face, and we wonder what is wrong now, we know in the next instant. Daddy is sitting exactly that way, and Timmy is mimicking. From now on he will watch us, scrutinize us, and then copy us; for he is an expert in the art of mimicry, of both the good and the bad.

With his developing physical coordination comes almost unending energy. Whether he has done it before, whether it is possible or impossible to do, Timmy wants to *do* something. Often he cannot tell the difference between what is physically possible for him or not. If it can be done, he wants to do it. Depending on his mood, he may want to do something useful, something interesting, or something else. During these years Timmy wants to be busy. He likes to be occupied every waking minute. But his busyness is not always boisterous activity. There are times when he chooses to sit quietly and look at pictures, or work with crayons; these periods of quiet concentration are short, lasting usually from five to fifteen minutes. In these three years, the activities with which Timmy can be busy are so varied that we have little difficulty finding interesting projects for him; and Timmy is full of energy and enthusiasm when he discovers all the things there are to *do* in life.

Many of the things to do have to be done outdoors. The whole new world of his neighborhood has opened to him, and slowly Timmy is getting to have confidence to be out in it without a parent in sight. Until now, his friends have usually been adults, and then the few adults who took care of him. Suddenly he finds someone his own age who likes to do the same things he does, and Timmy has a playmate! No more is he concerned only about his own needs and wants. He has begun to look out and become interested in the world around him, and the people in it as people.

His awareness of his environment and his slowly unfolding knowledge of it brings comments and questions. These years are years of learning for Timmy; and he learns by asking extremely many and extensive questions, almost continuously. Timmy has begun to think about the world outside of himself, and he discovers that there is hardly anything that he understands. Necessarily, his questions are as simple as his conception of his environment is, and he is usually satisfied with simple answers. Often his questions begin with himself: "When will I be as big as daddy?" "Why do my feet end in toes?" He is interested in his playmates: "How come Kathy can't live at our house?" "Why does Johnny wear glasses?" Constantly he bombards us with questions about his physical environment: "What is sand made of?" "Are these beans dead or alive?" When he questions us about things spiritual, usually related to one of the Bible stories we have told him, his little mind seems awed by the justice of the Lord in sending judgments. His questions are often voiced in this vein: "Is God sending this storm to punish the wicked people?" "Do you feel bad, Mom, because God took Adam and Eve out of the beautiful garden?" These are typical questions which Timmy might ask in this period of his life.

Endlessly Timmy needs reasons: reasons how and what and why and when. For at this age his time and space concepts begin to unfold; these concepts will not *fully* unfold for many years, but "large" and "small," "near" and "far away," "long ago" and "not for a long time" take on meaning for him. Because he begins to understand ideas and relationships, he can now understand our answers to his "how" and "when" questions. He can visualize something he has not seen: for example, if we tell Timmy that in a far away country the weather is very, very cold almost all the time, and the people wear warm suits made of the skins of animals, with fur lining and fur hoods, and if we describe a sled pulled by strong white dogs, Timmy will have a mental picture of an Eskimo. To prove that he has this ability, we can show him an Eskimo picture a day or two later, and he will open his blue eyes wide and enthusiastically shout, "I know about them! You told me about them one day! It's very cold there!"

Bible stories of "far away" and "long ago" now begin to have meaning for Timmy. And we do not limit our stories to the concrete, factual details, which the Bible relates as actually having happened. Timmy's mind can now grasp *reasons* and *results*—in other words, *concepts* or *ideas*. The idea of "far away" and "long ago" or of "sin," "disobedience," "justice," and "repentance," ideas which we often label *abstract*, can be made concrete realities for Tim. For it would never do that we teach him abstract concepts as abstract concepts, ideas as it were "pulled out of the blue." To illustrate, when we tell him the Bible story of David and Bathsheba, we stress David's sin and disobedience, not as an abstract concept, but as a concrete reality. We teach him what David's sin was by way of David's sinful *act*, his disobedience by way of his disobedient *act*. We teach the idea of courageous trust in the Lord when we use the illustration of Daniel's three friends who engaged in a courageous *act*, that of not bowing down to Nebuchadnezzar's image. Even we as adults learn ideas more readily by way of the example of the concrete realities involved; so our child must know that these ideas which he cannot see are real, and that they show themselves in our speech and actions. We teach them as concrete realities. It is in this way that Timmy learns to follow our teaching when we talk of forgiveness, repentance, love, joy. They are real for us and for him, and we show that we understand these concepts by our acts of forgiving, being sorry, loving, and being happy. Thus the Bible stories of "far away" and "long ago" also carry over into Timmy's real life of here and now.

We are not the only ones who tell stories. Timmy's active mind, drawing on the wealth of experiences and knowledge he already has had, creates stories, too. His "imagination" is at work, and he tells us stories about dreams he has had, or he presents his stories to us as his own actual, preposterous experiences.

Later, as we incorporate these characteristics into Timmy's life, we plan to see what Timmy does with these characteristics, and we will comment on their proper use. For the present, we only note them in order to know what kind of Timmy is developing in these three years. And we have not mentioned *every* characteristic which he will have; we will discover more as we follow him in these chapters. Besides, we could never exhaust the list, because each "Timmy" is different from other "Timmys."

* * *

The word "doing" is the key descriptive word for Timmy, aged two to five. At this age, however, and for many years to come, he does not always know *what* to do. He is not as aimless as he was before he reached his second birthday, but he lacks purpose and definite goals; he needs guidance and suggestions. He needs to be trained how to channel his energies properly. Since we are parents who work hard at being parents, and who are concerned far more with Timmy's training than with our own pleasure, we cannot get it over our tongues to say, "Don't bother me now, Timmy. Just find something to do. Go ahead . . . anything."

We will not even be *tempted* to say it if we continue our custom of preparing activities for him. Some of these activities fall into the category of "useful" tasks; and at this age both boys and girls generally enjoy helping with almost all chores without regard for the fact that later in life they will classify them as "men's" or "ladies' " work. Timmy is often begging to "please help you." Because we must say "no" to him quite often, we try to say "yes" to him when we can. Although we could finish the task ourselves with more speed and skill, we stop and say "yes," and take the time to teach him how to help.

A good start, for a mother, is to let him put away silverware or pots and pans after the dishes are done. Another challenging task, one that requires the skills of eye and hand coordination, is the folding of small towels and washcloths when they come from the dryer or the line. We will incidentally also be teaching him the concept of "half" and then "half again" (fourth). He will not fold very many at first, of course, because he cannot concentrate on an exact task for very long. But what he folds we expect him to fold carefully. Training Timmy to do this task and many other useful ones like it has these advantages: he is occupied happily for a short period of time; he is learning to develop powers of attention, concentration, coordination, and muscle control; he is learning that helping is a pleasant experience—that work is not distasteful—at least, that it need not be.

Daddy, too, in his after-hour chores around the home, will certainly have a small shadow who wants to help. The result is that, outside or in the basement, wherever daddy putters, our first reaction (if we are the daddy) is to say, "Now look! I've had a lot of interruptions at work today, and I've got to fix this faucet. The last thing I need is a little kid in my way." Really? We all know that there are some situations in which it is wise to keep a small child away. Is this one of them? Or is the problem in the mind of us as dad? Take him along, Daddy, and show him what is wrong. Tell him what you have to do to repair it. Very likely he will not quite understand. But he will understand something of infinitely more value than a broken faucet. He will know that you are so interested in *him* that you take the time from your work to explain the problem patiently to him; he will sense that you *want* him around. And if you hand him a tool to hold for you, he will hold it until his tired little arm trembles, because you *need* him. When you praise him for his help, he knows you care. You have done much more than repair a leaking faucet this evening, Daddy. You have been training your son.

Sometimes, especially when Timmy is three or older, we will give him certain duties to do on a regular schedule, whether he asks to help or not. Throughout his babyhood we have been periodically chanting to him, "We put it away," or "Put it in its place," and then we have put it away or put it in its place. Now it is his turn. Before lunch time, dinner time, nap time, we give him ten minutes' notice to pick up his toys and put them in his toy box. We have shown him repeatedly how to pick up the toys systematically. He knows how now.

When he undresses, he does not throw one shoe into the corner and the other under the table, but puts them on the shelf, or wherever they belong, because he has been trained to do it that way. He is easily able to put away his freshly laundered clothes in the drawers where they are kept.

Other simple chores, related to good grooming or good order, we can expect him to do with a little reminder. But any parent knows that at times Timmy needs more than a little reminder. There comes a late afternoon when mother or father says, "Time to put the toys away before dinner, Timmy!" And he says, "Not now, Dad. I not done playing." And he keeps on playing.

Psychologists in children's behavior advise a variety of methods for dealing with an answer such as Timmy just gave us. One solution is substitution: take his mind off this subject by offering him something else. Curti says: "The four-year-old engaged in pulling up pansies in the garden may be induced instead to play happily in the sandpile."[1] We could apply Curti's method and take Timmy's hand and say, "Let's wash the dirty hands, shall we?" and hope to induce him, after the bathroom break, to pick up instead of play with his toys. Thus, we could take his mind off the subject and use the "substitution" solution.

Another solution would be to reason with him. Curti also advises this method for some situations. She says:

To illustrate, a child of six begs to be allowed to wear out to play the new dress which her grandmother has sent her. The mother urges her to keep it clean until Sunday, when grandmother is coming to visit. The little girl, to whom Sunday is a long way off, insists until her mother explains how hurt the dear grandmother will be, and explains why the dress will not be so pretty after it is washed. Finally the child realizes in imagination the bad consequences of wearing the dress now, and adopts as a solution the plan of waiting until Sunday to please grandmother.[2]

Applying this principle to our problem with Timmy, we would explain to him that if all these toys are left out, someone might trip and fall and get hurt. Or someone might come to the door and see what a messy boy Timmy is. Or we can tell him that we have to go away after we eat dinner, and then there won't be time to put everything away. That would be the "reasoning" solution.

Another method of solving the problem is to have a certain sympathy for Timmy, to tell ourselves that he is only three years old and that we expect quite a bit of responsibility from him. Then we will suggest that we help him, meanwhile telling him how glad Bozo is to be back in his nice toy box. This is the "sympathy" solution.

We will not use any of these approaches. Not today at dinner time. Why not? Is there not a place in a child's life to have his attention drawn to something else, a time for reasoning, and a need for helping him? There is, we know. But *this* is not the time. When we were training him to put his toys away, we already gave him all these reasons and more. He does not need explanations now; what he needs is obedience. And I think that a failing of many parents, also covenant parents, is to talk too much and explain with too many words. Is not our word of command good enough? It is good that Timmy knows why we tell him to pick up the toys; but he must obey even if he does not know or refuses to see the reason.

Drawing away his attention or suggesting to do something else instead of having him pick up toys, after we have told him to do so, surely will not train Timmy to be obedient. Helping him when he is tired or when time is limited is good. Helping him in his disobedience is sin. None of these methods is the proper one for us, consistent, diligent parents.

Now we are back to the problem. What shall we do when Timmy says, "Not now"? The only right solution is the simplest one. We say, "Yes, Timmy, now." That is all. When he looks at us, our eyes and our whole mien convey to him the concept of authority, with love. No challenge to dare him to disobey, no anger, nor even frustration or impatience shows in our eyes, for there is none in our hearts. Timmy, brought up with quiet commands, knows he must do it *now*. If he does, we will have a talk with him after the clatter of dinner dishes is over; we will tell him again that he did wrong, and then have him repeat for us the answer of an obedient little boy. And he will promise to obey the next time. If, however, he does not obey our "Yes, Timmy, now," we will act. Using the rod of correction (our hand against his bottom), we will bring him to obedience.

Whether we ask him to pick up his toys, or whether he volunteers his help with a chore, we are insistent on high standards of performance in any of the helpful deeds Timmy tries to do. If he wants to do a task a bit above his ability, or if he is clumsy in a certain area of coordination, we will not discourage him—ever—by saying, "No, Timmy, that's all wrong!" It is just as easy to say in a pleasant, carefree voice, "Almost, Timmy, but not quite! Let me show you once more." Now he knows that we are not satisfied, but also that we really did not expect to be satisfied this time, and that we have confidence in his ability to do it satisfactorily soon. We have not shattered his enthusiasm and we have strengthened his incentive. How do we know that Timmy gets all this meaning out of our short remarks? By his high-pitched shout a few minutes later: "Quick, Daddy! I think I'm getting much better already. See?" His knowing that he will be praised for work well done, corrected for sloppy or inferior work, and encouraged to do better will create in him a sound attitude toward work well done.

However, engaging in helpful activities in the adult world occupies only a very small amount of Timmy's time. In the rest of his time he wants to be busy doing entertaining and interesting things merely because they are fun on his childish level of playing. In many of these activities he is learning, too, but he is not always aware that he is. Timmy will also know that every day there will be some time for a special project for him. On a beautiful, balmy summer day, we might not even use it, because Timmy is having so much fun outside. In fact, many days may pass when Timmy has so much of his own fun planned that he will not welcome any suggestions. But some days we will need several different ideas. At any rate, we have an activity to suggest, if he needs something to do. We also train Timmy to understand that we love him and enjoy surprising him, but there are times in our lives when we must not be interrupted. He may not ask for our attention at those times. He must play with his own toys and respect our preoccupation with our own duties. We will teach Timmy that these times are, for example, the pre-dinner hour for mother, or when she is baking or scrubbing the floor. Daddy is never bothered during a telephone call, or when he is getting ready for work or for a meeting. Our "Not now, Timmy. Soon—as soon as I have finished this," reminds him that we are his parents, not his servants.

If possible, we will reserve a special drawer for him, a low one, in the kitchen, his bedroom, or wherever is a convenient spot for storage for a small boy. In this drawer he will store scissors, a jar of paste, crayons, pencils, water colors, clay, and a roll of shelf paper. Timmy will soon be adding many treasures to its contents.

But before we let him use these media independently, we will show him the proper use of each. At first, at least, we will sit *with* him and oversee his progress, patiently suggesting improvements in his techniques. In his practice sessions we will use the shelf paper. We can cut off any size sheet of paper, and we always have a neatly stored, ready supply. His periods of learning to handle the new tools will be short, for his muscles tire easily from trying to manipulate these small finger-tools; and when he gets restless, we stop immediately.

After he has mastered the use of these tools fairly well, we can start longer, interesting projects. Because small children like to collect, we will start with a scrapbook and collect pictures. Timmy may choose the kind of pictures he wants to collect, and then look through magazines and papers for his kind. Now Timmy is learning to be selective—to cut out only the articles in his category. One four-year-old I knew, who liked to eat, chose her category and even suggested her own title for the scrapbook: Fine Foods. Another, showing a trait that would stay with her for life, chose flowers. Timmy will choose boats, and soon will be asking everyone he meets, "You have a boat picture for me?"

When Timmy tires of boats, we put the scrapbook away for

a time, and when, later, we bring it out to him, he will welcome it as a friend.

Coloring and painting books do not hold Timmy's interest very long. He is an active child who does not like to sit quietly more than a short time. So we tape a long strip of shelf paper at his eye level along the basement wall, and teach him what a mural is. This one will be done in crayon. Together we plan a beach scene, with the picnic table in the grass at the beginning of the paper. Over here the brown sand starts, and we will be sitting here, near the water, building sand castles. Then comes the blue water, with two sailboats out there, and, of course, his favorite, a Starcraft. Timmy is learning limitation, progressions, and probably size relationship. We are as eager as he to see the finished product. He works on it in many installments, whenever he feels like it.

Does this seem too hard for a boy going on four? Not if he wants to do it. His finished product will look like the picture of a four-year-old; Timmy is not an exceptionally advanced child, but he is learning much, and is so happy and excited about it. If we promise to keep it on the basement wall, he will be making plans for his next mural.

For a change, he can go back to pasting again, but not in his scrapbook. Our household has many small items that he can paste. We can find bits of ribbon, flat buttons, shell noodles, cereals, and a variety of other objects and have him paste them in whatever pattern he likes on a piece of construction paper. With a large wet towel nearby, he will keep his fingers free of paste, and will be delighted with the challenge of design and textures.

Timmy could start his next mural on the floor, and trace geometric figures. All three of us will enjoy going through the house finding things of various shapes and sizes to trace: pots and pans, bread tins, cups, utensils, books, toys—arranged in shapes of people and animals, or arranged at random. Or we suggest that Timmy go out and collect leaves of all kinds and sizes. He will enjoy that. We will press them until he is ready to trace them on another piece of shelf paper. Then he will color or paint them. As he learns to trace objects, he can trace attractive shapes or simple pictures onto strips of heavy cardboard. Colored carefully, these make bookmarks, which Timmy will be happy to make for any relatives and friends.

These suggestions do not nearly exhaust the possibilities of Timmy's use of paper in interesting and entertaining activities. If we temporarily run out of ideas, the obvious place to find a new one is in our own household. If we look through the house with Timmy's projects in mind, we will find many unusual surprises for him.

To keep our surprises for Timmy fresh and to hold his interest from project to project, we will have him work and play with more than paper materials. Timmy, like most children, likes to arrange; and he likes to work at his arranging in mild confusion. If we are mothers who sew, we will get out our box of leftover materials. If we do not, we will beg scraps from relatives and neighbors. Then, cutting the brightly colored pieces into squares, triangles, or diamond shapes, we will give them to Timmy to admire, sort, and arrange in patterns on the floor. Squares are easiest for a small child to handle. After he has enjoyed his arranging and rearranging in several sessions of play, we can suggest a final arrangement, which we will stitch for him into a—blanket? patchwork tent? Or Timmy may have a better idea.

If he is sick or for some reason must stay inside for a day, we can plan to make the household cornstarch-salt concoction, often known as magic goop. Timmy enjoys working with it and painting it more than he enjoys the modeling clay that we buy at the store.

If, when he may go outside again, he seems uncertain what he wants to do, we are ready with suggestions. Depending on the time of the year, we suggest a sandbox village, consisting of a series of buildings, streets, parks, made by molding wet sand in different kinds of containers and dumping them upside down. Or we suggest he get Kathy and make a small tent over a clothesline or spread over a couple of wagons, and using his very own patchwork cover. If we know someone at an appliance store (or even if we don't) we ask for a huge box or two, and some smaller ones. Then we watch Timmy and his friends build a playhouse, complete with a patchwork rug. In winter we encourage him to make simple snow sculptures, and go out and help him. The happiest part for Timmy is pouring water over the sculpture and watching it freeze.

As a break between the interesting projects, Timmy still has his "party." Varied with peanuts and raisins and shared with Kathy and his other friends, it is always a treat which he happily anticipates each day.

The preceding practical suggestions are only a few of the pleasant activities and the many happy times we have with Timmy. If we cannot think of a choice idea, we can go to the library and find dozens of suggestions under *Arts and Crafts*. The books, however, only tell us what to do and how to do it. They say nothing about the *motivation,* the *approach,* the *attitude,* or the *goals* of teacher and pupil (or parent and child). *We* know that these four basic principles, intangible, yet seen in every phase of our life with our child, make our homes different and distinctive from the homes of those whose lives are lived for themselves instead of to the glory of our sovereign God. In the next chapter we will explore these principles in the light of Scripture, as they affect Timmy in his first years of conscious self-expression.

In this chapter our purpose is to suggest and define Timmy's "things to do." Lest we get the impression that always in Timmy's life *we* are the ones who suggest, who supervise and guide, let us make sure we understand that he has much free time, as much as he wants, to invent new games with his friends, to make up his own songs as he sits in his sandbox, to follow a bug on the sidewalk, or to watch the clouds, whatever his inclination may be. Tim is no robot, going from one supervised surprise to the next. He is an individual who sometimes needs time away from us and time away from his friends to be alone to do what he wants to do, or to do nothing. He needs time to dream, to plan, or just to think. Or to talk little-boy-talk with little boys. Sometimes he needs to go downstairs to invent his own kind of boat out of bits and pieces in his corner. He may want to scowl and grumble and mull over the problems with his invention in his own mind, without outside interference.

He *needs* to develop as Timmy, not as a carbon copy of all

the neighbor boys, nor as a stereotype who plays what he is told to play. Free time, freedom to do whatever his mood or the weather suggests is a cardinal happiness for a young child. And we as parents are wise not to interfere, not to question overmuch.

But on the days when he is bored, when he cannot think of a thing to do, when his friends are on vacation, when the day is dull and dripping—whatever the reason—when he says, "I haven't got *anything* to do. What can I do that's fun, Mom?"—then we step in with our hoarded surprises. Even so, as we guide Timmy, we take care not to *regiment* him. Timmy needs our help to structure his days that need some structuring; he also needs his own choices to suit his moods, and, as we have said, much time for free play without overt adult guidance. If Timmy's days follow the above pattern, we all, parents and child, will make each day a happy day and a special day. There will be times when we do not feel as happy and enthusiastic as at other times; but, because the certainty that we are God's children is very vividly before our consciousness, we always have the knowledge of a deep undercurrent of peace and joy in our lives. For this reason we are cheerful and optimistic when dealing with our child. And thus we are able, day by day, to present our ideas with joy, enthusiasm, and help. The *way* in which we suggest the kind of day we will have today matters greatly: it will not be with a bright artificial gaiety or a fawning condescension, for Timmy will recognize its superficiality and respond in kind; but with a genuine loving concern, presented with unaffected light-heartedness, to which Timmy, trained for the element of anticipation and surprises, will usually respond happily and enthusiastically.

In newspaper and magazine articles we read repeatedly of parents who simply do not have the time to spend to teach, help, and play with their children. Curti also confirms this lack of time in the majority of parents. Speaking of children who want to "help Mother" or "work with Daddy," she says that "they are encouraged to want to help, yet are permitted to do but very little, and that only rarely—as a rule, when the busy parent has plenty of time."[3]

As Christian parents, we realize that parents' lack of time

for their children is a very real thing in the world. We see and hear examples of it every day. However, we do not agree that they *have* no time, but rather that they do not *make* the time. Their priorities are in the wrong places. They moonlight for a little extra cash, or entertain themselves with golf, bowling, and social affairs, or take part in various community projects, or work on extensive hobbies. None of these activities is wrong in itself, of course, if it does not replace the training of children. Usually, however, as parents become involved in a social or entertainment whirl, family life, at best, takes second place. At worst, home life becomes hectic, harried, and unpleasant.

In our covenant homes, we do have time or make time for our child. As a result, a surprising thing happens. We have a happy, contented child, fruitfully (and often quietly) absorbed in working on one of the surprises. He is not whining, teasing, quarreling, or getting into trouble. And because our life runs smoothly and more trouble-free, we actually do have *more* time for ourselves and our own extra duties and activities. Though our motive is providing happiness for our son, a by-product is more tranquility for ourselves. Try it. Many parents know from experience that it works!

After Timmy's work is finished, we expect help with the cleaning up. As we have done with Timmy's other chores, we ask help matter-of-factly; and we show, by word and example, that he must do it, as we do, with cheerfulness. If we teach him how to clean up quickly and efficiently, he will grow up to regard clean-up as part of the project. I remember that when an aunt said to a small boy one day as he hurried about his clean-up chores, "My, that's a big job for a boy like you, isn't it?", he showed his attitude toward clean-up in his answer: "Oh, Auntie, we don't make such a big deal about it in our house."

We tell our child plainly, "Some things that you have to do are not very nice to do. But there are not-nice things to do in your life, too. And if you hate to do it and grumble or even cry about it, the job seems even worse to do. Isn't that right? Now let me tell you how we do it, Timmy. We look at the job, then look at our two good hands, smile, and say,

'Why not?' And, Timmy, by the time we think about what a bad, bad clean-up job it is, the job is finished."

We can help Timmy in setting good habits of care for his tools and equipment by devising a small system of rewards as incentives—as long as the rewards are *given,* not *demanded.* If Timmy has his own drawer or cupboard, we can set up a semi-weekly or weekly inspection, with stars or badges for various degrees of cleanliness and order; and Timmy will try even harder if he knows he will get a whole dollar when he has ten gold stars or ten red badges.

His "spection dollar" (as the small boy I remember called it) is only an immediate reward, however. The long term rewards are those of training in good habits of responsibility and in caring for the earthly goods which God has put in our possession—in other words, the practice of good stewardship, and the training in the joy of giving of oneself to help another. This training of Timmy in helping is more than the application of the principle "do unto others as you would have them do unto you." It is the application of doing one's duty for God's sake, rather than merely of doing good to our neighbor or having him do good to us. If cheerful, obedient helpfulness becomes an integral part of Timmy's being, it will remain a part of his life. The principle of "help now, help later" means for Timmy that, if later in life he is asked to give energy, time, or talents in some phase of the work of God's kingdom, he will be glad to—in fact, if he is one of God's own dedicated servants, he will serve with eagerness.

Have we drawn too many implications from Timmy's help with clean-up after his project? Superficially, we are ready to answer yes. But when we remember that our whole life, in the looming crises and the paltry details, is lived for God's sake, we will take another look, the look of the sanctified Christian, at the small details, and begin to serve the Lord more consciously in these, too. And when we look at Proverbs 22:6, "Train up a child in the way he should go; and when he is old, he will not depart from it," and when we apply the knowledge about Timmy which we have gleaned from Holy Writ, then we are sure that no sphere of his life is too insignificant to be trained in the fear of the Lord and to have far-reaching results in his spiritual outlook later in life.

As we have drawn the picture of our son and his activities in this chapter, we have looked at the ideal situation. You and I know that our sinfully depraved natures always prevent us from reaching our ideal, which is living according to the precepts God laid down in His law. As parents we sin in being unduly cross and impatient and unreasonable with our son. He sins by being contrary and stubborn.

Besides, the individualities and personalities of parent and child strongly enter into our relationships. A method of discipline that brings the desired behavior in Timmy may be no good at all for Kathy. And the same method of discipline will not produce identical results in Timmy's behavior from one time to another. One day he may be in a soft, pensive mood, receptive to a quiet reprimand and an encouraging admonition. Another day his offense may be similar but his mood foul and defiant; then no amount of quiet talking will make him receptive to our words, nor repentant for his misdeeds. We Christian parents know how sorely we need rules to train our children; but we guard strongly against using rules with rigidity, with finality, as if they were ends in themselves. If we do fall into that error, our rules become a rather mechanical and magic cure for all the sins of our child . . . rule upon rule, precept upon precept.

Life, especially a Christian's life, cannot be pigeon-holed into neat categories. The rules have exceptions, lots of them, and our children have such diverse personalities and characteristics, so many quirks of imagination and rapid changes of mood that we discover that every rule cannot possibly fit every child, and that the same rule cannot always be used, even in similar circumstances, with the same child. And sometimes no rules seem to fit.

What then? Throw the rules away, and play it by ear? We know better than that. For if we throw our rules away, our standards are gone. We need those rules as helps and guides, to use with flexibility and love. They help us as we intensely study our child, not first of all to see how we can make him obey us, but to see what kind of guidance is best for him in his peculiar place in life. Is he soft-hearted, easily provoked to tears by a quiet talk? Sometimes? Usually? Then we use mild measures. Or have we discovered that he often likes to argue and talk back? Does solitude and a quiet time to think help him to realize his error? Is he at times a "hothead" whose unreasoning temper demands the rod of chastening? Or is he an enigma, so that we shake our heads because we don't know what procedure to follow next? We parents know that all of these characteristics are often present in one small child.

Again, what then? Scripture's answer is, "If any of you lack wisdom, let him ask of God, that giveth to all men liberally, and upbraideth not; and it shall be given him," James 1:5. And we show our child, all our children, by example and training, to live out of the principle of the grace of God. Even though they are all different and distinct individuals, they will all turn in faith and trust to ask their Father's guidance, so that each in his own way may glorify his Father in heaven.

* * *

It is in his pre-school years, from the approximate age of two and older that Timmy's "things to do" stretch out beyond "things to help" and "things to play." These latter activities are limited to the security of home and often are optional. Other "things to do" take Timmy into the busy life of the community and are often a necessity; and part of the process of Timmy's growing up is training in conduct in situations away from home. Before he was two years old it was hard to explain the reasons, for example, for taking him to the doctor when we all knew it was unpleasant for him.

As he becomes older and understands more, we gradually talk more and more to him about the necessity of visiting the doctor's office. We do not take him, as many parents do, and "cross our fingers and hope he will be good." He won't be. We will not let the doctor or nurse sneak a shot, either. That will not work more than once, anyway. And what will Timmy think of parents and doctor who resort to such tactics, at the same time they preach against them? Instead, we will prepare Timmy. Preparation to face a given situation is always a large percentage of our training. If he needs a shot, we explain in simple terms: "Timmy, the doctor will shoot a few drops into your arm with a needle. These drops will help you keep feeling well instead of getting a bad sickness. What, Timmy? Oh, I know you hate the shot. I know it doesn't feel good. But, Timmy, you need it. And remember what happens if you make a fuss? If you pull away and cry and fight the shot, you will hate to have the shot still more. After the fuss is over, you still need the shot. If you take the shot quietly, everyone will feel happy, and the shot won't seem quite so bad. And, Timmy, it will hurt a little. Now look at me. Can you take a little hurt?"

Timmy, having a trace of bravado in him, will probably brag, "I can take a *lot* of hurt!"; but in the gleaming white doctor's office, he will not be so brave. However, before we have left home, Timmy has promised that he will not cry or scream. He has fear, but we are training him to exercise his will over his fear and not give in to a violent outburst. We are not, to be sure, training our child to be a stoic. A stoic is not supposed to express feeling. Timmy does express his feelings in a calm, disciplined way, at the same time learning to regard a shot in its proper perspective—not important enough to make a fuss. If he passes the shot with flying colors, we will reward him with an ice cream cone on the way home. If he does not, we will talk to him at home, and chasten him for not having heeded our first talk.

It is wise, too, to prepare Timmy for an emergency. Often in connection with a local accident we can say, "We hope you never get hurt, Timmy, but . . . " and then explain that in case he ever has an accident, he must be separated from us for a time in the hospital. Then we prepare him for hospital routine. If we look ahead with Timmy to other problems which might arise, such as getting lost or his getting no response at the back door of our home, we teach him what to do; and we eliminate unnecessary agitation and foster a sense of security.

Timmy will go along with mother or daddy, or both of us, to the grocery store. But Timmy is not the kind of boy the personnel dread to see. We all know the kind. We see "dreadful" children like these every day in any given store. They touch everything they can, take off the shelf what they can reach, beg for what they cannot reach, open packages which a parent is buying or is not buying, cry when a parent refuses to buy what they want, scream when they are swatted, whine again to get their way, fight with brothers and sisters, and chase each other through the aisles if let loose. Yes, we all have seen the drama of the dreadful children. And I think we have all wondered why the drama had to be. It doesn't. For a few simple rules, laid down with characteristic firmness, and with an insistence on no exceptions in obedience to them, are the only necessary preparations for our child's shopping trip. They are: do not touch anything that is not yours, do not ask a parent to buy anything (*never* whine for it), and do not leave your parent's side. If our child obeys these three "do not's," the drama of misbehavior cannot be enacted. Of course, we know that there is no negative without the positive. The positive preparation for the shopping trip is the quiet talk with Timmy long before we leave, explaining that grown-up people can buy only what their money will pay for, and ending with a detailed description of the kind of boy we want to take along. Timmy now understands our high standards, knows we will insist on them and expect him to live up to them. And we all will enjoy our shopping trip.

When he faces any new or strange experience, we talk with Timmy. Talk, not preach. Much of what we say is based on good common sense, that is, Christian common sense. Rephrased, it would be applying to Timmy the basics of psychology as we find them in Scripture—applied Christian child psychology. Our tone and manner of talking with him is as important as our message: firm but not abrupt, insistent but not harsh, calm but not unfeeling, enthusiastic but not anxious. We talk often to him, and repeat our admonitions for his proper behavior as a Christian child from a Christian home.

When we do all this repeated talking to Timmy—and we must—we take care that we do not talk *at* him. We talk *to* him and *with* him. He talks, too. We ask him, often at first, and occasionally later, to repeat to us exactly what is forbidden and what is expected. If we are to have visitors, Timmy should be able to say, "I don't show off in front of them. And I never interrupt. I *do* be polite and shake hands." He learns that there are times when he is not the center of interest, or that he must do things he would rather not do. If we continue to stress (by example, too) that this is the way life is, that some situations are more pleasant and easier than others, but that our Lord sends it all, the big and the little things in life, the joys and the pain, then we also teach him to accept in his life what the Lord sends, with contentment.

We have not yet discussed one very important experience for our covenant child, namely, going to church. Parents often wonder at what age to begin taking him. Some say that the sooner he is exposed to the idea of worship and the communion of saints the better. Others think that their child should stay at home until he is able to understand the sermon. We, wisely, I believe, will again choose the middle path between these two opposite views. First, our child should be physically able to control himself for the duration of the service. He has to be old enough to understand that his "wiggly" muscles must remain quiet for a while, he must have good bladder control, and he must be old enough to understand that no talking is allowed. What age is that? There is no definite age in years and months which is correct for everyone. From my own experience I found that one of my children was more ready at twenty months than another at thirty months. A big part of the difference lay in the nature of the child, one being calm and placid, the other, high-strung and active.

As a general rule, we could try church-going at about two years old, usually not much before, and often somewhat later. Timmy, active, talkative, and irrepressible, will wait until he is a few months past his second birthday. Meanwhile we will prepare him and rehearse the order of worship. Using the method which has been successful in preparing him for other new experiences, we will impress on him the "do's" and "don't's," especially the "don't's." Timmy will repeat for us that: he must sit *very* still, must obey the *first* time he is told to stop something, must *never* talk or whisper, and must *listen*. In the next chapter I will discuss how we teach him to listen and with what attitude we go to God's house. Here, however, we will look only at the formal aspect of going to church.

How many times, fellow parents, have we left a service saying about some covenant child, "If that were my child, he would sit still! I just don't understand parents who do not or cannot make their child sit still in church. He really interfered with my worship."

This is a legitimate complaint, I believe. For, to our shame, many of our covenant children do not display proper Christian behavior in church. The fault lies with the parents more than with the children, for many parents allow or at least tolerate disobedient, unruly, undisciplined children to sit next to them. Why, with our richly developed view of the covenant and the importance we place on the spiritual training of the covenant seed, do we fall into neglectful practices when we train our children to worship their Maker in the communion of saints? There, in God's house, we should set the highest standards of sanctified behavior, and then maintain those standards rigidly.

Let us understand, too, that we have no choice but the choice of insisting on our son's exemplary behavior. For in the measure that we allow disobedience without correcting it, we are condoning it. We have already told him that we will not whisper. But, we are thinking, he is so small yet. Are we not being unduly strict? How can he communicate? When the sermon seems long, may he not ask to sit on mother's or daddy's lap, or have a piece of "church" candy? Now let us answer our own questions. He need not whisper except in an emergency. If we begin to allow whispering, we will be inclined to listen to his questions about when we are going home, and his complaints about being too hot or cold, or how his mitten disappeared, or his interest in how fast that fat man breathes. And if we look around us and at our own families, we know that we are often too lenient about allowing unnecessary conversation in church. Are we not? Therefore, if we make no exception to our rule, we have no problem. For my own children, I worked out the system of one tap on father's or mother's knee, which meant that the bench was getting so hard, and may he sit on a lap, please. A tap on mother's purse or daddy's pocket meant that a peppermint or lifesaver would be welcome. No more sign language or conversation was allowed, and none was needed. The rest was saved for the Sunday noon dinner hour.

Timmy knows that he may hold the song book with us during singing, but may not page through it during other parts of the service. We are supposed to listen then. He also knows that he may not turn around, wave at people behind him, or stand up in his seat. But it is not easy for active Timmy to behave quietly for the more-than-an-hour of the service's duration. He knows the song books are not playthings, but with characteristic quickness he pulls one out of the rack and lets it fall with a resounding bang on the floor. We look at Timmy with eyes full of warning as we replace the book. With defiance written on his face, he reaches for the book again. He wants it and will have it, his face says. What do we say? This is church and we don't want to make a fuss here? Shall we warn him again? No, Timmy has been warned, and we know and he knows that he is being openly disobedient. We act. Quietly we take him out of the auditorium to the car or a basement room, and give him the rod of correction. After he is quiet and we have talked about his disobedience, and he has made another promise to obey, we take him back into the auditorium.

Although he somehow may have had the idea that in this formal atmosphere, with all these people around, we would have to relax our insistence on obedience, he knows now that we will act quickly and take him out to chasten him.

Timmy does not do what some children do—strike back after a parent has tapped his hand or removed it from a forbidden place. Timmy also knows he may not ever strike back at a parent, for this action not only expresses defiance instead of obedience, but it also puts him on an equal plane with his parents: you hit me, I hit back. A discerning Christian parent never allows it.

But Timmy still finds it hard to sit still through a service. He taps his foot lightly—and annoyingly—on the seat in front of him. Mother puts the foot down. He taps again and gets the warning look. The third time he taps, mother decides to take him on her lap and hold him with firm, chastening arms. Instead of cooperating, Timmy holds his arms up rigid and straight, making it difficult to lift him. What does mother do when he stiffens in rebellion? She acts. She takes him out for another stinging spanking.

By this time, however, we are objecting that we can visualize the service becoming a parade of parents and disobedient children leaving and reentering the auditorium, more disruptive than the disobedience itself. If we stop to think, we discover that in reality it will not happen. For, remember, in the first place, that Timmy has been brought up with a combination of gentleness and firmness in a godly atmosphere. In the second place, when he knows that his parents will act quickly in insisting on obedience, often one trip out for a spanking is all that he needs to teach him that lesson. Some children need more. Timmy needed two trips.

We have never handled Timmy as if it were our purpose to be rigid disciplinarians, and although we insist on excellence in behavior in church, we *could* not treat him coldly. He is a little boy, just learning how to worship formally. We let him take a small cuddly toy to church at first. We take him on our laps and stroke his neck or back or arm. He likes that and will sit quietly for a long time. When he becomes restless, the gentle pressure from our arms and a reassuring piece of candy, plus a smile of encouragement usually calms him down.

Whenever we can, we praise him. If we take the time to count the forbidden things and how often we must say "no" to him, we will make a greater effort to praise him for doing the right or doing more than he was asked to do. We will reward him, too. Not always will we give him a reward—for then it becomes an expected payment—but often enough to stimulate him to try a little harder.

Always we will be alert to show a positive outlook in our training of Timmy. We will smile and laugh with him much, encourage and praise him often, and reward him with something special sometimes. As we watch Timmy we see the beginning of the regenerated life of the child of God and his striving against sin. We teach him repeatedly that an obedient child is a happy child, for an obedient child is doing the will of his Father in heaven. And because Timmy is a covenant child and begins to show it in his life, we know that in principle he wants to do the right; and by God's grace he will fight and overcome his sin, so that his sanctified behavior from his reborn heart will triumph. That is the way we view him, too, as daily we "train up a child in the way he should go," knowing that "when he is old, he will not depart from it."

NOTES

1. Curti, op. cit., p. 355.
2. Op. cit., p. 366.
3. Op. cit., p. 348.

8

THE CHILD FROM TWO TO FIVE YEARS (continued)

Furthermore, we have had fathers of our flesh which corrected us. . . . Now no chastening for the present seemeth to be joyous, but grievous; nevertheless, afterward it yieldeth the peaceable fruit of righteousness unto them which are exercised thereby.
—Hebrews 12:9a and 11

WHEN WE THINK OF DISCIPLINE WE USUALLY THINK OF the negative aspect of it, the "chastening" of the text just quoted above, which chastening is not "joyous, but grievous." We really know, of course, that chastening is only a part of discipline; but it is well to remind ourselves, as we live with our three-to-five-year-old Timmy, that discipline encompasses all of our handling of the child. Webster tells us that discipline is "treatment suited to a disciple or learner." He also defines discipline as "training, physical, mental, or moral." Further, he says that discipline is "developing by instruction and exercise" as well as "subjection to rule; submissiveness to order and control; habit of obedience."

It may be interesting and profitable to see what a psychologist, using a horizontal, logical approach, says about the subject of discipline. Engle says:

> Many persons use the word "discipline" and "punishment" interchangeably. We shall use the word "discipline" in its broad meaning of "the entire program of adapting

the child to social life." Punishment may be necessary sometimes in this program, but it plays only a minor and an emergency role.

Prevention of socially undesirable behavior is easier and more effective than the attempted correction of such behavior after it has developed. It is far better to place dishes on high shelves than it is to punish the child who breaks dishes easily reached on low shelves. It is far better to provide little sticks for play than it is to punish the child for playing with matches.

The ultimate goal of discipline is the achievement of self-control or self-discipline. . . . Discipline should be a matter of guidance, or leadership, and of example rather than of coercion. . . .

One fundamental principle of discipline is that treatment of the child be consistent. If one day we permit him to scatter his toys about the floor and the next day we forbid him to do so, how can we expect him to know what is desirable behavior?[1]

What shall we say about Engle's view of discipline? With some of his statements we can agree, at least as far as they go: we agree that discipline has a broader meaning than punishment, and that it is a matter of guidance, leadership, and example; we agree that good discipline is consistent; and we even agree that a goal of discipline is self-control—though it is not the ultimate one. We also believe in preventing misbehavior, but not in Engle's mechanical manner. I suppose that we could even say in a sense that we teach our child adaptation to social life. But the trouble with these goals and definitions of Engle is that they do not start out from our Christian perspective, do not proceed with the methods of Scripture, and do not attain any spiritual goals.

As we have said, in some formal aspects we agree with Engle. We know that when we and our child confront each other and rub elbows day after day, we use what Engle and many other authors call "psychology": we are reasonable, logical, tactful, sympathetic, understanding, encouraging. Any psychologist will tell us the importance of these virtues. But we are much more than that. Let us go back to that phrase

The Child from Two to Five Years / 161

of Webster about discipline: "treatment suited to a disciple or learner." Now in a sense our child is a disciple or follower of us his parents, and learns from us all that we are able to teach him. But he is ultimately and very really Christ's disciple, just as we are. Each day as we handle him, we guide him in the paths of righteousness by words and example. While teaching him to be a good citizen in the social community of this world, we teach him that this life is only a stepping stone to the life of the heavenly kingdom. Along the way we teach him "subjection to rule, submissiveness to order, and obedience" only for Christ's sake. The subject matter which we teach is *Christ's* teaching, as it is found in Holy Writ and as it influences and penetrates every sphere of our lives. Our philosophy of discipline—of handling our child—is so different from Engle's because our starting points are so different. His starts in humanism, ours in God's law.

Ours is a pleasant home. We have order without rigidity, flexibility without chaos. Timmy's physical surroundings are neat and clean without being sterile, and are as tasteful and comfortable as our budget allows. But the pleasantness of our home does not stem primarily from these comfortable niceties. It is the positive spiritual atmosphere which we work hard to maintain that truly makes ours a pleasant home. Just as certainly, our home is a home of wicked, horrid sins, which show themselves each day. But when God's law rebukes us for our sin and says, "Thou shalt not," we and our child say it, too. We try to *live* those "Thou shalt not's," too. But we say and live far more. We learn from God's Word the positive "Thou shalt," and teach it day by day to our child. The atmosphere of our home is not the somber, drab, joyless one of "line upon line and precept upon precept." It is instead an atmosphere of freedom in Christ, of obeying the spirit, not the mere letter of the law. It is a freedom within well-defined bounds. For example, the atmosphere of our home is not one in which we would find ourselves saying to our child, "Sunday is the Lord's day. You may walk, but not run on Sunday." Rather, we have an entirely different outlook. Instead of concentrating on what we may or may not do, we talk of the best ways to spend the Lord's day, and teach our child to fill it joyfully, in song and worship, in sitting at home, or taking a walk, with the service of God.

We show our child, also by our example—especially by our example—that we obey all God's commands, not legalistically or grudgingly, as a duty, but cheerfully and willingly. Our example, an imperfect one, nevertheless speaks loudly to Timmy. This example, set by both father and mother, further defines the home atmosphere which we share, and of which we have spoken before. In this atmosphere, love abounds. It is love for God and joy in His service first. Love for the family God has given us will be the basic ingredient in our entire home atmosphere. This will show itself in the very tone of voice husband and wife use to each other: genuine happiness in greeting one another, sincere interest in the affairs of the home, loving banter, lively discussions, and serious ones. Or it will show itself in arguments without caustic comments, in misunderstandings that are talked over in love, in hurts caused by sin healed by a forgiving grace. Timmy will see that his father and mother want to take time for one another, sometimes to discuss and decide issues, but often just to enjoy the other's fellowship. We as covenant parents begin to realize how needful for us this communion as husband and wife is. We cultivate it. And, as everything else which is cultivated grows, so our need to be close to one another, to share experiences, big and small, to love one another more deeply grows.

There are times in our lives when we consciously cultivate that closeness and love, such as when the nasty retort is at the tip of our tongue and we do not utter it, or when we are ready to confide to a friend one of the basic weaknesses in the character of our spouse, and then think better of it. We suppress these desires to sin with our tongues, to look instead at our own weaknesses, and to smile at or forgive those of our mate. For we do not want to backbite against the one we love most, do we? Nor do we want to do anything which will draw us away from a close spiritual unity with our mate. At other times we cultivate our closeness as husband and wife spontaneously, by a loving look, a sincere compliment, or outright praise. Timmy knows all about that. Just listen as he tells Kathy, "My dad *hates* potlucks, 'cause everybody takes stuff over there, and my mom is the only real good cooker in the world."

Our willingness to work at building a closely knit relationship as husband and wife—yes, it takes diligent, devoted work—will carry over to our willingness to fill our home with worthwhile periodicals, books, music. In our conversation about articles we read, about stories in the newspaper, about happenings in the neighborhood, Timmy will hear, perhaps without realizing it, our outlook on life, our reverence for things spiritual, the seriousness of our view of sin, and our reliance on Scripture.

Timmy could not explain this home atmosphere where the love of God abounds. In fact, it is not easy for us to explain it to others. But it is there, undergirding what we do and say. And I believe that also this underlying atmosphere of love is comprehended in the diligence—sometimes the almost unconscious diligence—which Moses describes in Deuteronomy 6: "And thou shalt teach them diligently unto thy children . . . and thou shalt bind them for a sign upon thine hand, and they shall be as frontlets between thine eyes."

We might consider this kind of atmosphere the indispensable background for our specific talking of the precepts of the Lord when we sit in our house or walk by the way.

For we persevere in teaching Timmy an understanding of *how* to view all the "do's" and "don't's" in his life. We tell him what he is doing wrong when his friend leaves his shiny new firetruck in our yard and we watch Timmy tiptoe down the basement with it and stow it noiselessly in the farthest recess of his favorite cupboard. Step by step we show him that even though Johnny left his toy in our yard, the firetruck is still Johnny's. To take it is stealing, and God's law says, "Thou shalt not steal." Further we explain to Timmy that he may not obey God's law with a sullen face, for the Lord wants His children to obey willingly. We tell him how much we care (and God cares) that he acts like a child of God.

Although he is far too young to understand any discourse of ours on love, that it "suffereth long," and that it "seeketh not her own" (I Corinthians 13:4, 5), he will understand our manner when we correct him in love. He will also understand something like this (after he has done a wrong): "Timmy, you did a very wrong thing. I wouldn't be a good mother if I didn't talk to you about it (or spank you so that you learn not to do it again)." Or, better: "Don't you see, Timmy, how naughty you were? The Lord tells Christian mothers to teach their children not to be naughty. And He says right here in His Book that sometimes mothers must use the stick on their boys, so that they will learn to obey. Now do you see why you must be spanked?" He doesn't, really—not fully. But he is living with a love that corrects him, and he is learning the beginnings of obedience for God's sake.

One of the most difficult tasks for the covenant parent is to teach his child to *want* to obey. And yet . . . he *does* want to obey. That is the tension of our regenerated child. His old nature wants to live in rebellion and sin; his new man in Christ lives in loving obedience to God's commands. The trouble is that we see so much of that sinful old nature. His thinking and his actions are so steeped in sin that often we, steeped just as deeply in sin, see little else. We see his swift reaction of striking back to our hand of correction, as we described it in the previous chapter. By nature he wants nothing to do with obedience to our authority. He might first show his rebellion by his angry, resentful face when we correct him. Not satisfied with that, his show of rebellion increases. He tries to demonstrate his equality with us and his spurning of our authority by striking out physically—with hands or feet.

Or he shows his defiance in another way. He rebels secretly (he thinks) behind our backs. While we watch, he goes through the motions of obeying with a pious face; but when he thinks we are not looking, he does the thing we have just told him not to do. His sinful rebellion has taken the form of sneaking, and that hypocritically, too. With this kind of sinful disobedience almost always goes the sin of lying, too. To cover up his dishonesty, his cheating, or sneaking, he denies it in order to escape the consequences.

To take a concrete example, suppose that we put Timmy to bed for his afternoon nap. Soon we hear a few suspicious stirrings upstairs. Investigating, we find him quietly in his bed, his face serene, his eyes closed in mock sleep. We remind him,

"Lie still and go to sleep, Timmy." He does not answer. Can we not see that he is already asleep? As we go down the steps, the telephone rings and we talk a few minutes until a small crash makes us hang up hastily and find out what happened. Upstairs, Timmy is too carefully composed in pseudo-slumber, including his rigidly-controlled facial expression. In the bathroom, we find his small drinking glass smashed in the sink, and in the wastebasket several soaked cotton balls—some of Timmy's favorite things to touch—his wet "marshmallows." On one of the balls is a tinge of red. We call, "Tim, you'd better come here." But he is "sleeping" and doesn't respond. We go to his room and say, "Sit up, Timmy." He sits up, wide-eyed and alert. As we confront him with evidence, he has lies ready. The glass "just fell." He didn't even hear it. The cotton balls were in the wastebasket long ago. Kathy gave him that cut on his finger, which has stained his sheet, and is still bleeding.

What should we do? We know he likes to play in the bathroom before he naps; and we know he was there, quietly sneaking his disobedience, giving meanwhile a hypocritical show of perfect obedience. We know, too, that he is lying. What is more, Timmy knows all this, too. Shall we dismiss the episode, bandage his finger, and tell him to stay in bed after this? No, we shall not.

If we drop the matter here, we will be wrong on several counts. First, our lack of pressing for the truth and correcting Timmy will show that we condone or at least fail to criticize his disobedience. No disobedience or lying is too minor to correct. Second, our sinful natures—and Timmy's—are so corrupt that, after we initially disobey, we find it easier to disobey the second time, and often to a greater degree of wickedness. Third, we are allowing Timmy to cultivate an attitude and a habit of trying to see how much he can get away with—stealthily, hypocritically, dishonestly. No, we do not want such a situation to have the smallest opportunity to arise.

As serious, loving, covenant parents, we talk to Timmy and remind him he *must* tell the truth. Not only we, but God demands it. (We cannot use language such as this for a three-year-old, of course. In this situation, too, we use a vocabulary to fit his level. I have found that a good opener to get a small child to tell the truth is to get him to admit a little at a time. The procedure goes something like this: "Did you look in the bathroom for just a *little* minute?" If he answers yes, and he often does, go on with step by step concrete questions until he has told all the truth: "Did you think you were just a wee bit thirsty? And you thought about taking one more drink?" . . . etc.)

After he has confessed to all his wrongdoing, we show him the evil of it. We tell him he must obey even when we are not there, for God is always there with him and knows what he does. We will be careful, though, not to use God's holy presence as a "scare tactic" or a "big stick" to our small child. We will teach him that a loving Father wants loving obedience. To cultivate a spirit of trust, we tell Timmy plainly that we want to be able to know that he will do the right even when we are not looking. Then we explain that the only people we can *truly* trust are God's people, because God's people fight hard against sin and try hard to do the right, because they want to obey. We tell him firmly, "Timmy, if you play with cotton balls and water only if mother or daddy is not watching, and if you quickly stop doing it when we come, you are not obeying us. Timmy, little boys who really want to obey God and daddy and mother do not sneak. They try hard to fight their wicked sin. They do the right because God's love is inside them, right here" (we point to his heart). "And God's love inside them makes them *want* to do the right thing instead of the wrong thing. Do *you* want to do the right? . . . "

And therein lies his struggle. He does and he doesn't. It is our weighty calling as parents to help him with his struggle, to lead him on the right path of obedience and to cultivate a spirit of trust between our child and us for God's sake. To do this, we repeat for Timmy the Bible's instruction in obedience for the covenant seed. We tell him over and over that we *expect* to be able to trust him, not because he is always so good, but because he is God's child. At first he will not understand it all. But he will become accustomed to this kind of spiritual talk and will slowly perceive what we so earnestly are teaching him.

To be sure, he will not always prove himself worthy of our

trust. He will sin over and over again. When we discover that he has not proved himself trustworthy—and we are alert to discover it—we will act as we feel: sorry. Harshness and severe scolding will not prove as effective as a genuine godly sorrow when we tell our child that we found out that still he cannot be trusted.

When, by the grace of God, he fights his sinful nature and does obey for God's sake, we share our joy with him and praise him and encourage him to go on in the right way.

Gradually, if our child obeys from a regenerated heart, we build up a quiet trust in all our lives together, from the minute details to the grave crises. Take, for example, the candy dish episode. In my own family, when the children were young, we had a candy dish, with candy, within reach on the coffee table. The children asked and received a piece after meals and at various other times. We had the understanding (of trust) that though it was possible for them to help themselves when I was not looking, they would not take a piece unless they asked. Then one day the aunt of the previous chapter came over again. She gave one of the children a bag of candy and said, "Tell Mama to hide it on the top shelf of the cupboard." With a look of amazement one of the small children answered, "Oh, no, Auntie. My mom would never do that. She puts it right here in the dish and we don't take it without asking. She trusts us."

Later that same child said to me, "Mother, if auntie is a Christian, how come she thinks she can't trust us?"

Admittedly, a piece of candy is an insignificant detail in life. But the principle of trust is not. We will dedicate our efforts to create and maintain a spiritual attitude of openness in our dealings with each other. We will strive for a candidness whereby our child will tell us (with fear in his voice) of his misdeeds, knowing that though he will be chastened, the chastisement will be administered by understanding, loving, devoted parents. Timmy will also tell us his joys and disappointments. Cultivating and continuing this rapport, this spiritual bond of trust, is not easy. There will be many failures and heartaches. But we will never stop trying.

A. N. Martin, in *The Banner of Truth,* offers some valuable insights into this subject of dealing with our child in love. He says: "There are probably four or five governing principles of the Christian life which meet you at every turn, and this is one of them: the consequences of my implicit trust in and obedience to God are not my responsibility but his. . . . If we carry out our disciplinary influence upon our children in the consciousness that we do it in God's name, then it will keep us not only from indifference to this responsibility, but also from fearfulness of the consequences in the performance of it."[2]

Next, Martin examines the love for his child from the viewpoint of Proverbs 13:24: "For he that loveth his son chasteneth him betimes." And he discusses that love as follows:

> I like to define it this way, and it is a workable definition for me, and has been of some help to people over the years: Love is that selfless affection which seeks the good of its object even at personal cost. To love my children means that I want their good even at cost to myself. I know from Scripture that discipline is for their good. There are many verses which show this, but we may use Proverbs 29.15 as an example: 'The rod and reproof give wisdom; but a child left to himself bringeth his mother to shame'. Do I want my child to be wise? The rod and reproof are the means to make him wise. So if I love my children I will discipline them, not with tyrannical cruelty, nor will I refuse them to discipline them by reason of unprincipled sentimentality, but I will apply the rod and reproof of correction with firmness, suffused with true love. You want to declare to your child that you hate him? Then refuse the rod of correction.[3]

Because the author of this article closely examines the context of the verses with which we head this chapter, I would like to quote one more worthwhile paragraph.

> The most vivid statement concerning this kind of relationship is found in Hebrews 12.9. Notice what the writer says about parents who stand in responsible relationship to their children but do not discipline and chastise them when needed: 'Whom the Lord loveth he chasteneth and scourg-

eth every son whom he receiveth. If ye endure chastening, God dealeth with you as with sons; for what son is he whom the father chasteneth not? But if ye be without chastisement, whereof all are partakers, then are ye bastards'—you are illegitimate children—'and not sons' [Heb. 12.6-8]. What is he saying? He is saying that if God were to say that he loves you, and yet had such a relationship to you that your good did not mean enough to him to take a course of disciplinary action that would move you into the way of obedience, the only way of good and blessedness, you would be like bastard children. To be without the sanctifying influence of the rod is to be like a bastard child running loose, whom nobody claims and nobody loves. Parents who feel that they are surrounding their children with love because they let them do as they please, are treating them like bastard children. That is the emphasis of the passage. If you are without chastisement, you are without one of the most necessary helpful influences of parental love—you may as well not have anyone to claim you as their child. If you look at the Christian families and the Christian homes in the best of our evangelical and Reformed churches, you see children turning out as though they never had the influence, or very little of the influence, of a loving father and a loving mother. We must never set up a dichotomy between faithful discipline and love, as though these things stood in antithesis one to the other. No, we must set up the antithesis between tyrannical administration of the rod and loving administration of the rod. But never between love and discipline, as though the proof of one's love is the infrequency of one's correction.[4]

Then he underscores what we have been saying about the mutual relationship between Timmy and us:

We can set this in a larger context. It will be hard for children to believe that the discipline that we say is administered in love is genuinely administered in love unless they can see this experience in the larger context of our demonstrated love to them. The parent who never has intimate, close dealings with his children except in the situation of discipline is putting a big question mark over the reality of his love to his children. But that parent who takes time to cultivate interests that to him would not be natural but, because they are things of interest to the child, pushes aside his own schedule that is 'important' and says, I am going to give myself to spending time with that child, and demonstrates in many specific ways his love and his concern, his selfless affection for the child, then, when he must administer discipline, it will be much easier for the child to know that what is done in this situation is not in contradiction to this, this and this, but is simply another expression of the same love.[5]

Each parent, making the most of his own personality traits and those of his child, will acquire the method of training his child in obedience that works best for him in his specific situation. All personalities cannot use the same approaches, the same phrasings, the same facial expressions. Some of us are phlegmatic, slow-spoken; others have lively, louder ways; many have an irresistible sense of humor; some are nervous, rapid-fire talkers; and others ponder their words. But with all of our individual differences, the basic tenets for training obedient children are the same in all of our covenant homes.

The rules are few and simple. First, we remind ourselves that we are still working to achieve a relaxed attitude and an untroubled atmosphere, as we have been doing ever since Timmy was born. In unharried surroundings, free from hectic pressures and tense situations, we cultivate the habit of giving orders in a kindly, matter-of-fact voice. Second, we expect and demand obedience promptly, the first time Timmy is told, with no exceptions and no compromise. Third, we ask for obedience with a happy heart and a cheerful face from our son. Does this sound like stern, unbending authoritarianism? It is not. It is Scriptural: "Children, obey your parents in the Lord: for this is right," Ephesians 6:1; "Children, obey your parents in all things: for this is well-pleasing unto the Lord," Colossians 3:20; "Correct thy son, and he shall give thee rest; yea, he shall give delight unto thy soul," Proverbs 29:17; and, "Thy testimonies have I taken as an heritage forever: for they are the rejoicing of my heart," Psalm 119:111. In these few selections from the many Scriptures which speak of our child and his obedience, the striking note is the brevity of God's command to obey. Without qualification, children must obey because "this is right" and "well-pleasing unto the Lord." Necessarily following obedience for God's sake is the delight of the parents in their obedient child, and the joy in the child's heart as he obeys God's testimonies. That is why unquestioning obedience and cheerfulness go hand in hand. For if a child wants to obey because "this is right," his face will reflect the "rejoicing of his heart" as he freely does as he is told.

When we ask our child to pick up his toys now and he says, "I'm almost ready to, Dad," is he obeying? His "almost" can mean anything from two to thirty minutes, I suppose, but it does not mean *now,* and Timmy's answer is not an obedient one. But if he does not even respond to our order to pick up his toys now and we ask him why he has not answered, he may often say, "I didn't hear you, Dad." We are charitable, of course, and reason that his little mind was filled with his play. At the same time we are alert to see if he is deaf to us rather often, especially when told to do something he would rather not do. For he can cultivate this kind of deafness. Another name for this kind of deafness is disobedience, and it is our duty to train him to use his ears also in the service of the Lord in the sphere of obedience. If we impose a penalty for this type of deafness, his hearing improves. If Timmy does what one small boy I know did when asked to put away his toys promptly, and he says "oka*t*e" (with a grinding emphasis on the *t*), is his "okay" obedience? We know that any grudging, unwilling compliance is not true obedience.

If Timmy, at age three, has been saying a short mealtime prayer for some time, and then one mealtime claims, "I can't say it," he is not only disobedient, but stubbornly so. If he persists in his stubbornness and says he cannot say it, we, who are sinners ourselves, probably feel anger welling up in us. If we do, we will leave Timmy in his high chair, or put him in another safe place, and leave him for a few moments. This gives us a chance to become calm and think about our next step, rather than act on angry impulse. When we come back to Timmy, we first talk to him. If, as we talk, we see sinful stubbornness instead of obedient penitence, anger may well in us again. A good rule, I have found, is: the more angry we are, the more quietly we talk. This device helps us to regain control of ourselves, keeps us from shouting raging words we will be sorry for later, and gives a tone of seriousness, with quietness, to our rebuke.

If Timmy does not listen to us—and one of the sins Timmy has to fight hardest is stubbornness—we chasten him immediately. But not if we are still angry. Consciously we ask ourselves if we are. If we are hot inside, or feel like giving him the "spanking of his life" because he dares to defy us, we go away again and think and become calm. We do not whip him to vent *our* anger. When we go back to Timmy, who also has had a few minutes to think, and he is still unwilling to obey, we chasten. Without threats of "next time" (it is the *present* that matters to both of us), or waiting until the other parent hears about it (Timmy knows what cowardice is), we act.

At Timmy's age, three or four, what is a chastening suited to this offense, to his age, and most conducive to bringing results? A curt banishment to a chair in another room or to his bedroom with orders (which we check on) to fold his little hands and think, may soon bring an "I'm sorry, Mom. I can say my prayer now." Some children respond to chastening which deprives them of a pleasure, preferably connected with the misdeed. The logical one in this instance, I suppose, is to deprive him of food (or a favorite food) until he asks a blessing. If our Timmy is still stubborn—and he may be—a series of smart slaps on his bottom with hands or paddle may be the next step. If, at this stage, he works himself up into a rage, if he wills to have an angry tantrum, we will use the glass of cold water, our seldom-used severe chastening, for severe wilful disobedience. The form of our chastening will be determined, at least in part, by the type of our son's misdeed. Our common sense and sanctified Christian judgment, which are what we are called to use, tell us not to make a mountainous issue out of every petty quarrel or misdeed of our son. At times a curt rebuke or "That's enough!" is all we need say. But we are also called to use our knowledge of Scripture's descriptions of the blackness of sin and the awfulness of straying from the path of obedience and to recognize those sins and strayings in the life of our son, and bring him back, with admonitions and the rod, to the right way. A. N. Martin adds this touch:

> Our discipline must always be within reason. How does God discipline us? With perfect knowledge of who we are and what we are at different stages of development. The words of the Psalmist in Psalm 103:13-14 form the Biblical basis of this aspect of God's discipline of his children. 'Like as a father pitieth his children, so the Lord pitieth them that fear him, for he knoweth our frame, he remembereth that we are dust'; and remember that, in the context of the thought of his sovereign concern in verses 9 and 10, 'He will not always chide, neither will he keep his anger for ever. He hath not dealt with us after our sins, nor rewarded us according to our iniquities.' God's discipline of us takes into account all the variable factors. So as we administer discipline to our children let it be reflective of his discipline of us in this respect. . . . It must be within the framework of the child's mode of co-ordination, in terms of the child's natural temperament. All of these are variables, so you cannot set up rules and say, 'At age 9 months I will administer the first spanking, at age 12 months this and this etc.' There are variables, and as concerned parents we must seek to take all these variables into consideration in the administration of discipline in God's name, in love, with sufficient firmness, but always within reason. And only you as parents, prayerfully concerned about your children, can know these variables. We must be careful not to judge one another.[6]

In a covenant home we place the emphasis on the positive. Without preaching it, and more by our attitude of simply *expecting* it, we "set the stage" for obedience. If Timmy hesitates to obey us when we tell him to do an unpleasant duty, or something he would rather not do just then, we can understand that he would rather not do it, and sympathize with him. We can tell him that, too. When it is past his bedtime and he is still having a happy time with his friends, but is tripping and falling from fatigue, we tell him, "Timmy, we know what a good time you are having. But our eyes can see that you are too tired and must go to bed now." If tears well in his eyes we remind him, "Tim, you may not make a fuss. You must obey mom and dad anyway, and making a fuss first is not obeying." Tim, trained in cheerful, prompt obedience, will come in cheerfully and promptly. We agree with Martin when he says:

> One of the pivotal issues in consistent discipline is always to keep your word. It is not the severity of the punishment which is most significant—it is the certainty. Never, never make a threat or promise without following it through. Never do it. You will break down every foundation upon which respect can be built if your children know that your words are nothing but idle threats. If you have to raise your voice to gain attention for the obedience of your children, you have missed it. If you have got to say the thing twice, you have missed it. The child should respond to the first statement which is an expression of your will, and know that obedience should be based upon, not loud tones and big threats, but 'Mummy has spoken and she means what she says,' 'Daddy has spoken and he means what he says'. You come then to the most essential place of teaching them submission to authority simply because the authority has been expressed, and it is right for them to obey.[7]

In this atmosphere, chastisement is the exception, not the rule. Again, Martin says:

> Our discipline should always be proportionate. The rod is medicine, one has said, not food. And if you turn medicine into food you destroy its remedial quality. So with our discipline; there are some things that warrant just a sharp glance from the parent; there are other things that warrant a word of rebuke. There are some things that warrant a normal kind of spanking; there are other things so serious that the discipline ought to impress the seriousness of the issue.[8]

However, even the thought of our being a "slapper" or a "shouter" as our fearful or crafty child skillfully ducks out of reach fills us with horror. We do not bring up children who want to "get by" with something or try to "get away" with mischief. We do not, if our home is a spiritual home and if we are earnest, diligent, believing parents.

We hope and pray that our child may be a spiritual "Jacob" and not an "Esau," who was in the covenant line outwardly, but not in his heart. Because we trust that he is showing signs of being a "Jacob," we talk much with him after he has sinned. For, as the historical Jacob, he has certain weaknesses, and sins much. Especially if a sin is frequent or great, we choose a time to tell him, in a childlike way, by story or illustration, what God's Word says about it. This chosen time is not mealtime. We make mealtime a more lighthearted, happy, humorous time, a time of cheerful Christian fellowship. The proper time will often be before bedtime prayers. If Timmy is able, we have him learn how to ask God's forgiveness for his sin. Above all, we teach him from God's Word and from his own experience that an obedient child is a happy child. For "no chastening for the present seemeth to be joyous, but grievous: nevertheless, afterward it yieldeth the peaceable fruit of righteousness, unto them which are exercised thereby."

* * *

Now Timmy is talking. In his waking hours he hardly ever stops. And he has learned it all from us. He watches us and listens very closely; and at this highly impressionable age not a detail of expression, pronunciation, or tone escapes him. He is an expert mimic, too, we remember. He speaks with a Midwestern twang, an Eastern slur, or a Southern drawl, depending on where he lives. Best of all, he enjoys mimicking the ways adult have with language. "Do you want me to tell you a story?" he asks, with proper condescension. Then he spins a run-on tale about the snakes and bears in the woods behind Kathy's house. As we listen, with appropriate comments, we are evaluating his imagination at work. When he finishes, we ask, "Did you make up that story?" If he answers, "Yes," we could ask, "Why don't you tell me a true story now?" Then he will probably say, with a laugh, "We really played with trucks in Kathy's sandbox."

If, when he tells his preposterous story, he insists that everyone of his experiences in it truly happened, we have some correcting to do; for if Timmy tells as truth what is false, he is lying. And there lies the danger in Timmy's imagination. It is not permissible for him to accept for himself or present to us the yarn-spinning of his imagination as truth. Any psychologist will agree with this. He wants Timmy to know the difference between reality and fantasy. We do, too. But we go a step further. We want Timmy to know the difference between the truth and the lie, and to live the truth. It becomes an ethical matter, one of his relationship to God's law. As a general rule, we listen with interest and amusement to his imagined world, peopled often with his imagined friends, but at the same time we watch that he does not present it as true or use it as an escape from the real situations of life. I have found that a suitable reply often is, "Now tell me a true story."

Because our own example, also our language usage, speaks louder than our intentions, we are aware of our manner of speaking to our son. Do we ever take the time to examine the thousands of words which flow in communication between us and our son? What else, besides the overt meaning of our words, are we telling our son as we converse?

Scripture teaches us much about our speech, and how we use it—also how we do not use it. Three brief selections will satisfy here: "The preparation of the heart in man, and the answer of the tongue, is from the Lord," Proverbs 16:1; "Let your speech be always with grace, seasoned with salt . . . , " Colossians 4:6; and, negatively, "Excellent speech becometh not a fool . . . , " Proverbs 17:7. If we were more spiritually sensitive to these truths of Holy Writ, would we be aware that the answer of our tongue is from the Lord? Would our speech be always with grace? Would it, contrary to the fool's speech, be excellent?

Even formally our speech should be excellent. When the Lord made the languages at Babel (we do not believe, do we, that they just evolved, outside of the hand of the Lord), He created order and logic and rules in each one of the languages. Whether men have corrupted this order is another subject. Be that as it may, we are called, as covenant people, to have excellence of speech, also from the formal point of view.

If we want our son to learn proper grammar, we will speak correctly to him. And it is better, generally, to speak adult language. Every family has its pet names, its nonsense words, and its ungrammatical constructions, usually with a family history behind them. Ordinarily, however, let our little mimic imitate correct usage. He is not too small to have his grammar correct. In fact, if we say to him, " 'He don't' isn't right, Timmy. We say 'He doesn't,' " Timmy will grow up with correct usage long before he learns the rules behind it. To Timmy we also speak slowly, usually softly, brightly, and cheerfully. We also speak kindly to him and kindly about others.

Although the above paragraphs have viewed our speech formally, we cannot compartmentalize our speech any more than we can any other sphere of our lives. The formal often blurs into the material content of our speech. How, then, do we train Timmy to speak as befits a covenant child? A small child is a vibrant, bouncing, bubbling individual; and spiritually minded parents are cheerful, peaceful, content people. When these two get together, laughter and happiness and family jokes follow. Scripture says, "A merry heart maketh a cheerful countenance," Proverbs 15:13. What a sorry sight it is to see a child who cannot sense humor or roar with gales of laughter at a joke. We encourage this lightheartedness in a Christian context, for we know that we are the only truly happy people on the earth.

Because "A wholesome tongue is a tree of life; but perverseness therein is a breach in the spirit," we teach our son to have a wholesome tongue. We have already begun to teach him that a wholesome tongue is a reverent tongue; never "by rash swearing" may we "profane or abuse the name of God," but "we use that holy name of God no otherwise than with fear and reverence."[9] That is not nearly all, however. We teach our child to abhor the minced oath, the "Gee" and "Gosh" of unbelievers; for the reason they use these oaths is to get as close to using God's name lightly as they can, without actually saying His holy name. Rough talk, slang, expressions that border on smut are incompatible with covenant speech. That does not mean, of course, that Timmy will not hear them and repeat them—even with a certain bravado. Something about the aura of coarse language has an appeal to a small boy's sinful nature, and he knows more of this language than we think he does. Do we immediately reach for a bar of soap and say, "I'll fix him"? Not we. At least not yet. We tell him seriously about a clean heart that makes our tongues clean, and we tell him that sin got in again—and he *likes* to let sin in—and his tongue is filthy now. If he does not listen, and repeats his foul words, we will use outward cleansing or the rod of correction as well.

Often God's people hear remarks from those outside the church such as this: "Christians are boors, fifty years behind the times"; "Those do-gooders are so intent on witnessing that they have no time left for manners"; or, "Polish? They're upright people with good intentions, but stiff and introverted, with little refinement." Do you resent these accusations as much as I do? Do we resent them because in part they may be true? Surely, we of all people, who try hard to be God-centered in all areas of life, do not want to be rough-hewn clods. We should not, anyway. We want to be shining lights, examples of love, meekness, lovingkindness, and sanctification of life. In Scripture we learn how God's Word affects our lives, also our behavior toward those whose lives touch ours. Psalm 119 is a classic example of God's Word and our lives. There we say that we "hate vain thoughts," and that we have "chosen the way of truth," and we pray for "thy merciful kindness," and "good judgment and knowledge." The Psalm points us in each verse to God's precepts, His holy law, and His righteousness. In its refrains the Psalm shows how our hearts are changed. When our hearts are changed, our conversation will show it. Not only will we be careful *what* we say, but also *how* we say it; for "A soft answer turneth away wrath: but grievous words stir up anger," Proverbs 15:1; and "O that my ways were directed to keep thy statutes! *Then shall I not be ashamed,* when I have respect unto all thy commandments," Psalm 119:5, 6.

When we train our son in good speech habits, we are teaching him something that comes directly from the heart. The choice of his words, the tone, the manner in which he speaks them reflect his inner life. At his young age of three to five years, much of Timmy's speech mirrors his respect. And does not "respect" underlie the refinement and polish of his manners? Most of the people with whom he speaks are older than he is. This is the age when we teach him how to talk to the aged. All old people love small children. When grandfather comes and Timmy says, "H'llo," without looking up, or runs from the room and hides, or makes a silly, self-conscious remark, we can attribute these actions to preoccupation, shyness, or nervousness. Our knowing the causes does not make Timmy's actions right. He is taught to leave what he is doing, come up to grandfather and greet him with a handshake or a kiss and a "Hi, Grandpa!"

We teach Timmy the same kind of respect for us. While he is listening and replying to us we teach him to look at us, consistently, all the while. Is it not frustrating for us as parents to speak to a child (no matter what the subject matter) and have him look around the room, smile at something out the window, trace an interesting pattern with his finger, and dart a glance toward us occasionally? It is not only frustrating. It is wrong. Attention and respect which come from Timmy's heart are reflected in his listening posture. This posture does not just happen. We teach it to him. Then, whether we give him directions for what he must do, or whether we reprove, we have a child who looks at us alertly, respectfully, obediently.

How does he respond to us? If we say, "Wear your heavy cap this morning, Tim," and he says, impatiently, "I'm *getting* it," are we satisfied with his answer? If father says, "Tim, I hear you threw stones at Kathy," and he says, "Yup," is that good? If a neighbor stops by, and Tim comes in from play and wants cookies with us, and he says, "Hi," to our neighbor, does his greeting meet our standards of respect? In all three examples, Timmy has fallen short. We train Timmy, when told to get something, to say, "All right, *Mother.*" To father's question, he says, "Yes, *Daddy.*" To our neighbor, he says, "Hello, *Mrs. Stone.*" When we teach him to use our name with his answer, we are teaching him much more than outward polish.

We teach him respect for our office as parent. No, we are not militaristic parents. How could we be? And Timmy is no puppet, sprinkling every phrase with a "yes, Mother, no, Daddy," ending. We use our judgment and common sense here, too. What is more, we will discover that if we insist, consistently, on respectful answers, Timmy's whole tone and manner become more wholesomely obedient and loving. Try it. It works.

The same rules apply to the niceties of "please, Mother," and "thank you, Dad," the "I'm sorry's" and "excuse me's." We teach him to keep his speech free from impulsive interruptions of others' speech, of cruelty ("I'm going to wring Fido's neck") and of wickedness ("I hate Kathy!"). For "A wholesome tongue is a tree of life: but perverseness therein is a breach in the spirit," Proverbs 15:4.

Our speech—and Timmy's—reflects our outlook on life. Because our contacts with our neighbor are expressed through the medium of speech, this speech reflects what we are. We teach Timmy, through speech as well as acts, the love of the neighbor. As he follows us through the house, "helping" with little chores, we will want to chant to him the beautiful Scripture found in Matthew 22:37-39: "Jesus said unto him, Thou shalt love the Lord thy God with all thy heart, and with all thy soul, and with all thy mind. This is the first and great commandment. And the second is like unto it, Thou shalt love thy neighbor as thyself." Timmy will also understand what Romans 13:10 means: "Love worketh no ill to his neighbor. . . . " Not yet will he understand the terminology of the beautiful Answer 112 of the Heidelberg Catechism, in response to the requirements in the ninth commandment: " . . . that I do not judge, nor join in condemning any man rashly, or unheard; but that I avoid all sorts of lies and deceit as the proper works of the devil, . . . also that I defend and promote, as much as I am able, the honor and good character of my neighbor."[10] But we can explain to Timmy what this answer means. We train him so that his speech reflects true love for the neighbor, a considerateness, a selflessness, a kindness, rooted in the love of God. Repeatedly we tell Timmy that only Christians can really love their neighbors, and even they cannot do it *nearly* perfectly. And we explain the cruelty in the world of sinful men on this basis alone—not that they do not know any better, but that because of their sin they do not want to and they cannot love their neighbor.

Again, we are objecting, all of the foregoing, though it may be true, portrays too much idealism and does not work well in practical life, at least not for a child under five years old. Is it not true that Timmy, though a covenant child, is totally depraved and sins in all that he does? Are not the remembering and practicing of all the details of a godly relationship with his friends and neighbors tremendously difficult for him? If we have ever carefully observed any child of Timmy's age, certain characteristics are striking: he is immensely self-centered, he has no outward polish, he is often sadistically cruel to his playmates, and he is a tease and a toy snatcher. Psychologists, of whom Curti is one, bear out that all these characteristics are present. Curti reports on an experiment with four- and five-year-olds:

... there is more grabbing (not mere taking). In the four-year-olds, competitiveness in this situation is seen to be at a high point. After quoting remarks made by the children the author says, "Perhaps the reader can gather something of the tenseness, the speed, the competition in the air. Note especially the kind of personal remarks made, the grabbing and hiding of stones, the increase of muscular tension, and the final out-and-out quarreling...."

The numerous studies on competition which have been made indicate clearly that competitiveness or aggressiveness is no definite something, no particular behavior possessed by all children—an instinct![11]

We would not call it an instinct. We would call it sinful selfishness. And, surely, we do not believe it is easy to train our little boy not to be a self-centered, cruel, taunting clod, but rather a loving, kind, considerate, spiritually sensitive covenant child. By our example and by firm discipline we show him how wrong is the sinful way, and how to walk in the right way. However, if we taught only by our example and discipline, we would still not achieve the goal of covenant parents. We could not do all this by ourselves. We covenant parents cannot bring up our small child, in this sphere either, without the grace of our God, given us through daily prayer for and with our son. Timmy, too, could not respond to us as a covenant son, were it not for God's regenerating grace in his heart.

* * *

These three years of Timmy's life, while we have him at home with us and under our influence all day and every day, are the priceless years to teach him things spiritual. He learns both formally and informally. Let us look first at the formal training Timmy will be receiving in these years.

By the age of two (with some variations) he will be able to learn a simple prayer. As we teach him the words, we insist on proper prayer posture. We are teaching him much more than words—we are teaching him to pray. Certainly he will not understand the import of all the words we ask him to repeat after us. But some day he will. And, remember, we are teaching him how to speak to his God; this we will do with the diligence of Deuteronomy 6, wherever and whenever we can.

The whole concept of reverence is not so easy to teach a small child. How can he reverence One whom he cannot see, and that with his eyes closed? Yet, for a covenant child, renewed by the Spirit, with the hearty confidence of faith, we need not define it. He knows his heavenly Father, and by His grace bows before Him in reverence. Although he knows that he has a Father in heaven, he needs to know so much more. We talk to him often about God's majesty, and tell our three- or four-year-old that He is the only King of all the heaven and earth. And we try to portray to his little mind, through Bible stories and picture language, the other attributes of God: His holiness, omnipresence, fatherhood, love. Almost certainly he will say at some time during the conversation, "Jesus is God." Then we teach him the wonderful mystery of the trinity, and end by saying, "I'm big, but my mind is not so great. I don't understand it all. Do you?" And he will say, "No." Then we can say, "But the Bible teaches it, and I believe it. Do you?" And he will solemnly nod his little head. He is learning that faith is "the evidence of things not seen," Hebrews 11:1.

As he begins to understand more about the holy God he worships, he begins better to understand the reverence due Him. We parents teach him by example, by insisting on reverent words and reverent posture at devotions at mealtime, or any other devotional time. When Timmy was under two, we taught him what we expected during devotions. We have made a good beginning. Let us carry it on consistently, and never allow walking around or any kind of playing during devotions. If we do not allow it, Timmy will not ask for it, for he knows nothing different. By our firmness, cheerfulness, and calm expectation of reverence at all times of worship or devotion, we show Timmy that this is the *only* way a covenant child worships. We remember, too, that outward signs—the humbly bowed head, the undistracted folded hands, the bending of the knees—set the stage for the inner experiences of communion with God.

Do we encourage him to make his own prayers? Not yet. Not for a long time. He is too young yet to know the art of true prayer. In accordance with Scripture's principles, we instruct him over and over, for many years before he has the knowledge and the maturity to make his own prayers. The danger is not that his prayers will be too simple, but that they will be contrary to the rules laid down in God's Word. Too often we hear of small children praying unsupervised, silly—or worse—sacrilegious prayers. In the September-October, 1972, issue of the magazine *Liberty,* are spine-chilling examples of prayers of children with some religious background, but who nonetheless make a mockery of prayer. Some examples are:

Dear God, Why did you put in tonsils if they just have to take them out again.

Why did you make so many people? Could you make another earth and put the extras there.

I'm afraid of things at night more than in the day. So if you could keep the sun on longer that would be a good thing.

If you made the sun the moon and stars, you must of had lots of equipment.[12]

Never, never would we want words such as these passing over the lips of our child. Rather, in this "intake" period of his life, we will be diligent each day to pour into him the wealth of instruction from God's Word. After he has learned much of things spiritual, including the art of prayer, he will be able to express his experiences distinctively, reverently, Scripturally. But let us wait a few years for that.

Another part of Timmy's spiritual training is in going to church. In the previous chapter we viewed the formal side of Timmy's church-going, his attitude and behavior. But if that is all the training we give Timmy, we are neglecting a large area of our responsibility. Not only do we teach Timmy that we are quiet, reverent, and attentive, but we also teach him what church is. And the age of two to five years is not too young for this. A small child can understand when we tell him that God made one day a week a day of rest, when we must worship Him. But we do not worship Him *by ourselves*. All God's children go to God's house to sing, to be happy, to pray, to listen, to learn.

Next we explain to him what a sermon is. Too hard for Timmy to grasp? Not at all. We do not underestimate him. We teach him that the minister studies God's Word and then tells it to us. We tell him how Christ speaks to us through those words of the minister. That is *preaching*. The preacher takes only a little part of God's Word each Sunday to explain to us. That is called a *sermon*. Each Sunday we hear a new sermon and we learn more each week.

Later we question Timmy about our instruction and reinforce the gaps in his memory or understanding. Now that he knows that a sermon is preaching on a portion of the Bible, we are ready for our next step in our preparation for church-going. If our minister is preaching a series from a certain book of the Bible, or if he is preaching from the Heidelberg Catechism, so that we know what is coming next, or if we can find out the text before the service, we read the text to Timmy. We tell him what words the minister will use, and ask him to listen for them. To cultivate an early habit of attentive listening, we ask him to tap our hand, lightly, unobtrusively, when he hears the text and the words he was told to listen for. We can vary this tapping by asking him during another sermon to press our hand when he hears a whole sentence he can understand. But is this not annoying to us parents and to our fellow worshippers? Not if Timmy is taught the difference between poking and gentle pressure. The pressure is not a noticeable act, and is felt only by the parent to whom it is applied. Speaking as this parent, from experience, I learned that my young child kept my own mind from wandering, and made me more attentive to the things in which I had instructed him.

One danger is that in his joy that the minister is saying "just the right thing" he will forget the no-talking rule and whisper his joy. Although inwardly we are elated with his attentiveness, we discourage his verbalizing it, and tell him that we will talk about it after we get home. The benefits of this method of learning to listen are great. What better time is there than in our child's tender years to teach him to listen to God's Word and worship actively? Why should not our child listen actively, interestedly, and joyfully? The alternative, covenant parents, is occupying our child during worship with nothing, or with candy, or with wishing that the service were over. When, then, will our child begin to learn to listen? At seven? Or ten? Or will he never learn really to listen?

This method takes preparation, time, and patience. This preparation, time, and patience are spent in teaching our child to worship. After services we do not forget the sermon, but question Timmy and answer his questions. Church-going becomes, for all of us, a joyous, fruitful experience.

Other aspects of training Timmy in growth in spiritual life we often teach informally. Authorities sometimes call it incidental learning. It is not incidental in the sense that it is unimportant, but incidental in that it is taught in connection with another subject, or alongside it. For we know, and Timmy must be taught, that we are no dualists, with one time and one area for the natural and another for the spiritual. We teach him that we look at our lives differently from the way most people do. We look at them through the eyes of God's Word.

Our wish to teach him a God-glorifying life will not make the formulation of answers to his numerous questions easy. We answer his questions when he asks them, even though we may think we are busy. We really are not too busy for him, are we? For our outlook, especially as mothers who are with him all day, is always that Timmy's education is far more important than getting a room cleaned in thirty minutes, or the dishes done on time.

If his question seems trivial to us, we will not dismiss it with a wave of the hand; for we are trying to learn to know how a little boy of three years old thinks, so that we will better be able to understand him. When we view the world on Timmy's level, the question may not be so trivial after all.

When Timmy's forthright questions become embarrassing to us, many of us would rather hedge on the answers. When he asks, "Why won't you let me go into the bathroom with Kathy?" or "Did God send me down from the sky or did you buy me from the hospital? Tell me *now*," tell him now. Now is the right time to give Timmy a pure, Biblical view of the way the Lord made the sexes, and how He provided for reproduction. We will remember not to preach to Timmy. What he wants is information. We give it to him briefly, simply, and Scripturally.

When Timmy is afraid, and when he persists in being afraid of certain things, what do we do? Fear has a real place in our lives. Some fears are of our own invention and are not founded on reality; other fears are occasioned by the real dangers present in our earthly surroundings. Each day as we face reality, we face fear: fear of a car accident, fear when a tornado is sighted in the vicinity, fear when a loved one is struck down by a serious illness. Many things we should fear. Our child has these fears, too. His may be the fear of dogs, of being in a dark room alone, or of thunder. Do we say, "Look, Timmy! There's nothing to be afraid of. Forget it"? We agree with Jersild that this is not the approach:

> Many social pressures are brought to bear upon children to get them to conceal or disguise their fears. Children themselves taunt each other with epithets such as "Fraidy Cat." Adults also, in many ways, discourage the display of fear, not only by practices such as asking the child to "be big" or to "be brave," but also, sometimes quite unintentionally, by the practice of telling children that there is

really nothing to fear. What an adult thus says to reassure a child may fail to dispel the child's fear and only give the child the impression that it is cowardly of him to be afraid.[13]

An important element in handling Timmy's fears is for us to understand that whether they are legitimate fears (fears grounded in reality) or not, to Timmy they are very real fears. For that reason, we will never stand in his dark room among the horrid shadows cast by the corner street light and say, "See, Tim, Daddy isn't afraid!" That isn't the problem. Timmy is the one who is afraid. How then do we help Timmy to overcome these fears? Even though he fears when there is no good reason to fear, we will not ridicule or "pooh-pooh" his feeling. That is not our way of handling Timmy. Instead, we will teach him, speaking quietly, and often admitting that dad used to be afraid of funny shadows, too. We reassure him that we would never leave him alone in his room if it were not safe; and we tell him firmly that he must fight hard against being afraid of things that really will not hurt. Most important we remind him that his Father in heaven is always there, and He holds Timmy in His hand. Never do we present our Father's care as some kind of magic that will make everything turn out all right, but we present it so that Timmy will learn humble trust.

Timmy will soon learn to come to us with his fears, great and small; and each time he comes we will teach him to view them in the light of Psalm 27:1: "The Lord is my light and my salvation; whom shall I fear? the Lord is the strength of my life: of whom shall I be afraid?" Timmy's trust will be childlike and imperfect, just as ours is. He will be like the small boy who told me, "I heard the loud, loud thunder and saw all that lightning when I was in bed last night. But I wasn't afraid, because God was right there with me. But I got up quick anyway and went to my big brother's room just . . . just to see if he was okay."

Mothers, those of us who have the priceless privilege of being with our son through most of his waking hours, occupy many of these minutes with the abiding truth of God's Word. These are the only years in which we can teach our child in this particular way. And why should we, dedicated, believing parents be always concerned with the earthly, the transitory, the trappings of our pilgrimage? Prepare for this part of our day, too, mothers. And as we dust and scrub and wash the dishes, we will chant a verse from Scripture; then two, three, until we and our son are happily reciting a whole passage. We do it happily, spontaneously, never as a chore, and our joy catches on. Timmy will soon be saying, the moment he has finished his breakfast milk, "The verse, Mom!" In choosing songs, we will learn those often used in our worship services, so that Timmy can participate, too. In my home, ironing time was often Bible story time. Our child would settle himself on a small rug, his Bible-story rug," he called it, and enjoy stories as long as the ironing or mother's voice held out. Timmy cannot understand much chronology or space relationship, but it is wise, anyway, to tell the stories generally in order, from the beginning to the end of the Bible; by this method we will include all the stories our small child can understand. As we study these stories beforehand—for we do—we are amazed at the benefits of knowledge and spiritual insights we reap for ourselves.

In all of Timmy's training in these three years, when we teach, rebuke, or chasten him, when he learns obedience for God's sake and the use of a sanctified tongue, or when we stress the formal and informal aspects of his spiritual training, we show him how serious and important these truths are. When he wilfully or stubbornly sins, we make him know why we swiftly correct him, even though "no chastening for the present seemeth to be joyous, but grievous." Yet we teach him, not with long, somber faces, but we make his spiritual training as much as possible spontaneous, joyous, corrective, and reverent. We do this in the knowledge that "afterward it yieldeth the peaceable fruit of righteousness unto them which are exercised thereby," Hebrews 12:11.

NOTES

1. Engle, op. cit., p. 528.
2. A. N. Martin, *God's Directives for Family Living* (London, Eng.: Banner of Truth Trust, April, 1972), p. 9.
3. Ibid.
4. Ibid., pp. 10-11.
5. Ibid., p. 12.
6. Ibid., p. 13.
7. Ibid., p. 15.
8. Ibid., p. 15.
9. Heidelberg Catechism, A. 99, p. 14 in Doctrinal Standards of *The Psalter* (Grand Rapids: Wm. B. Eerdmans, 1955).
10. Ibid., p. 16.
11. Curti, op. cit., pp. 377, 378.
12. Jersild, *From an Article by Robert Nixson* (Washington, D.C.: Review and Herald Publ. Assoc.), pp. 10-12.
13. Jersild, op. cit., p. 264.

9

THE KINDERGARTNER

... for the children ought not to lay up for the parents, but the parents for the children.
—II Corinthians 12:14

Before we leave behind a period of close contact between parents and child, a period of almost constant fellowship, intensive training, and rich associations, let us, with Dr. Wurth, view it in retrospect. Dr. Wurth has a high regard for the place of the child in the God-fearing family.

The child is born into the family. And at least in the first years of his life the *family* is the fellowship in which the entire life of the child rests, whereby it is borne, led, ruled inwardly as well as outwardly.

With the animal it is entirely different. Very soon after birth it must leave the nest and it seldom returns. With an animal a family tie is almost unheard of. As soon as we leave the world of the animals and return to the realm of men we note a natural difference. The child, under normal circumstances, is born from two parents who possess, by reason of their marriage, a lifelong bond. And the child at his birth (or actually before) is immediately received into this bond, and remains there for a long time. This family, the communion of father and mother and possibly brothers or sisters, is temporarily for the child "his world." Particularly at the beginning of his life he does not have nearly enough independence. He does not live his own life as yet.

He cannot go his own way, as the animal does. The child's rightful home, for the time being, is the family. That family is for a long time almost exclusively the sphere and mainstay of his life.

The child has his own destiny, his own independent, individual existence; that is, he must make of himself that which he basically is. But, in fact, he is not yet there. It will be a long time before he realizes his potential.[1]

Dr. Wurth sums up his observations by saying:

In closing, with regard to the subject of the family, we draw attention to a few special points by which spiritual training can be of great value. All proper spiritual training, we have already pointed out, must bear with the character (of the child) through training to freedom. If we are to attain that goal, however, then it is necessary that the climate of the family itself breathes genuine freedom. This does not constitute a plea for license or a disregard of rules. Here, too, freedom is understood as bound to standards; but it is nevertheless a free, inner bond.

It is to be understood that, as one watches the spasmodic sphere which characterizes so many families, in these families not much proper training toward freedom is given; spasmodic training, which usually follows from the fact that in family living the ethical norms are not truly integrated. God's law, instead of inwardly ruling the relationships, is borne with difficulty only as an outward yoke and an oppressive burden. How necessary it is, therefore, that in family relationships, the liberating operation of the Holy Ghost —"where the spirit of the Lord is, there is liberty" (II Corinthians 3:17)—should reveal itself among us! Then only our children will get the opportunity to develop as truly free. . . .

Not of least importance is the training in the family in fellowship. If one later wants to be in a position for the giving of a love which indeed deserves that name, which does not seek itself, which believes and hopes and bears all things (I Corinthians 13), which is prepared for genuine service (Galatians 5:13), then it comes down to this, that he has not merely theoretically learned, but knows by actual experience what this love includes.

And what social communion is more fit for this purpose than the family where people of different sex, different age, different disposition, different character live so intimately with one another, continually, day after day. Here a child or a growing youngster experiences and enjoys not only the mystery of love, but also receives the opportunity to learn what it means to give himself, what reciprocation means, what mutual service means.

Especially from the viewpoint of character formation is this lovely fellowship of life in the family so indispensable. Not for nothing has a great poet said:

'One builds talent in quietness,
Character in the storms of the world.'

A man never becomes a character in the ethical sense in isolation but in the continual contact with and meeting of 'the others,' where one must constantly learn to adapt himself, to bear with the neighbor, to deny himself, to hold in check all kinds of inclinations and passions, and not to give in to all possible wrong sentiments or resentments.

Over and above the bonds of blood proceed relationships of spiritual and ethical nature, virtues such as reverence, obedience, loving inclinations and a readiness to serve; and still more—communal piety, a living faith in Christ and a love proceeding from the Holy Spirit, on which the essence of unity depends.[2]

These excerpts, I think, restate the principles which we as believers and our seed confess, and which we have expressed as our belief and our way of life in previous chapters.

But now as we again center our interest on Timmy in this chapter, we see entering his life some of the "training toward freedom" mentioned by Dr. Wurth. For a part of each day Timmy will leave the shelter of his nest and go to school. He is soon to start kindergarten, a new and a special phase of his life.

Long before the day that our shiny-eyed, brand-new-clothed five-year-old starts out for his first day of school, we have been working toward this day. Living according to the Scriptural principle that it is the *parent's* duty to educate the child, we have been educating him continuously at home, and now have made provisions to further his formal education.

In a sermon on Deuteronomy 6:7 ("And thou shalt teach them diligently unto thy children, and shalt talk of them when thou sittest in thine house, and when thou walkest by the way, and when thou liest down, and when thou risest up"), Herman Hoeksema tells parents about this duty.

> Notice . . . that the parent is held responsible for the training of his children. Moses does not at all address the congregation of the people of God in general, but emphatically he speaks in the singular. He addresses the individual parent. There is no one that has more right, more God-given right to the child than the parent. . . . But especially is this so with the covenant-parents. They are the believers, and they are the ones that are held responsible, and that express the promise before God and His congregation time and again that they shall see to it that the children are educated according to the doctrine of the covenant. . . . He may perhaps perform that duty through someone else, that is his servant, but that does not make any difference. Not the teacher, private or public, has any duty regarding your children. The duty to educate them is yours, and it can only become the duty of the teacher by your employing him.
>
> And from this follows that you are responsible for all that your child is taught. It is not thus, that you are responsible for what it learns directly in the home, and someone else for what it learns in school, and again someone else for what it learns in the catechism and in the Sunday-school, but you are responsible always and everywhere. Not as if these other persons that teach your children have no responsibility. Surely they do. But their responsibility is entirely different from yours. You are responsible for all that your child is taught, responsible before God. . . . Es-

pecially in the school the child receives the lion-share of his education. The school it is that trains the child, that practically shapes him, and the words of the teacher have more authority for him than any other. And the result is that we begin to feel and to act more and more as if we were not responsible for that part of the education of our children. And that is a mistake. All these institutions are merely extensions of the home, the teacher is merely the servant of the parent, and even as the boss always remains responsible for the job his servants perform, so the parent is absolutely responsible for the education of his children by the teacher.[3]

Fellow parents, we who are serious and conscientious about our responsibilities, we will ponder these our duties before God, which duties have not changed since the words of this sermon were spoken in the year 1916. It follows, from the paragraphs just quoted, that if we are responsible before God for the instruction the teacher gives, we will choose the very best school with the very best teachers for our child. I quote again from Herman Hoeksema:

. . . As Christian parents we cannot be indifferent with regard to the religious instruction of our children. Religious instruction they certainly must have, and they must be brought up in the fear and admonition of the Lord, our covenant-God in Christ Jesus.

. . . As Reformed Christians we will also insist that our children must receive a religious education of a very marked type. That we agree on this is evident from the confession we repeat every time we offer our children for baptism. We promise to bring them up 'in the aforesaid doctrine, or help or cause them to be instructed therein to the utmost of our power.' Now this is very significant. For this doctrine is the Reformed doctrine. And one of the characteristics of the Reformed faith is, that it confesses that all things exist for the glory of God, that even our salvation is not the ultimate end of all things, but that it is a means to an end. It is, for the Christian of the Reformed type, not sufficient to know that his sins and the sins of his children have been washed away in the blood of Christ Jesus, and that now he and they are marching heavenward. On the contrary, his covenant-God did save him, in order that with his children he might be to the praise of His glory, here in the church-militant and in the midst of the world, and presently in the glory of heavenly perfection. He must fight the good fight. He must walk in the precepts of his covenant-God. He must reveal himself as a child of light in every sphere of life. Now, this conviction has a definite influence upon his conception of the task of education. Were it different, it might be an irrelevant matter to him, as to what sort of education the child might receive to help him through this world, as long as he is saved. But entirely different it becomes if also the salvation of your child is in view only the means to the highest aim: the glorification of the Most High. Then you will aim in your education at the perfect man of God, knowing the will of his God for every sphere of life and for every step he takes upon the path of life, and you will take care that in his life he is well-equipped with a clear and concise knowledge of all the precepts of the Most High.[4]

We have confessed that this is our purpose in life. We also want our child, by the grace of God, to make this confession. Therefore, we cannot choose just any school as our child's educational home. We cannot even choose just any Christian school. We will choose, in the first place, a school organized and operated by a society of parents, a "parental" school. In the second place, we will send our child to a parental school operated by parents from our own denomination, if that is possible in the area in which we live. That is the ideal. In that way, we have unity in all the phases of our son's training. We also have a voice in the society which runs the school, and the privilege and calling to keep that school doctrinally pure.

This is the only choice we have—to send our son to as doctrinally pure a Christian school as we can. Another Scripture, besides the one we quoted from Deuteronomy 6, tells us about our parental duties. It is the text quoted at the heading of this chapter: " . . . for the children ought not to lay up for the parents, but the parents for the children," II Corinthians 12:14.

This verse tells us not only about our monetary and material duties to our son, but to our much more important spiritual duties. In the context of a chapter in which Paul tells of his revelations of the glories of the third heaven and of his thorn in the flesh, he speaks also of material gains, and pledges not to be burdensome to the church of Corinth. The thrust of the chapter, however, is on spiritual gain. Paul tells us in verse 19 that "we speak before God in Christ: but we do all things, dearly beloved, for your edifying." When we send our child out to begin his life's formal education, we are admonished that *we* are the ones who "lay up" for our child, not the other way around. Surely, there are formal, material benefits which will accrue from our son's schooling, for we live in a material world. But let us take the "laying up" of a spiritual heritage for our son very seriously, covenant parents. We will try to lay up and build up this heritage for our son in all the years of schooling to come.

But now Timmy is only five years old and about to enter the "readiness" period of his education, namely kindergarten. Because we have used the time God has given us during Timmy's first five years in trying to train him well, we believe that Timmy is ready, formally at least, for school. We have seen to it that he can dress himself. That includes operating zippers, buckles, and shoe laces. He knows good health habits and we have taught him the rules of civic safety. With his name, address, and telephone number firmly implanted in his little mind, he is ready to give this information in an emergency. To his teacher we will leave the task of showing him formation of letters and numerals, and any other readiness skills necessary before he enters first grade. For this kind of teaching Timmy's teacher is specially trained and is usually more qualified than we are, and we entrust this area to her.

In another phase of preparing Timmy for his first year of school, we will have a series of chats with him about this unknown realm of kindergarten. Not in anxiety, but setting a comfortable tone of joyful anticipation, we will talk with Timmy about his conduct as a God-fearing little boy among other God-fearing children in a God-centered school. Many children, unlike our son, are timid, clinging kinds of children, terrified at the thought of separation from their parents. These children will need more encouragement to further independence than will our out-going, talkative, mischievous son. We will talk seriously with our son, nonetheless: we will show him that it is time that he must take care of himself for a part of each day (on his way to and from school); and at school he must go to another, who at first will be a stranger to him, for the help he usually gets from his parents. Timmy will nod sagely to this, and in theory be ready and eager to trust all his school life to his "mother-away-from-home." In the novelty and strangeness of entering school, however, we know that his confident little face will reflect perplexity, confusion, and possibly fear. Until now he has run to the safe familiarity of father and mother with all his problems; and if you would ask him, he could predict the method we would use in treating his problems. He knows us and trusts our consistency. But to trust a stranger, or even guess how *she* will react to one's troubles will not be easy at first for Timmy.

And Timmy is accustomed to obeying us. Although we have taught him that the Lord tells us that we must obey all in authority over us, he has had little experience with obedience to authority other than ours. He is too young to know, without being taught, that he owes his teacher, who is guiding him for a few hours a day, the cheerful, prompt obedience he also must give to us. We do not take it for granted that he knows this. We teach him, every time a different situation arises, respect and obedience to authority other than our own.

Neither do we assume that, since we have tried to teach him to use his time well, to do his best when asked to help with a task, that now he will naturally be a diligent worker in school. Certainly, it is also his teacher's task to teach him careful, diligent work habits, but it is our duty first of all. We will prepare him, with firmness mingled with kind concern, to pay attention always, to try to do his best, and to work with diligence, from lowly kindergarten up through the grades.

Although Timmy will learn through actual classroom experience the "give and take" with children his own age, the consideration he must have for the feelings of his classmates, the injustices, real or imagined, under which he will smart, we will still do our best to prepare him to get along with many children of his own age at the same time. It may be necessary to spend a little time with Timmy here. Quick, impulsive, and without the advantage of learning the restraint which comes from having younger brothers and sisters, Timmy, still an only child, is likely to be somewhat self-centered. It is easy for him to know the love of the neighbor in theory (as easy as it is for us, his parents); but when his classmate neighbor crowds him out, then, in practice, that love will not be so easy for Timmy. And it is true that we are not able to prepare him nor shield him from unpleasant experiences or his own wrongdoings. We would not want to. Timmy must live his own life and must be tried and molded through its pleasures and its trials. There is a difference, however, between hovering protectively over Timmy to shield him from life's difficulties, and gently but enthusiastically preparing him for some of his first experiences away from home. If we do the latter, Timmy will view kindergarten as he has viewed all the other "firsts" in his life, with eager anticipation and a measure of confidence, replenished by our consistent guidance.

All these aspects of preparing Timmy for his attitude toward school are closely interwoven with our spiritual perspective. In fact, they embody our spiritual outlook. How could it be different?

Our spiritual outlook (and Timmy's) in starting kindergarten in a Christian school is that he is beginning another calling in his life in the fear of the Lord. This calling is his formal education, as far as he pursues it. If he is truly spiritually responsible, he will know that in the years to come he does not have a choice to be diligent or not to be diligent, to try or not to try, to study or not to study. He has only one choice—to serve the Lord in the days of his youth—and that means in diligence, effort, and perseverance.

But today, the first day of kindergarten for our first child, we will not send him off with preaching. Probably we never will. We hope, instead, to make our whole life our testimony. But, with a prayer and a pit in our stomach, we will wave a cheerful good-bye that we do not entirely feel.

Timmy, too, possibly has mixed feelings about the cheerfulness of his good-bye. It is with a certain reluctance that he leaves the arms of his parents and the security of his home. Yet, he is ready psychologically, physically, and mentally for separation from his parents and for formal learning. This thing called "readiness" does not just happen. The Lord plans it that way. At a given time in his life, all of Timmy's faculties unite toward a readiness for his next advance in life. So often we talk about growth patterns and maturation as if they are automatic and expected developments in a child's life; we fail to see that the Lord brings all the aspects of his being to the proper point of development at the exact chronological age which is the time for our child's next undertaking. Thus, at age five, his tremendous babyhood growth has leveled off, and our child is ready to sit still for a short period of time. He is able to take care of his own basic physical needs, is ready for separation from his parents, and is eager for a closer association with children his own age. Usually this separation from parents (particularly mother) is without trauma, at least on the part of the child. However, too often I have seen well-meaning parents, concerned about their child, hovering at the school-room door, or promising to wait in the hall, or saying, with ill-concealed tears, "I'll be right outside if you need me." These parents, the "hovering," overly concerned kind, are not doing the right thing psychologically. Worse, they are not doing their duty before God. If the time has arrived for our child to start school, we choose a school in the fear of the Lord, and we bring or send our child, and entrust him to the care of the school. If our child senses that we have doubts or fears about his well-being there, he will begin to doubt and fear. If he knows that we are within calling distance (and that we really want to feel needed) he will call us or cry for us. If, however, we leave him with finality and no hint that we are available until after school, he will accept the fact, and enjoy school without a thought of lonesomeness. In all my years of experience as a teacher with beginners at school, I have never had an unhappy child after a parent has disappeared; and I am quite sure that the hovering parent usually *creates* the situation which leads to the crying, parent-clinging child.

When it is time for our child to begin to learn the approach to reading and he is ready physically and psychologically for it, he is usually ready mentally, too. This period of time when he asks questions about "how many" and "what does it say," and the period when he is enthusiastic about starting school is not definable in terms of months or weeks. Neither is it a very short time which, if we are not wide awake, will escape us, and our child's readiness and interest will disappear. Rather it is a budding awareness, earlier chronologically in some children than in others, more marked in some than in others, an awareness of the whole world of learning which is opening before them. Our child's interest in symbols (numerals, letters, words) may span a time period of more than a year, and may fluctuate between avid delight and inattentive indifference. Some children must be made aware that they *are* ready; because they do not *seem* to be ready does not necessarily mean that they are not. In our age of easy labels, we may fall into the error of shaking our heads and saying that Suzy is a tomboy and Joey is mechanically minded, and probably they never will be good students. Have we sat down with them, systematically, with picture books, story books, ABC books, counting books? Have we tried to rouse their interest? Are we trying to cultivate an interest in learning?

Timmy is ready and eager to start school. Through the last year or two we have read to him, showed him a great variety of books, fostered his ability to color and "write" without pushing him. Forcing a child to be interested in something for which he is not ready is worse than indifferent neglect, I think; for in forcing an interest he does not feel, he not only will be bored, but will rebel, at least inwardly. In this area, too, we are gentle and relaxed as we open the wonders of the world of books. We keep the atmosphere pleasant, and we suggest short, frequent periods of readiness work. For this is the start of our fostering a lifelong enthusiasm for books and for learning.

How do we know that Timmy is ready to begin school? Always alert and inquisitive, Timmy asks more questions now than he ever has. He is thirsty for knowledge, often for the knowledge that is found in books. He asks, "What does this say, Mom? What does b-a-n-d-a-i-d spell, Dad?" He practices writing his name and the letters of the alphabet. He is ready to go further.

In the next two or three years he will learn more than in any similar time period in his life. We must not forget that the Lord has created him in this way, that he is able in these first years of his formal learning to assimilate knowledge like a sponge. In these years he is blest with great powers of memorization and marvelous powers of retention. In my many years of teaching beginners, I have never ceased to marvel at their avid propensities for learning. Often in the beginning reading class I sense that I am the one being propelled faster and faster into new areas of learning by the pupils. The magnitude of these gifts of memorization and retention is heightened by the spontaneous exuberance of early childhood. Also, the child has had no previous experience with formal learning which might create associations and crowd out his present learning. He is like an open well, waiting to be filled, or, as an unusual first-grader aptly put it, as he rubbed his short blond hair, "There: now my mind is as clear and shiny as a piece of glass. Let's learn to read today." He knows he will, for he has a naive acceptance of all that his teacher says, and an implicit trust in her wisdom. By the time he is five, the Lord has given our child the ability for the first glimmerings of the abstract. In kindergarten Timmy will learn that a symbol called a letter stands for a sound, and he will be able to hear the three "b's" in "bouncy baby." He will understand it, too, for the Lord has given the average five-year-old this ability. He will be able to put five pegs on a peg board if his kindergarten teacher flashes a numeral "5" on the flannel board. He is translating the meaning of an abstract symbol to a concrete number of pegs. And he likes immensely to do it! He can hardly wait for each new day of school. He is ready!

Already, as responsible parents, we have been training Timmy to be able to think for himself in emergencies. We do this in two ways: first, we furnish him with memorized information—name, address, telephone number, and possibly grandmother's telephone number; second, we test him with hypothetical situations such as, "What would you do if you thought you could not cross the street alone?" "What would you do if you feel sick at school?" "What would you do if mom or dad were not at home, and you couldn't get into the house?" Learning to foresee a possible difficulty is part of Timmy's education. Having him learn to face an emergency without panic is one of our contributions to his kindergarten education.

Now our happy son goes to kindergarten. Not immediate is the danger that he will grow away from us; he is still our small, loving, confiding son. But we don't want him *ever* to turn away from us, nor ever to stop trusting us or confiding in us. We will never stop working to keep open the lines of communication between our son and us, the lines of communication rooted in a parent-child love in a natural sense, but above all in a spiritual atmosphere of openness and trust and confidence; for both parents and child are working for the higher goals of walking in obedience in the path of the Lord's commandments.

That is the way we try to send him off to school each day—with an undercurrent of spiritual peace. That is not always so easy. The small irritations of life get in our way and make us impatient or short tempered. When it is time to get Timmy ready for school, he may have been disobedient and not come in from playing soon enough; he may complain, with an edge on his voice, that he can find only one shoe; or his milk may spill all over his spotless school pants. We scold, more from irritation than from principle. He defends himself while we further accuse, "Why are you *always* sloppy and careless?" (Is he?) Timmy cries, we rush, and he goes to school with anything but peace.

Not always will life run smoothly while we get Timmy ready for school; but it is possible to manage our time and our routine so that many of the small irritations of life are prevented, and unpleasant hassles are the rare exception. If he goes to afternoon kindergarten, we teach him to be aware of the passage of time during the morning. We teach him approximately how long an hour is: as long as it takes us to eat, do dishes, and clear the kitchen; as long as his bath (when he plays in the tub); as long as our weekly shopping trip to the grocery store. Then we ask him to report his whereabouts every hour, just so we know that he is all right and that he is available. After a few too-long "hours" and some that last only fifteen minutes, Timmy becomes so accustomed to the "feeling" of the passage of sixty minutes that he becomes uncannily accurate about popping his head around the corner of the door and piping, "Is it an hour?" And, if we digress a moment from getting Timmy ready for school, we will know, after we have tried the system of reporting, that it is an excellent practice, both for parents and child. For parents it is good because we can question him about his doings and early detect and discourage any mischief; we can take care of his physical needs—a drink, a bathroom stop, or a scrubbing; we save ourselves uneasiness and worry because, if he is safe and well, we will see him approximately every hour. For our son it is good because he learns a responsibility for his activities, and learns to give account of his doings to his proper authorities; he learns that we his parents have a loving concern for his well-being each hour of the day; he enjoys, too, the little hourly visits—for a snack, a smile, or comfort for small troubles. Only in certain situations (ball games, hikes) do we suspend the "report-every-hour" rule. Until our son reaches his teens and must, in the nature of the case, become more independent in his activities, we will not suspend the reporting rule during his playtime. As he nears his teens, our rule is more flexible, but we still know where our son is.

If Timmy's school sessions are in the morning, we get him up early enough so that we do not have to hurry him while he is getting ready. Creating a relaxed, unhurried atmosphere is certainly worth more than the ten or fifteen extra minutes of sleep in the morning—or it will be after we have tried both ways and evaluated the results from our Christian perspective. Our before-school conversations will be cheerful and enthusiastic—but not artificial—and filled with lighthearted "school talk." "What do you think you will do today?" "Do you want to take your new book for 'show-and-tell'?"

Sometime, before he has been in kindergarten very long, and when we are having a leisurely conversation about school, we will ask him if he thinks he will tell us, when he comes home, if he has misbehaved on a certain day. If he readily agrees, and says he will truly tell us the first thing when he gets home, we probably have reason to be skeptical. We know that Timmy is impulsive and more ready than his neighbor for mischief, but his impulsiveness does not always extend to ready confessions. If he wavers in his answer, and is not sure that he would like to tell us, we can be sure that his answer is more honest—even for a covenant child. Our sinful nature (and his) is such that we would rather cover up or ignore our misdeeds than confess them. Timmy must hear this truth about his nature and must know that the right way is to tell his parents that he has done wrong. We will tell him that the Bible says that the *right* way is to say that we have sinned, even though it hurts to have to tell what wrong we did. We will tell him, as we have told him so often in the past, that, because he trusts us and loves us, he will come to us and tell us about his sins. In case he still has doubts about coming to us, we will make clear to him that we will make it our business anyway to find out about his behavior. Then we will tell him why we will find out. He really knows: he knows that we promised God to bring him up to the best of our ability in the fear of the Lord; he knows that if we are to do this, we must correct and chasten him often; and he knows that if there is the right spiritual attitude between parents and children, there is openness and candid confidence. Timmy also knows, without being able to articulate it, of course, the difference between suspicious, prying parents who rob a child of his privacy, and parents who basically trust their covenant child, but who, with a full knowledge and experience of sin, have a healthy skepticism, and who care enough to find out the truth.

Timmy knows, too, when we are asking prying, nosy questions for our own ends, and when we are asking from the motive of our child's own best interests. If we are wise, we will not question him overmuch. Seldom will we ask him immediately upon his arriving at home, for we consider his fatigue and we respect his inclinations to tell us his stories when he is ready. When he does talk about school, we listen intently and with interest, especially to his Bible stories, so that we can note his progress and prod his memory, if necessary. If we do question him, a good way to start is, "And what was the best thing that happened at school on *this* day?" Not only do we get a picture of Timmy at school, but we also watch him make judgments and evaluations of the new events in his life. We can learn much about our son in his reactions to the situations he experiences and observes. His reaction to his teacher is especially important to Timmy's life at school. If he says, in response to our question, "What do you think of your teacher?", "She's soft," we know he is happy with his "mother-away-from-home."

If, one day after he has settled down to his school routine, he tells a highly improbable story as true, what do we do? Accept it as he tells it? Express utter disbelief? Probably neither. Rather we may express mild skepticism at first. We might ask, "Are you sure?" "Did it happen *just* that way, Timmy?" If he persists in maintaining the truth of his story, we may want to carry our skepticism a step further and say, "Well, if it really happened that way, Tim, I think I will talk to your teacher about it this evening." Then he may begin to soft-pedal his original version. "Jackie didn't exactly *hit* teacher. Teacher didn't chase him *much.*" Finally, he will retract the whole thing and tell what, if anything, truly happened.

Why do we bother to go through this whole process with Timmy? Why not dismiss it as one of the fantasies of childhood? Why not rationalize that it makes Timmy feel important to have a big story all his own to tell? Why spoil it? The answer, we as covenant parents know, is that "lying lips are an abomination to the Lord: but they that deal truly are his delight," Proverbs 12:22. As we train Timmy to be spiritually sensitive and penitently responsive to God's law, we show him, first, that the line between the truth and the lie is straight and definite. There is no gray area of part truth, part lie, and part fantasy. God's law demands truth in the inward parts, and condones no lie. Therefore we teach Timmy, by our questioning and by our discussions, that a statement or a story is either the truth or a lie. Second, Timmy must learn to recognize a big story, a gross exaggeration, or a distortion (told as truth) for what it is—a lie. Whether his lie is told to get attention, for entertainment, or for mischief, it remains a lie and a sin. Third, we remind ourselves that we chasten in love: a love that will not overlook or condone the lie, a love that does not express itself in harsh accusations and threatening recriminations, but a love that leads him to see that his story is a lie, that a lie is a sin in the sight of God and that "they that deal truly are His delight." This love understands that kindergarten is his first real opportunity to come home and tell his own unique experiences. At the same time this love forbids and chastens lies and takes the time to correct and to lead in the paths of truth according to God's Word.

When Timmy comes home with the story that Scott threw stones at the girls during recess and teacher really scolded him, and if he waxes eloquent on the dire results of throwing stones at the girls:—"You could hit their eyes and make them blind," or "Once a girl swallowed a stone a boy threw at her," we would do well to maintain our questioning attitude and ask, "Who else threw stones, Timmy?"

Or if Timmy comes home with bright cheeks, rosier than usual, and says, "I had to hide my face today, but I don't know why. I didn't do anything wrong. Teacher just made me," we could choose to laugh, or become angry and demand the truth. Again, probably we will do neither. Instead, we may stroll over to the telephone and say with a casual air, "That's strange. I never heard of a teacher doing that before. I think I will ask her why she did such a thing." Most likely a surprised Timmy will come running and begin to explain that he was only a "little bit" naughty. And soon he will tell the whole story of how he was warned not to squirt water in the boys' bathroom, but he did anyway, and got Scott's shirt and pants all wet. Again, our method of calm questioning, implying our disbelief, has solved the problem. When Timmy comes home with many protestations of innocence, we will not be too "gullible." We know, and he knows we know, his weaknesses. And we both know, that for Timmy's sake, we will find out the truth. In all our dealings with him concerning his life at school, we remain healthily skeptical—in love.

Throughout Timmy's year in kindergarten, both of us parents will daily reinforce all the covenant training we have given so far in his life. During this year, when he attends school only part time, we have more time to exercise our calling to train our son for a godly life than we will next year. Therefore, we will arrange our schedules to be at home, if at all possible, when he comes home from school. He needs us then, not only to listen and rejoice or sympathize, but also to guide and correct and chasten, if necessary. At this age, he is also old enough to understand why we have always—as long as he can remember—told him to trust us. As we mothers work, we can chant the text in Proverbs 3:5, "Trust in the Lord with all thine heart; and lean not unto thine own understanding." And as we dust and sweep we can explain to Timmy that, though mother and dad are big already, we cannot understand everything as well as we should, and we don't always know what is best to do. Then we ask him how we can find out what is right to do, and he will have the answer: "Go find out in the Bible." And we will tell him *that* is what trusting in the Lord is: knowing from His Word that He takes care of us, finding out what He wants us to do, and how we must live, instead of following our own understanding, which is a very poor understanding. Applying this Biblical truth to Timmy's life, we tell him that his understanding is very poor, too, and he always must trust in the Lord's way. How does he know what that is? He must ask us, his guides here on earth, to find it for him; and because *we* go to the Lord to find the way—because *we* trust the Lord—Timmy trusts *us* to show him the Lord's ways.

If a new baby is coming—and a baby girl named Sarah will arrive this year—we prepare Timmy, just as we have prepared him for the other "firsts" in his life. Because he has been the only child for so long and has not by experience learned the meaning of sharing with brothers and sisters, having a new child in the family could cause jealousy and a sense of rivalry. But if we tell Timmy that there will be times when the baby's needs come first and his come second (and that it is sometimes good for us to come second); and if we explain that he will be needed to help more because a new baby is so helpless, he will be prepared even though he does not understand it all. This, of course, is not enough. This is only a formal preparation. We are a God-fearing family, and we and Timmy accept our new child as a gift of God, as another covenant child to love, and with whom we share, and sacrifice, if necessary. Timmy will welcome the news, for his friendly nature will go out to the new baby, and he can hardly wait for its arrival, even though after she arrives he may have periods of frustration when mother is more preoccupied than Timmy would like her to be.

Toward his covenant school mates, too, Timmy is learning the importance of Christian behavior. With many failings and often with chastenings, he is learning the virtues of kindness and consideration, selflessness and generosity, patience and restraint. It is not so easy for impulsive Timmy to let his light shine wherever he is, but our standards (because they are God's standards) remain high, consistent, and Scriptural. On the day when he comes home and says with a beaming face, "My teacher says the same things you do, Dad. . . . She talks the same way about 'love our neighbor' and 'be kind' and 'obey God's law' . . . , " then we are happy. Timmy is experiencing covenant education in another area of his life, and it all speaks the same language.

Most schools schedule periodic parent-teacher conferences. All schools schedule them on request. When we confer with Timmy's teacher, and she says, "Do you have any questions?" we want to ask the right ones. Our first ones will not be: "Can he write his name?" "Does he know his numerals?" "Does he recognize his letters?" These questions may be important, but for us they are not first. Rather we want to know: "Does he listen?" "Does he follow directions (obey)?" "Is he kind?" "Is he reverent?" "Is he selfish? Stubborn?" "Does he cheerfully obey?" "Does he use his time well?" Then we will carefully note the teacher's answers. But why are these questions the important ones? These questions and their answers are so important to us because, in this pre-academic grade, it is essential that Timmy sets right habits for school-going. We need to know whether he follows his right habits—or his training, if you will—consistently. For these right habits of Timmy follow covenant lines of training; and, if he is spiritually responsive and has no physical or mental impediments, he will use his time and his talents well. However, in all our efforts, we will never forget how sinful he is, nor how imperfect our training is. Nor will we forget that neither of us will succeed in our own strength, but that daily we will beg our Father in heaven for help and guidance.

In summary, we view Timmy's life in kindergarten as a unique age with unique experiences, as setting the stage, with good attitudes and good effort, for future academic life. Throughout this year we will notice our son change. Through contact with many other children and through disciplined experiences at school, Timmy will begin to mature and gather knowledge and insights which were not possible before. He will come home with stories of many "firsts" in school life: sports with children his own age, working on projects with a group of children, singing new songs, attending school chapel services, sitting quietly for longer periods of time, paying close attention. Often he will do his share of complaining about situations that are not fair or do not seem fair to him. Naturally sympathetic to our child, our only one, we may be ready to step right into the situation and correct the wrong. If we are wise parents, however, we will first calmly assess the situation; we decide if it is an engulfing wave or only a ripple in his life. We do not want to be overly protective parents, shielding Timmy from all unpleasantness. If he is to grow up able to bear with his neighbor, to deny himself, to hold in check his sinful passions, and to possess a love which bears all things, he must know from experience the unpleasantness, the pain, the cruelty, the unfairness of the world; and he must learn, through our guidance, how to cope with the "hard knocks" in his life in order to discipline himself and to overcome his weaknesses.

Another change we will notice after Timmy has been in school for this first year is that he acts or tries to act like the rest of the boys. He is in a group now, and he does what the group does. In other words, a process of conforming has set in; and this has both its bad and its good sides. To be a member of the herd could mean that Timmy's unique individuality, his desire to express himself in his own special way is suppressed. To be one of the group can mean that it is thought strange to be different and to show a distinct individuality. The tendency to view all in the group as equal and to treat them as such, so that the group begins to think alike and has the same goals in life, is typical of the spirit of the age in which we live. The world of today likes conformists, for conformists are easy to mold into a pattern; the Antichrist, too, at the end of the ages, I think, will strive for all to conform to the mass. That is conforming in the bad—in the worst—sense. And there is a danger here for Timmy. We don't want him to be a mere cog in a wheel. We urge him to think his own thoughts, speak his own mind, express his own God-given personality.

But the fact remains that Timmy is a member of society, and a pupil in a class. He may be a rugged individualist, but he must be a rugged individualist within bounds. For, in his dealings with his neighbor, Tim must love his neighbor, be limited by him, and at times suppress his own desires in favor of those of his neighbor. When Timmy enters a group of his neighbors, this kind of conforming sets in. Under the hand of a wise teacher, this is good. We may want to call it a process of refining, of polishing, of learning the niceties of living in society—or, to put it in Scriptural language—of loving his neighbor for God's sake. This kind of conforming to the group will not rob Timmy of his character. It may discipline it, and "civilize" it, so that, also in group action, Tim may assert his individuality for the good of his neighbor.

In Timmy's formal and informal training, in all his work and play, in his routine home life and in the rare emergencies, we will be continuing our previous methods of training. In our words and works, the attitudes and atmosphere we foster, we will remember the words of the Lord in II Corinthians 12:14, " . . . for the children ought not to lay up for the parents, but the parents for the children." We will be especially busy laying up his covenant heritage.

NOTES

1. *Zedelijke Opvoeding* (Kampen, The Netherlands: J. H. Kok, 1960), pp. 150, 151, translated.
2. Ibid., pp. 157-161, translated.
3. *The Standard Bearer,* Vol. 3, p. 534.
4. Ibid., p. 532.

10

THE CHILD'S EARLY PRIMARY YEARS

Thy wife shall be as a fruitful vine by the sides of thine house: thy children like olive plants round about thy table. Behold, that thus shall the man be blessed that feareth the Lord.
—Psalm 128:3, 4

IN THE PREVIOUS CHAPTER WE NOTED THAT WHEN THE three major forces in Timmy's life—his home, his church, and his school—all rest on the same foundations, his training from start to finish is sound, consistent, and unified. This is ideal. If we find ourselves in circumstances less than ideal—if our church as denomination is departing from the solid truths of Scripture, if our Christian schools are Christian more and more in name only, or if we have failed to make our homes strongholds of godliness—then we are called to purge the evil and to right the wrong in the area in which we err. A lengthy discussion of the three spheres of influence on our child does not have a place in this chapter, for we are primarily interested in our calling as *parents* in the home throughout the childhood of our son. But as the man "that feareth the Lord," quoted in the text above, we are alert to make sure that we find and belong to the church that is the purest manifestation of the body of Christ here on earth, that we establish spiritually distinctive covenant schools and maintain them, and that we maintain righteousness in our homes. If one of these areas is weak or teaches principles inconsistent with the other two, the result will show in Timmy's life. Probably we will not be able to see it immediately; but at best it will confuse Timmy, and at worst it will lead him on wrong paths. Take, for example, a home, a Christian home, but a weak Christian home, where parents do not insist on obedience. When it is time for their son to go to bed he says, "No, not yet," the parent says, "Why not? Aren't you sleepy?" The son says he will go after one more short game. "Now up to bed with you," says the parent after the game. But the child stalls, and the parent says, "But you promised. . . . How about after a nice little snack? . . . " At his covenant school he is taught to obey his teacher *the first time*. At church he hears Sunday after Sunday, "Children, obey your parents in the Lord; for this is right." How will this inconsistent training end? With an obedient child? Or will he more and more walk in disobedience?

Such a child will not be as beautiful, as spiritually beautiful, as one whose training in all three areas speaks the same language. For if his training is imbued with spirituality in all areas the child will be like an olive plant. Why this figure? The olive plant (or tree) and especially the olive grove is known for its flourishing, dark green foliage, its health, its vigor, and its beauty. Scripture in other places uses the figure of the olive plant in this way. In Hosea 14:6 the Lord promised concerning Israel, when healed of its backslidings, that "His branches shall spread and his beauty shall be as the olive tree. . . . " In the beautiful picture at the head of this chapter we see the portrait of the God-fearing family, the man who walks in God's ways (verse 1), whose wife is a fruitful vine and whose children are spiritual olive plants, reflecting in their health, beauty, and vigor that they have been securely planted in the fear of the Lord in a devout Christian home.

Day by day, however, in our sin-weary lives, we don't always walk in God's ways, and our children often look more like thistles than olive plants. We become discouraged when we do not see the fruits in our children which we had hoped to see. But let us not lose our spiritual sights. Let this text spur us on to new effort and hope in obedience to our God.

We will pray, as Timmy starts his full-time primary schooling, that we may see him, fed by God's precepts, grow to be a healthy olive plant as he lives round about our table. Our home, without doubt, is most important in molding his life. But we are also aware that we send him to school for most of his daytime hours. Because he is six years old now and has an enthusiastic interest in new experiences, especially in learning to know the whole new world of reading, he is eager to spend every day at school. School is an important factor in his life in primary years because the novelty of each uncharted experience impresses him deeply. In his primary years especially he awakes from the misconceptions of early childhood to the realities of the world around him. He comes to first grade saying, "Just skip me with that reading book, teacher. I don't know how to read yet." When the teacher answers, "Don't worry, my boy. You really do. You just think you don't," he still shakes his head skeptically. Not many days pass before the light dawns and he says, with shining eyes and eager face, "Teacher, do you promise me that reading is just putting the sounds together by the rules and then we read words? Promise that's all there is to it? And I thought it was going to be hard! Do you let us go ahead by ourselves if we want to?" This knowledge hits most first graders with a tremendous impact; we sophisticated adults, having lived with the printed word for almost all of our lives, tend to forget that the whole obscure, meaningless world of symbols suddenly opens for him, and he begins to know and to understand.

Primary schooling impresses the small child because it is a new way of life for him. He learns with his peers, competing with, helping, or sympathizing with his classmates. Gradually he learns to think and to work more and more independently, and we notice at home that the influence of school makes him more mature; and we note that he has developed a better understanding of the love of his neighbor as he has had to practice it at school.

Because school has such a great impact in the life of our small child, and because (as we have established in the previous chapter) school is the extension of our home, we are concerned that Timmy has a qualified teacher. His teacher must have the academic qualifications which we as parents lack, and the spiritual outlook which is the extension of ours; for his teacher is called to follow, with Timmy and his classmates, the lines of covenant instruction.

Now we can see more clearly than ever the advantages of operating a parent-controlled school. By electing responsible parents to the school board, we have a choice in hiring teachers that meet our high standards. And they are high. They must be! And even though the subject of the qualifications of teachers for our child is at the periphery of our treatment of the child in the covenant home, we will take a brief look at those qualifications, because of the effect they have on Timmy.

In order to attain the ideal harmony between home and school, we hire teachers who have shown a good academic record themselves, and who have the background necessary to teach given subjects. In other words, our Christian teachers must be academically able. Just as important—probably more important—they should know the covenant child. From many years of experience in grade school teaching, I have noted that the study of the *covenant* child is too often neglected. Aspiring teachers have plenty of exposure to the volumes of worldly psychological principles governing the child, but they have done too little research and too little study on the Biblical principles of the psychology of the child. More important than knowing at exactly what stage of maturity the child is at the current moment, is the knowing him as a saint and sinner—at the same time, in the same person. And I think that our teachers, as well as parents, should view him more often than is done, as a *covenant* child. The easy part to see is the misdeed, the sin, the sneaking, the disobedience. And the natural reaction is lashing back and "chewing him out," and then severely chastening this sinner. I grant that it is often necessary to chasten him (severely, too), but I also maintain that we (parents and teachers) all too often leave it there. That is our failing. We all too often treat covenant children as heathens. Wrong-doing . . . punishment . . . period. Either before, during, or after the chastening, have we consciously asked the Lord for the grace to talk, question, admonish, or heal? Have we used Scripture as our guide? If he is a true covenant child and not a rebellious son of Esau, he will surely repent and show amendment of his ways, even though he may often slip back into his sins. Teachers, as well as parents, could learn to use the spiritual and Scriptural approach much more often, not merely because it brings the desired results, but because it is the right way to deal with covenant youth.

A good teacher needs many virtues, of which the most important probably are: patience, diligence, consistence, orderliness, firmness, kindliness, cheerfulness, and enthusiasm. This is quite an impressive list, for a beginning, I know. But here is an awesomely difficult task. Together with the parents, each teacher is God's tool to be used in molding the child's future. Consider the influence of the teacher in the interpretation of the many materials taught, or the influence of her personality and conduct in minor classroom crises. Someone has once said that there are no insignificant crises in first grade. All disputes are earth-shaking . . . to first-graders. When we view the following episode from the eyes of a first grade girl, we can judge, with her, the influence of her teacher. Two first grade boys, both self-styled "baseball players," argued much about being up to bat first. Complicating matters, they allowed one of their fellow classmates to have his hits only by special coercion from the teacher. He was a poor hitter and a no-good player, they said. After many talks about unselfishness and love of their neighbor, the problem was still unsolved, and the boys still fought about being first. The playground arguments increased. One noon hour the first grade teacher decided to have the quarrels settled. She called in all the offenders and with firmness, mingled with understanding, she laid down rules and extracted solemn promises, with a promise of her own of swift chastening if the rules were not explicitly followed. Then she rather curtly dismissed the baseball players. Meanwhile the first grade girl, waiting to take a test she had missed, was the quiet audience to the proceedings.

"Now, Suzy, to your test," the teacher sighed to the patiently waiting girl.

"Not yet, Teacher. Where's your record book?"

"My record book? Why?"

"Where's your red pencil that you mark with?"

"Here on my desk. What are you trying to do, Suzy?"

Solemnly the little girl opened the record book to the first page, and drew a neat "A" in red pencil.

"There, Teacher, that's for you. It's your mark."

"My mark for what?"

"Why, for scolding those boys. You're the best scolder I ever heard. When I get big, I'm going to scold my kids just that way."

If we multiply that example by the thousands, we realize the influence of the teacher over her class. It matters not so much *what* she says but *how* she says. She works, too, for a *class,* not a conglomerate of individuals, but for children in a group who work together, pull for one another, shield and protect one another, and share one another's joys. Always she looks for the method that will be the best way to teach attitudes and skills to the covenant child.

As parents, we expect highly qualified teachers for Timmy. We pay for them, too. And we are charitable. When we consider what sinners we are, and how miserably we fail in our duties of Christian parenthood, then we are not the first to cast a stone at an unwise teacher. By grace, too, we have learned to heed the words of Galatians 5:15, 16: "But if ye bite and devour one another, take heed that ye be not consumed one of another. This I say then, Walk in the Spirit, and ye shall not fulfill the lust of the flesh."

The Lord expects us to use our common sense, too, in our dealings with school personnel. Then, on the one hand, we can send Timmy to school responsibly, not anxiously, and not interfering needlessly with the numerous trifles in his school life. On the other, when communication between parents and teacher is needed, the relationship should be easy and spontaneous. Initiated by either the parents or the teacher, conducted formally or informally, as soon as any problem may arise, ease of communication prevents misunderstandings. Just as we follow the principle that preventing an unhappy situation in Timmy's home life is easier and better than repairing it, so we deal with his school life. Often a quick telephone call clears up a misconception and prevents a potential problem from arising. And the best part is that our child is not caught in the middle of an unpleasant situation. But (are we objecting) we hate to be teacher-botherers? Or, if teachers, should we call the parents about *that?* I do not think the danger for most of us lies here. I don't think we tend to communicate too much. I think (also from experience) that the danger is the opposite. We are too reluctant to communicate; when we do, we find it is later than we had thought.

Besides communicating directly as parents and teachers, either socially or if problems arise, we communicate much to our child by our approach and attitude toward one another. Let me explain. The covenant teacher is called to show respect toward the parents. I believe that *respect* is a better term than *cooperation,* for cooperation could be forced and mechanical, but respect is an attitude of the heart. Spontaneously, as situations come up in class, or outside of class—"my mom read our whole memory chapter with me last night," or "my dad 'splained why he spanked me last night, so I wouldn't grow up to disobey God"—the teacher will praise, *in so many words,* the efforts of godly parents, and tell her pupils how blest they are. Using examples from Scripture as they occur in Bible lessons, she will confront her pupils with many examples of godly parents—Moses' parents, who hid him three months because they saw he was a proper child; Hannah, who prayed in faith for Samuel, and dedicated him to the Lord—and she will not fail to apply it to their godly parents of today, who also dedicate their children to the service of the Lord. The teacher will take the attitude that mother knows best—even though she doubts that the child needs that wool scarf in forty-degree weather, or if she knows that boots *would* be better than gym shoes on the muddy playground. She will not contradict the home or criticize it when mother asks if Suzy may stay in at recess today because she had a cough last night . . . and Suzy seems to be in perfect health. She shows her pupils by her attitude how much she respects their parents.

We parents, too, by our example of speaking highly of Timmy's teacher, show respect to one worthy of the calling of Christian school teacher. When Timmy comes home with the story that teacher punished all the boys and that he *told* her he didn't throw snowballs at the cars, but he had to hide his face anyway, what do we do? Take Timmy's side, and say that it was grossly unfair of his teacher? Say nothing much, but *think* that it was unfair? Call the teacher? Definitely we would not do the first two. Before we call the teacher, we will sit down with Timmy and get the setting, the action, and Timmy's involvement. Gradually the picture changes. Timmy was in the setting, in the action . . . and involved. All the boys were throwing forbidden snowballs into the street—Timmy, too. Some boys deliberately aimed at passing cars and scored direct hits. Others did not aim, but scored hits anyway. Timmy just threw without scoring. He did not throw *at* the cars, but he threw. And we happily tell him that his teacher's chastening was right, and none too severe. We are happy because we want to take her side.

Probably one of the failings of most of us parents is the use of our tongue with respect to Timmy's teacher. Certainly, we defend her, especially in Timmy's presence. We think highly of her qualifications. But when Timmy comes home and says, "Teacher was crabby today," our unsanctified tongue is quick to say, "Probably got in too late last night." Then to our husband, in Timmy's hearing, "I understand she keeps late hours quite often. I don't like it. And if you ask me (he didn't), her dresses are somewhat on the short side for a person in a position of leadership." Timmy brings us up short with, "But they're pretty, Mom," and we remember that it is evil to backbite, especially because she is Timmy's teacher. And we resolve anew that, though we know she has shortcomings, we will not discuss them, not before Timmy, not before anyone. For "if any man offend not in word, the same is a perfect man, and able also to bridle the whole body," James 3:2.

In the lower grades, it is not so difficult for Timmy to show respect for his teacher. Repeatedly we have taught him he must obey his teacher with cheerfulness for God's sake. And, in usual situations, this is not hard for a child in the early primary grades. For these children enjoy their schooling and love their teacher and look up to her as the end of all wisdom. Very freely they come to their "mother-away-from-home" for help with a frustrating math problem or for a safety pin or a band-aid. But we know we cannot relax and say: "There! Now for three years at least I won't have to bother with teaching Timmy respect for his teacher, because he already does respect her." What about tomorrow? Tomorrow he is in intermediate grades. We want our olive plant to flourish. Therefore we feed him spiritual admonitions. That is not all we do. Teacher, parents, and child pray for one another. We pray in the presence of the child, so that he also learns how to pray for his fellow saints. Each prays for the prospering of the school, for the reason that it is a distinctively Christian school. Teachers have beautiful opportunities for these prayers, especially at the beginning of each new school day. We parents will find that the child's bedtime prayer is the ideal time for instructing our child in the art of praying for those in authority over us. But we will discuss this prayer more fully later in the chapter.

Before we examine Timmy's progress in the first three grades, we will look at the characteristics which he as a primary schoolboy possesses. Generally, he is still a dependent child. He depends on parent or teacher to tell him what to wear, how to proceed, what to say. Except for a characteristic spurt of independence in the first grade, when he suddenly realizes he has entered the adult world of words, and tries to demonstrate that he, too, "has arrived," our child depends on us for most of the details of his life. In his year in first grade, he needs much guidance. Parents and teachers can take little for granted. Those who have truly taken the time to observe and study these little ones understand that the logic in first grade is not adult logic on a small scale. It is a quite different logic. A teacher outlining a precise procedure quickly discovers this logic, as the following illustration may demonstrate.

She says, "To make the small 'd,' draw a circle first, then a line."

But Suzy's always comes out wrong. In the air, Suzy draws a circle and then a line. On her paper, it looks consistently like this: b.

"First the circle, Suzy, *then* the line."

"I did, Teacher."

Teacher is ready to grasp her pencil-hand and help, when Suzy says calmly, "I did what you said, Teacher, but I think I put the stick on the wrong side. Could that be my trouble?"

With patience and careful directions, we still guide his way each day. He is an uncertain child, unsure of his next step, often asking, "Now what do I do?" The early primary child is not very sure of his brand of logic. Especially in school, he will repeatedly ask, "Am I thinking the right way, or am I wrong again?" Needing constant reinforcement, he looks to his parents or teacher for encouragement so that he can carry on. He is a joy to teach at this age, because, whether he is doing a math paper at school or an intricate chore at home, he will almost outdo himself in trying to do well if we praise and prod him by simple exclamations: "Great! Keep it up!" or "You're doing better than I thought you would!"

Also in his relationships to others, Timmy depends on our initiative and leadership. Constantly he is asking, "What shall I say?" or "What should I do if. . . ?" What he really wants to know is how he is expected to behave in a given set of social surroundings. How often have we not witnessed the drama of a small boy entering a room filled with adults, standing still for an uncertain moment (an hour for him?), and then doing something inane such as grabbing a handful of candy or jumping up on a chair and shouting. Or we watch him greet a strange new boy with a swift punch in his stomach. Though there may be the element of humor in such situations, we are mortified to be the parents of a boy who behaves in such a way. He needs us to train him so that he knows how to act properly in society. From our instruction and example he learns manners, polish, poise. Putting ourselves in his place, we try to feel the awkwardness that Timmy feels in a social gathering, probably filled with strangers twice as big as he is. Sometimes we prepare him by rehearsing situations: we are Mrs. Smith or Mr. Jones and he is Timmy, in varying sets of situations. Thus prepared, Timmy usually comes through the actual social test fairly well. And we need not resort to silent embarrassment or scoldings in public.

In his primary years, Timmy has not only the ability to absorb knowledge readily, but, under normal circumstances, has a will to learn. He truly enjoys it. Often, in first grade, I have seen a child struggle to figure out a new word, finally pronounce it correctly, and then giggle with the sheer joy of learning. One small boy showed his delight in learning by saying, as he left the classroom for a short dental appointment, "Promise not to learn any new words while I'm gone, Teacher?"

"If we do, I'll help you with them later."

"No, Teacher, that's not what I mean. I'll miss all the *fun* when you teach them."

Their constant thirst to know more they show at school by asking, "When can we read our *next* book? May we *try* to learn the words in the next story by ourselves?" At home, they want to know, "When will you teach me to run a jig-saw, Dad?" "Am I old enough to bake cookies yet?" "Please, may I take piano lessons?"

The primary child's great interest in and capacity for detail is necessary at exactly this stage of his learning. In school and at home he is absorbing all the knowledge and information on which his further learning is based. Without fail, the primary child, glancing at a blackboard *filled* with instructions, will say, "You made a mistake, Teacher. There's no dot on that 'i'!" When telling a favorite Bible story, such as the one of Noah and the ark, haven't we all as parents had the experience of telling every detail just right and being self-satisfied with the fine job of telling it, only to have our Timmy say, "You told the story quite well, Dad; but you forgot to tell that the ark was three stories tall." Timmy didn't forget.

But probably more important to remember than any other element in Timmy's formal learning process is that Timmy, in his primary years, is a *responder* and an *absorber*. Nowadays especially we hear so much about urging the child to express himself and to learn *what* he wants the *way* he wants to. What proponents of this theory overlook is that first there must be something put in before it can come out—an impression before an expression—and, that before Timmy knows what he wants to learn, he must be taught the ability to judge. Of course, we don't go to the other extreme and treat him as a characterless vacuum. Surely, he expresses himself—but, in these years, mostly as a responder to the material taught him. Never do we want to forget that these are the foundation-laying years, especially for his formal learning. It is educationally right and proper that he does much listening and heeding in these years. It is Scriptural, too. David says in Psalm 34, "Come, ye children, hearken unto me: I will teach you the fear of the Lord." Solomon, in Proverbs 29, says, "Hearken unto thy father that begat thee. . . . "

Timmy's will to learn, his interest, and his response are not always consistently good. Part of the reason is that he does not yet have the capacity for steady concentration. Although his attention span becomes longer each year, he still has a relatively short span, and his body calls for a change of position or some exercise between spans. His ability to pay attention and to concentrate can be improved by coaching from his parents and teachers. We have already developed Timmy's attention span to a remarkable degree in church, so that he is able to listen well for a much longer period of time than a nontrained child could. We have taught him, too, that listening in church and listening in school are basically the same kind of listening.

We know that his attention span is longer now, and his powers of concentration are much greater, but that he can go off on a tangent at any time. Although we think that we are prepared for his quick shifts of thought and his injections of completely extraneous thoughts—quite sensible to him, but without any logical reason to us—he often brings us up short. All of us have had the experience, when having a serious talk with our Timmy, that he says, in his own very serious tone, "Know what? Scott's daddy has a big wart on his forehead." His sudden change of attention and shift of thought has caught us by surprise again.

The other part of the reason that Timmy does not always listen and respond as he should is sin. He knows what his calling is. He knows that he must use his time and his talents in obedience to the Lord. But he is a weak and frail sinner. And we have to help him see that he is a disobedient covenant child again; then he must repent and fight to do the right in the fear of the Lord. So his battle continues.

Another characteristic of Timmy in early primary years is his enthusiasm. In his work and in his play he is either frowning and biting his lips in intense concentration and effort to succeed, or shouting and laughing in wild abandon with the joy of what he is doing. What he is doing he is doing better each year; his smaller muscles are better developed, and he has the opportunity to flex and control them in the many competitive pastimes he enjoys with his classmates. School helps his eye-to-hand control, and before he enters second grade, he can copy from the board or compose his own thoughts and set them on paper, precisely, on proper lines, and with even spacing and size. On the playground he learns to judge the height of a pitched ball with his eye, and then hit it with a fair average of accuracy.

The early primary child, at home or at school, can refine his skills by working with a rope. A length of rope about four feet long will help him develop almost all of his muscle skills. Folded in half, then in half again, and then tied in a knot, the rope becomes a perfect tool for throwing. Timmy will try first to throw it up to the top of his head and then catch it. He will hold it at shoulder height and drop it into his other hand, held at knee height. Next he tries to throw it over his head, with his right hand, and catch it with his left, or he slips it, with his right hand, under his left knee, and catches it with his left hand, and quickly reverses the process. If he has a companion, he will play catch with it, gradually increasing the distance between him and his friend. Then he and his friend will compete in throwing it at a target or through a ring. All these exercises test and develop his judgment and dexterity. When he tires of these games he may open up the rope and lay it out straight on the floor and try to walk it, hop it on alternate sides, or crawl its length with two hands on one side and one foot on the other. His other foot he holds high in the air. His friends may hold the rope low and taut while he jumps over it without tripping, or he goes under it without touching it. Or, if he is in a quiet mood, Timmy may want to make letters or intricate figures with his rope.

He will enjoy any new challenge, with his rope or without. Though he enjoys his old games, the primary child is eager to try a new skill and plunges into it with his whole being. Have you ever seen a brand new first grader handle the challenge of beginning to read? He reads with his whole body. He taps his feet, or moves them swiftly back and forth, he scratches his arm, rubs his eyes, and as he frames each successive word, his whole body moves in a backward-forward rhythm. His small fists clench as he says, "No, don't help me!" And he will keep trying until he is reading unaided. After having reading and math and phonics through most of his school day, plus fast-paced games on the playground, it is no wonder that he comes home from school very tired. A primary child needs much rest—rest for his developing bones and muscles and rest from the tensions of the new experiences of each day.

In these years we will see a change in the way Timmy expresses himself. His delight in expressing overt affection wanes. He has to be reminded to kiss us good-night at times, he doesn't sit still and cuddle on his parents' laps as often, and he tries not to be seen in public holding our hands. Instead, he gets up early and surprises us by bringing us a wobbly breakfast tray of spilling juice, instant coffee, and soggy cereal, accompanied by a beaming face and solicitous attention. If our primary child is a girl, she may (depending on her character) cling to overt affection a little longer than Timmy does, but she, too, will express her love by arranging a beautiful bouquet of wild flowers for us, and by making potholders by the score, and surprising mother by cleaning the playroom cupboards.

While we are living through Timmy's first three years of formal instruction in the covenant school we have chosen for him, it will become a way of life for us to create an encouraging atmosphere for his academic excellence. Never prying, quizzing, but always interested and helpful, we will unobtrusively oversee his progress. When Timmy is slothful and puts mischief before good grades, we are quick to notice and to remind him of his duties to use his time and talents in the right way. And we do encourage good grades. Why not? They are the rewards of diligence. But we ask him to work for much more than good grades. We encourage him to work for an understanding, for order in his work and system in his thought progressions. If he is able, we want him to do more than he is asked to do—whether it is an extra poster for science, the starred problems for extra credit, or reading a book simply to know more. What we want to accomplish is to make Timmy a willing and able student. Of course, we can only help him. The Lord has given him his potential. Not every school boy has the ability to be an excellent student, and some school boys are very poor students. That does not change our responsibility; we parents are called to make him try to do his best, and we will work to implant a godly attitude toward the work which he as pupil must do. He is old enough now to understand that his calling before the face of God is to work hard at being a good student. A parent who is vitally interested in his son's schooling, who teaches him not to be afraid of hard work, who insists on his son's best efforts, who sets high standards of behavior, and expects diligence from his son, and who does this with a loving, quiet insistence is training his son in the proper spiritual attitude in which to pursue his whole further life as pupil.

Remember, in these years of training and foundation-laying, we prepare our son for the rest of his life. To do this, our basis and our outlook is soundly Scriptural and deeply spiritual. And we take issue with Editor DeKoster who, in an editorial about Christian education, says, ". . . schooling without religion to establish who the child is, and Whose the child is, whence he comes and whither he goes, Who creates and sustains all things and why, Who recreates and how: without all this, schooling is simply training."

The editor is trying to say, I believe, that education asks all the basic, important questions from a religious point of view, and answers them, too. Education, and necessarily educators, view the child from a spiritual and an ethical perspective. Training, according to this quotation, is outside this sphere. It seems that the editor sees training as the mechanical end of schooling. What Editor DeKoster fails to take into account is that training has more than one aspect: training can be formal or mechanical, and it can also be ethical or spiritual training, as in Proverbs 22:6, "Train up a child in the way he should go; and when he is old, he will not depart from it." Seen in the light of this text, Christian education in the schools is but one phase of the child's covenant training. Training and education are very closely related. They are two aspects of the same idea, and both lead to the same goal. We parents are "trainers" who ask who and what the child is, whence he came and whither he goes, and we consult our "Source-book" always as our only infallible guide in our training course.

While Dr. DeKoster maintains that mastery of skills and subject matter is training, a training that is merely mechanical, he still faces the question: what, then, is Christian education? This is the way he answers it:

> ... do not expect to define Christian education in terms of a so-called 'Christian math,' or 'Christian science,' or a 'Christian antithesis in the arts.' You can stir up hot and fruitless arguments if you take this tack, but the Christian school will get lost in all the wind and noise. The Holy Spirit graciously enlightens secular man with much that is true. Einstein led us to atomic fission, and Jonas Salk to the cure of polio; while St. Paul quotes a pagan poet to make his point at Athens, as Calvin quotes Cicero and 'the philosophers.' Don't hope to go Paul one better by inserting an 'antithesis' into subject matters, with secular education on one side and 'Christian' education on the other—you will simply drive a wedge into a Christian community which ought to be united in support of true Christian education. What then? ...
> For me, the key to the essence of Christian education is the recognition that the school is not only preparation for life, but it is life itself. ... Love alone educates.[1]

The article expands on the idea of education in the sphere of love, in the context of morality, and with a spiritual consciousness; but the above quotation expresses the author's basic idea of Christian education, I think. How do we evaluate this philosophy? According to DeKoster, the subject matter in education is not necessarily Christian or non-Christian; education is neutral, and can be set in a Christian or in a common-grace-secular context. Let us not be taken in by this view. For us, Christian education is Christian in its essence, its substance, and its perspective; the approach, method, and content must be Scriptural and spiritually distinctive in order to meet our definition of Christian education. Of course there is a Christian science, a Christian history, and a Christian antithesis in the arts, even when we quote pagan philosophies. We quote them with a spiritual perspective and with a critical evaluation. Surely, if our Christian education were not Scripturally based in every aspect, if it were neutral as to its essence, it would not be the kind of education we would want for our covenant seed. Also, we cannot agree that education is life itself. This little phrase is bandied about by educators these days, and at first glance seems harmless enough. But if we think of its implications we will note that, because education is life itself, the one who is educated may govern that life and that education as he sees fit, for this education is his life. He may decide. He may have the say-so. Who are we to lord it over him? In this education which is life he is free to express himself and to choose what he will do. Do we sense all the overtones and dangers of the unscriptural view of our child's learning here?

Heartily we reject this theory, and acknowledge that, though we are teaching *living* children, this education is a *preparation* for the rest of their lives because childhood itself is a period of preparation. Therefore, education is a *preparation* for life. And, surely we agree with Editor DeKoster that love alone educates . . . and trains. It is the love that sees our child as a depraved sinner, a covenant child, and a redeemed saint. In love, *we* make the choices for him, and *we* are his guides. And in love which holds fast to the standards of God's Word we prepare him, in all facets of his education, for this life and the blessed life to come.

* * *

So far in this chapter we have concentrated on Timmy at school. Yet it is our home which is the meeting place and the basis of unity for the spheres of school and church in Timmy's life. It will always be the most important place for his covenant training; for, just as we received Timmy from the hand of the Lord, so we seriously assume the responsibility (also delegated from the Lord) of his covenant upbringing. We care, and we try.

But our handling of Timmy does not stay the same. Slowly we are developing and adapting our training to fit the needs of our growing child. When he is in grades one through three he does not have so many physical dependencies as formerly. In fact, he brags about his abilities to lace his own ice skates, to untie the hardest knot, to carry a heavy load. We find that we do not have to "talk down" to him so much anymore, nor give such long, patient explanations. His vocabulary and his comprehension are broadening.

New kinds of faults emerge. Now that he has come to complete awareness of himself as a separate individual and since he has tasted the beginnings of learning, Timmy wants others to know about it, too. He likes to lord it over his classmates or his small sister, if he can. Bossiness, we might label it, or pride. Also, with the greater measure of freedom he has gained in these years goes a degree of irresponsibility. He may thoughtlessly stop at the home of a classmate "for a minute" on his way home, to ask permission for his friend to come along home with him; and his "minute" becomes an anxious half hour for mother at home. Or he may call, after giving mother another hour of worry, and say, "I'm at Scott's house, and may I stay awhile?" This tendency may be more characteristic of primary girls than of boys; but each in his own way will show, at one time or another, a thoughtless disregard of his responsibility. And though he has plenty of time for play with his classmates and friends, he often has a definite impatience when he must find time for the essentials we insist upon: to come in after school before he plays, to change his clothes and put them away, to discuss his school papers and explain his errors and correct them to our satisfaction.

Parents of the primary child will, I think, recognize these faults as typical of their child at this age. A little later in this chapter we will try to determine the wisest way to handle these new weaknesses of our son, along with other kinds of shortcomings which we had not seen before in Timmy's life.

Now he is bringing into our home the evidence of outside influences in his own life. He mimics his friends, or one special friend who is his particular hero. New thoughts, new words, new actions enter our home by way of Timmy. Some of these intrusions bring fresh viewpoints, subtle humor, or serious insights. Some of these influences are good. But not all of them are. Timmy, sinful Timmy, likes to repeat the questionable words, to imitate the improper actions of one or more of his heroes; on the playground he learns the dirty words and stories that little boys like to repeat. All of these tales do not come home, of course; but we are realistically aware of what Timmy hears on the playground—even though it is the playground of a covenant school.

We hear words which embody ideas which we have never taught him. Arising partly from his maturing sinful nature and partly from associations with other sinful children of his age, these words often take the form of disobedience: "Aw, Mom," or "Jimmy may. Why can't I?" or "Do I *hafta?*"

Although from now on we will have to fight Timmy's use of his tongue because it is so easy for his sinful nature to express itself in the disobedience to which he is so sorely inclined, yet, because he is a redeemed child of God he is sorry, and grows in grace after each battle with his disobedience. He *knows* what is right and we encourage him to discern what is good and what is evil in each of his various contacts. Especially precious to us are his reactions after visiting in other covenant homes. His wonder and amazement at other ways of doing things will secretly amuse us. He will tell us, after a dinner invitation to Scott's house, "Scotty's mom is real nice to their baby, but she doesn't make him sit still like you make Sarah." And, "Scotty may walk around with his dessert. And when Scotty said, 'Pooey!' to his mom, she didn't even scold him."

When Timmy tells of his experiences in other homes, we listen; these stories tell us the things which have really impressed him, and show us what he thinks about his own home. For as yet the only standard of comparison he has is the home in which he was brought up, and he measures all the other homes he visits by that standard. Not only do we listen intently to see how he really feels about what he sees and hears in other homes. We answer his questions. He will surely ask: "Was she being a good mother? Do you like Scott's daddy? Do you think Scotty's home is a good home?" Answering his questions will give us the opportunity to teach him that just because a family does things differently does not mean that their way is worse than our way. If, however, that family is lax about living the right way, about bringing up their children in the fear of the Lord, we show Timmy that some aspects of their lives could and should adhere more strictly to God's law for our lives.

But we will tread carefully here. At this age Timmy is a little absolutist. To him, things are right or wrong. A person is good or bad: he wants to categorize everything by stark black and white contrasts, and fit people's lives into one or the other category. No tempering judgments, no sympathy for weaknesses in some aspects of others' lives, no insights into the tensions of sin and grace enter into his simple standards. Thus, if in answer to one of Timmy's prying questions we admit that there is a weakness in Scotty's home, we temper our criticism by reminding Timmy that this is basically a good home, with some weaknesses, just as ours is. Our home and Scotty's home, because they are Christian homes, are good. But they are not perfect Christian homes, because all the people who live there are sinners. If we need any examples to convince Timmy, we can remind him of our conversation of yesterday, which went something like this:

"Mom, was King David good or bad?"

"What do *you* think?"

"Well, in one story I thought he was very good, but in today's story, Teacher said he was a wicked sinner because he married another man's wife."

"Maybe he was both."

"No, Mother. He couldn't be. . . . "

"Tim, aren't you? Don't you try to obey and to love God all the time, and do what He wants?"

Tim nodded solemnly.

"How come, then, that you told that lie to your teacher and to me, and we had a hard time making you tell us the truth? Tim, are you good or bad?"

After a moment's reflection, Tim had answered, typically, "I think really good, Mom, because I *was* sorry. But I get what you mean."

The severity of Timmy's judgments of others does not extend to his own faults. One of the hardest faults for him to conquer is his selfishness. It comes out in personality clashes at school. When assertive Timmy and insistent Suzy both want to be the leaders and both want to win, they will surely quarrel. When Timmy brags about his accomplishments over and above those of his classmates, and when we hear about his bossiness from his teacher, we know that he will not change his ways after only one heart-to-heart talk.

Timmy will need repeated teaching to love his neighbor. Our talks will teach him to try to put himself in his neighbor's place—not so easy for a first grader—and see how he would feel if he were bossed by a loud-mouthed classmate. That is not all. When he shows his self-centeredness, we let him tell us if these thoughts and deeds come from a heart that truly loves the Lord and wants to do His will. In other words, we teach him the Golden Rule: "Therefore all things whatsoever ye would that men should do to you, do ye even so to them," Matthew 7:17 . . . for God's sake. We do not stop there. We teach him to be a Christian who does more than is asked of him in relation to his fellow Christians—to be "kind one to another, tenderhearted, forgiving one another, even as God for Christ's sake hath forgiven you," Ephesians 4:32.

If Timmy has understood all this, we tell him about the exercise of *humility,* a virtue quite foreign to our unsanctified natures; but following Paul's instruction, we heed the admonition, "in lowliness of mind let each esteem other better than themselves," Philippians 2:3. After all this instruction, will Timmy stop his selfishness as he uses it to push his way and boss his classmates? Most likely not. Most likely it will be a lifelong fight to dedicate his assertiveness to the glory of God . . . in humility. Sometimes a story from God's Word speaks most vividly to a small child. From a classroom experience, I remember the day that we had the story of Miriam and Aaron rebuking Moses for his sole authority, and their coveting some of it, and Miriam's subsequent punishment of leprosy for seven days. At noon hour of that day, a pushing boy and a shoving girl were struggling for first place in line, when suddenly a small classmate's voice rose above the noise. "I'd quit thinking so much of myself, if I were you. Remember what happened in our Bible story to Miriam when she tried to be the whole cheese?" The subdued quarrellers both walked silently to the end of the line.

Another decision we must make—which our parents did not have to make—is the decision about the place of television in our home. A teacher-colleague once remarked, after listening to conversations on the playground and in lunch-hour groups, that he wondered what *he* talked about during his free time as a youngster. He grew up without television. Timmy knows about all the programs. Even if we severely restrict his watching of television, he hears all the programs discussed by his schoolmates. And then *he* wants to see those programs, too. Needless to say, Timmy needs some firm guidance rules. But before we lay down his guidelines, we will closely examine our own attitude toward television.

That television is not wrong in itself we take as a premise. Just as alcohol in itself cannot be considered as a sinful substance, so no inventions made under the providence of God in the world are sinful as such. The fault comes in their misuse. If we, as Timmy's parents, decide to bring television into our home, we will ask ourselves just what it is that is intruding itself upon our lives. Before we turn on any program, we will remind ourselves, as we do in all the other spheres of our lives, that we are *different,* that we are not of this world, that we are pilgrims whose interests tower far above the here and now. Negatively, we are ready to turn away from sin, from watching God's laws being trampled under foot, from filling our souls with light vanity. Already we are setting up high standards for ourselves over against any television program. We and our children do not want to disobey our God in this part of our lives, either.

Next, we will take a look at the fare that is offered on the programs. Because we are devoted children of God, without being overly "pious" in a rigid, narrow way, we will not pick at small details to criticize, not measure by "precept upon precept, line upon line." We will look at the philosophies governing these programs on television. Most are materialistically oriented: that is, they have to do with *things.* The programs are about amassing things, preserving things, loving things, stealing things, coveting things, killing for things. Again, *things* are not wrong if they are not an end in themselves. But will our young child be led astray by watching their misuse?

Many, if not all programs are man-glorifying. Not just the glaring examples such as Super-man, but more subtly, the "doctor" programs, science documentaries, and even soap operas enhance man's progress or man's dignity. A discerning Christian knows that they stem from the insidious evolutionistic philosophy that exalts man in a world without God.

The drama on television portrays a non-sanctified life at best and lewd wickedness at its worst. We watch actors and actresses play at sin and occasionally pretend the sacred. Do we enjoy this? Does our son grow up with this? But, you may interrupt, what about the innocent cartoons? Shall our son watch them? Maybe. Or do they, too, mock at obedience, at authority, at a sanctified use of the tongue? And are they worthwhile fare, or empty vanity?

If, then, we agree that so much of the programming that *could* come into our homes *should* not (and I think that if we are godly, we will agree), what is there left to do with our television set? Probably not much. Probably we will decide against having television viewing available in our home. And our decision will be wise. If we *do* allow a set in our home, we surely will limit our watching and our son's, to a bit of sports, education (?), news, and nature films. Even in these areas we may have to say no.

But, because of our whole outlook on life, we are not unhappy that we cannot be television watchers. We are not unhappy because television is not a great concern in our lives. While many around us magnify the value of entertainment, we are asking different questions. We are also teaching our son to ask these questions. The questions are these: in the small but precious amount of time the Lord has given, how can I best use it? How can I be a better steward? Am I using my God-given gifts by staring at pictures hour after hour? Could I do something more worthwhile? Would I do better to read, to practice a musical instrument, to work at a craft, to help a friend, to work, to study God's Word? As we order our lives away from the vanity of the world's empty entertainment, and as we teach our son to seek for higher, lasting values, we do not walk around with long, stiff faces. We will not let Timmy do it, either. We are not Christians who feel constrained in our calling. Even when Timmy says, with a long face, "Scotty may watch that program," we will explain with patience and love and a God-fearing cheerfulness why Timmy may not. In the area of television watching, when we are unsure of whether to allow our child to watch something or not, the rule holds here, too—when in doubt, don't. We will not be sorry.

What, then, will Timmy do with his "spare" time? He will have some, but not much, after he has mastered his catechism lesson, Sunday School material, and any work he may have taken home from school. Our active son needs the outlet of working with his hands. If he is motivated and supervised, he will probably be interested in some woodworking. With dad's help, our primary child will have his own little putter corner in the basement, equipped with his own tools, and probably his own jigsaw. If our child is a girl, we mothers start to teach her weaving or simple embroidery. Always cooperating with our child's "secrets" and "surprises," we are encouraging him to work diligently and well in order to give to others.

When he is not working or playing—and he still needs his free, carefree, playtime—we suggest reading. When he goes to the library, we try to arrange to go along so that we can guide his choice of books. Though he will want all horse stories or all dog stories, we urge him to choose from broad areas in the field of reading. And he will be surprised that he enjoys most of our choices. He enjoys them because at this age his interest in almost any subject is easily aroused. Let us make the most of this trait during his primary years.

When Timmy was quite a bit smaller, we often found it necessary to talk *to* him. We spoke and he listened and obeyed, but rarely responded, because he was too young. Now there are times when we still talk *to* him. Usually, however, we talk *with* him. Undoubtedly he will still have to listen much, for he is a young child in the home, and he has much learning and obeying to do, but his developing understanding and reasoning powers have enabled him to begin to express his thoughts. And although there is a time for the lecture in his life, there are more times when conversation is the better method. In explaining a concept or solving a problem or disciplining for a misdeed, we are usually wise to discuss. In this discussion, of course, we are careful that we do not set up a free situation, that we do not sit down as equals. Though we are clearly his guides, he asks questions and expresses his opinions, and also his willingness to have them corrected. When he has done something wrong, often a good opener is to ask him, "Do you have anything to say?" If he responds freely, we can keep up our questions, ending with, "What do you think you should do about it?" Often a child, when soberly relating his own wrongs, condemns himself more severely than we would.

To keep a wholesome atmosphere of open communication, we are parents that keep his trust. We show this by our actions and also—and some undemonstrative parents forget this—by our words. When once I scolded a first grader rather sharply for more than his share of mischief, I ended by telling him that I liked him, that I hoped he would be an obedient boy in the Lord, and that I cared almost as much as his mom did. His reply startled me. "You got her all wrong, Teacher. She don't care at all about me. She never, ever told me she cared." Happily, the mother, made aware of her lack, told her child, and his attitude improved. By our I-love-you-and-I'm-all-for-your-good attitude, we invite his confidences. Then we respect them. By our enthusiasm, we share his joys and triumphs. In all his experiences, we try to keep our psychological and spiritual equilibrium. If he is fresh and loud-mouthed, we are not going to dismiss it with a shrug and "it's a stage he's going through" excuse. Nor, if we are not ready to laugh at it, will we flippantly disregard our parental duties by saying that he'll laugh about it when he is older. The answer is not always to preach to him, either. A child is adept at turning us off. We need wisdom and judgment to know that some things in life are minor, not worth fussing over; some things are better handled by a good sense of humor or a good-natured tug at his hair; the serious wrongs we chasten.

During these years Timmy will ask questions and offer unexpected comments which show that he now can understand deeper Biblical and spiritual concepts. He may ask a question such as, "Why did God say Achan had to be stoned to death for stealing some gold and silver from Jericho, and David might live, and even marry Bathsheba, after he stole her from her husband, who he killed? Wasn't David's sin worse?" This problem—of unbelievers who are punished and of believers who are forgiven, all in the sphere of the covenant—is typical of the kinds of questions Timmy asks. He will ask many more questions about his life as a Christian, most of them concrete and practical, dealing with everyday life; and he will be better able to grasp the spiritual concepts in our answers. Now he knows how to express his spiritual life more ably. Because he can speak knowingly of God's law, of obedience, of God's Spirit in his heart, of sin and forgiveness, it is time that we teach him how to pray his own prayers. Soon, too soon, his memorized bedtime prayer becomes a trite ritual which he rattles off at high speed before he makes his flying leap to beat his shadow into bed. And too often our thoughts are far away, and we don't notice that tonight Timmy's prayer was only a pious formality. When this happens, we know it is time to change his bedtime prayer from a routine to a time of spiritual petitioning.

Also in the realm of prayer, the atmosphere of our home has long been Timmy's silent but eloquent teacher. Because we are praying parents and a praying family, Timmy will already know much about the art of prayer. From his Christian home environment he will have observed parents who have tried to have the whole family present for as many meals as possible, because mealtime is also devotion time. He will have listened to serious discussions about prayer, about what we should pray for, and how. Certainly, he will not have understood all those discussions; but he has heard them, and listened. And he has, for a long time already, understood our seriousness in trying to pray aright, our reverence when we approach the Holy One, and our sense of deep need for the comfort and solace of prayer. This is what our home life of devotion has taught Timmy. Now, at the age when Tim begins to be able to express his thoughts and feelings, he is ready to join us in taking an active part in the prayers which rise from our family to our Father.

Prayer, to be thoroughly Scriptural and a true spiritual art, must be well taught and well practiced. The "sentence prayer" fad, popular in some households, in which each child prays whatever comes into his head in whatever order the prayer happens to proceed, is to be criticized on at least two grounds: the child often asks for superficial, materialistic, and even absurd things; and an informal prayer thus prayed has no unity, order, and usually little reverence. When Timmy is six or seven, some evening when we are not hurried, we will ask him what he thinks he would like to pray about before he goes to sleep. "To forgive my sins," "to keep me safe tonight," "to bless us all," he may venture as a start. Drawing him out, and suggesting some ideas ourselves, we now have many phrases to incorporate into a prayer. Now what? We have been taught that prayer is necessary for the Christian "because it is the chief part of thankfulness which God requires of us," and that we are to ask for "all things necessary for soul and body," which Christ has patterned for us in the Lord's Prayer.[2] Now we teach it to our son. And, from experience, I know it will be a good refresher course for us parents. Two or three simple statements are enough for Timmy's first prayer. We can guide him to a good beginning—praise to our God or thanks for His goodness. Suggesting, prodding, rehearsing, we prepare him for his short prayer. Periodically, we discuss what should be included in our evening prayers, and gradually make them longer, so that they express more elements of praise, joy, trust, need, petitions for the needs of others, and sorrow for sin. Before Timmy prays, we ask him to sit quietly and organize his thoughts for his prayer. When he is ready, we listen attentively and critically. Sometimes it will be necessary to correct a superficial statement or a wrong petition in Timmy's prayer. Usually we will be leading him according to Scripture's guidelines in the art of true prayer. This will not make Timmy's prayers less spontaneous. He is a small child, and his words will flow freely and in a childlike manner with a fresh beauty, earnestness, and trust unmatched by the prayers of an adult. Prayer is one of the great beauties of the young covenant child.

* * *

Timmy is also making progress in listening in church. Building on the good habits we have been trying to instill up to his primary school years, he has learned to sit quietly and to give his full attention to the sermon. Of course, Timmy does not *always* do this. No child does. We do not have perfect children. That is why we must teach and re-teach, discipline and reinforce. But we do not excuse his lapses. We teach, chasten, and try again for better attention from a more devoted little church-goer.

Now is a good time to teach him not only what a sermon is (he knows that already), but how it is constructed. If our minister follows the logical method in his exegesis of a central theme with two or three sub-points or divisions under that theme—and that is an excellent, true and tried method of sermonizing—we explain, possibly by a diagram, what we mean. Using a situation with which he is familiar, we show him how we could make a speech on it, with a theme and two or three divisions. *Timmy learns in school,* we write on the *theme* line.

1. What does he learn?
2. How does he learn?
3. Why does he learn?

He will delightedly answer our questions, and probably even ask us for more diagrams. Then our next step is easy. We tell how a minister explains his text in the same way.

During the service, we will operate our pre-arranged signals. A pressure of our hands on his means the theme. Then come the fingers, one, two, three. When the minister finishes talking on point one and begins point two, we signal again by a gentle pressure of our hand on his. After a few church services of this kind of listening, we will reverse the procedure. Timmy will listen for the theme and apply the pressure; he will put out his fingers—one, two three. There will be some false starts when he tries the hard part—trying to find where point one ends and point two begins, and he will need our help there for quite a while, but he will *listen*. And he will try. From one of my own children's complaints that she couldn't find the beginning of point two because she couldn't remember for so long a time what point two was, came a system of mnemonics. We remembered the first letter of each point as a helper to remind us later on in the service. It helped me, too, and I still listen that way. So does my child, now grown up. And it has led to some strictly esoteric humor, such as the times the letters spelled IRS, ESP, and FOG. Our close attention to the structure of the sermon will be the springboard for our post-sermon discussion of the content and spiritual message. This is a time of explaining concepts at his level and demonstrating, concretely, how the truths of the sermon fit his little life.

At first the exercise of close attention and of proper sermon-listening will seem difficult to Timmy. And the last thing we want to do is make church-going a chore. We want our son's attitude to match ours, to be one of joy—of joy and gladness in the wonderful salvation that is ours. Nowadays, however, in the church world there is often an overemphasis on the element of joy and celebration, a superficial joyousness, which is more dangerous to our child than an emphasis on sober attention. We must teach our child that true joy is deep, because it is joy in the Lord. And that is not merely a superficial happy "feeling," but is the result of heeding, studying, and understanding God's Word. Scripture says so in Proverbs 3:13-17, *"Happy* is the man that findeth wisdom, and the man that getteth understanding. For the merchandise of it is better than the merchandise of silver, and the gain thereof than fine gold. She is more precious than rubies: and all the things thou canst desire are not to be compared unto her. Length of days is in her right hand; and in her left hand riches and honour. Her ways are ways of pleasantness, and all her paths are peace."

Throughout all our happy life with Timmy, in our lighthearted humor, our conversations, our work, and our play, in our rejoicing that we are God's covenant people, chosen for salvation in our Lord Jesus Christ, we keep an undercurrent of seriousness, of admonitions to holiness and warnings against sin, and of the importance of doing whatever work God has called us to do. We teach these undercurrents to Timmy as the foundation of our lives. This is what David meant when he said, "Teach me good judgment and knowledge: for I have believed thy commandments," Psalm 119:66. Building on the solid foundation of the commandments of our God, we will establish our covenant home where "thy wife shall be as a fruitful vine by the sides of thine house: thy children like olive plants round about thy table. Behold, that thus shall the man be blessed that feareth the Lord," Psalm 128:3, 4.

NOTES

1. *The Banner,* vol. 107, no. 44, p. 4; no. 54, p. 4 (Grand Rapids: Christian Reformed Publ. House).
2. Heidelberg Catechism. *The Psalter,* op. cit., pp. 16, 17.

11

THE CHILD IN LATER PRIMARY YEARS

Little children, let no man deceive you; he that doeth righteousness is righteous, even as He is righteous.
—I John 3:7

Y ES, OUR CHILDREN IN THE LATER PRIMARY YEARS ARE STILL "little" children: little in maturity, little in knowledge and wisdom, and still little in spiritual understanding. True, our children in the later primary years, usually called the intermediate years of grades four, five, and six, are no more *very* young children. Physically, they are growing. Spiritually, too. At this age, they can easily understand the above text; they know what righteousness is, and they know it is their joyous and yet difficult calling to *do* righteousness, for their God is righteous. In these years of development, our children learn that, as they begin to evaluate situations in life for themselves, they must analyze and judge all things in the light of God's righteousness. Applying the standard of God's righteousness to their lives, they say, "Behold, I have longed after thy precepts: quicken me in thy righteousness," Psalm 119:40. And then, even at such a young age as this, they understand by experience the last verse of the chapter quoted above: "And he that keepeth his commandments dwelleth in him, and he in him. And hereby we know that he abideth in us, by the Spirit which he hath given us," verse 24. Our children begin to feel in their lives the paradoxes of keeping God's commandments and breaking them, of longing after His precepts and longing after the world. They can talk about it, too, and pray, as children who have God's Spirit abiding in them, "Quicken me in thy righteousness."

To understand Timmy in the years when he is nine, ten, and eleven, we will have to look at many changes, some of them drastic, in his appearance, his abilities, his behavior, and his problems. First, we will see how he is changing physically. Timmy, along with most children of his age, will have a growth spurt during these years. His appetite will be almost unsatiable; for he is a half-grown child and needs so much sustenance, not only for his boundless activities, but also for his amazing growth. Not all children of this age grow rapidly physically. Some late maturers save their growth spurts for junior high and even senior high years. Regardless of his rate of growth, Timmy will begin to be an awkward and gangling boy, unsure of what to do with his hands at the ends of arms that seem just too long to be graceful. They are quite suited, though, for home runs in the noon hour ball games. When he comes into school, however, those feet that flew over the bases cannot walk through the rows of seats without bumping into desks or sending notebooks flying. Have you ever watched a group of intermediate children climb a small flight of steps into school? Someone (sometimes several—girls as well as boys) always trips and falls, scattering books and parcels through the hall and back down the stairs. The kindly classmate who comes to the rescue invariably suffers the same accident. He cannot even help his friend without awkwardness. Usually the child of this age is quite nonchalant about it all. "Just stumbled over my own feet," he mutters in passing to the hall teacher. He doesn't seem to mind.

Sometimes, however, our son is embarrassed by the prepuberty changes that subtly begin to take place. When he intends to shout to his friend on the playground and just squeaks instead, and when he tries again and his voice sounds lower than the voice he recognizes as his own, he is uncomfortable. When his vocal chords play tricks on him as he responds in class, and his classmates snicker, he feels very uneasy, and

The Child in Later Primary Years / 247

wishes his voice would behave consistently. But it won't. It will continue changing and deepening for several years. Yet he feels a certain elation as his voice tone drops several notches. When his intermediate choir teacher at last assigns him to the low tenor section, he knows he has arrived. He is growing up.

If our pre-adolescent child is a girl, she sees her body losing its straight, childish lines. Signs of hair where no hair was before, signs of breast development bring mixed feelings. She welcomes and fears these changes. Probably this is the reason that a girl at this age is easily provoked to gales of loud laughter or torrents of bitter tears.

Our child is not quite sure of himself. He knows he is not a small child. He does not altogether want to leave childhood. Yet, in a sense, he is eager to. And he does not quite know how. If he tries to act "grown up," he fails at that, too. With his lack of security goes his awkward, gangling body, and he usually succeeds in doing just the wrong thing.

His mental abilities are changing, too. Now he knows what continuity in learning is: building and expanding on what he has already learned in his earlier primary years. He is ready for systematic and systematized learning: he discovers basic structure in words, sentences, paragraphs, chapters, and begins to experiment with systematic outlines of his own. Time and space relationships come alive for him: he can project his thoughts back hundreds of years and form mental concepts of life in time far removed from his own; he can also form judgments about relationships of distances, whether in his own land, on another continent, or in outer space. Only because he has the ability to deal with abstract ideas can he understand and imagine objects and places he has never seen, and ideas of which he would never have dreamed. His ability to deal with the abstract enables him to interpret maps, charts, and graphs, and extract useful information from them. In simple doses, he is being taught concepts and the logic necessary to form them. In Biblical history, for example, he learns that God's plan of salvation followed the national line of the people of Israel. After he has learned this, he is able to trace this line and build further concepts of the antithesis between Israel and her godless neighbor countries. Then he can take the concepts of Israel's ceremonial laws, of Israel's symbolic worship, and understand them in the light of the larger context of Israel's unique place in history. Equipped with his greater mental abilities to understand concepts, to see relationships, and to interpret facts, he sees isolated incidents as part of a whole. His thought processes are broadening. Arthur Gates records a series of graded reasoning tests for children from seven years and older. We may be interested in the types of reasonings that challenge the nine- to eleven-year-olds:

9 Years

Three boys are sitting in a row: Harry is to the left of Willie: George is to the left of Harry. Which boy is in the middle?

10 Years

There are four roads here. I have come from the south and want to go to Melton. The road to the right leads somewhere else: straight ahead it leads only to a farm. In which direction is Melton—north, south, east or west?

11 Years

Where the climate is hot, aloes and rubber will grow: heather and grass will only grow where it is cold. Heather and rubber require plenty of moisture: grass and aloes will grow only in fairly dry regions. Near the river Amazon it is very hot and very damp. Which of the above grows here?[1]

Generally he enjoys using his sharpened reasoning powers to the best of his ability, and accepts challenges with equal enthusiasm, whether it be to delve into the complexities of math or the early Egyptian civilization. At this age our child is still rather easily motivated to learn new things, and is genuinely interested in knowing more. Because our child is able to respond, question, and converse, and because he is beginning to use an adult vocabulary, it is a pleasant experience to teach him, both at home and at school. He likes projects for extra credit at school and he wants to putter for the joys of challenge and success at his work-area at home.

The area of his formal education is not without its problems, of course. Nothing is, in our sinful lives. Timmy likes to show off his intellectual growth. Often he acts "big," important, and proud of the small advances he has made in the field of learning. He has a beginning of knowledge in some areas, and he thinks quite a bit of himself. As a result—and partly, I think, because he wants to show his increasing independence—he becomes careless and sloppy in his academic work.

In our child's overt behavior in these intermediate years, we see traits and acts which surprise us. We are not ready for Timmy's extremes of behavior, and are often caught off guard by an exhibition of rude, rough behavior toward a playmate or his little sister, followed the next morning by a surprise snow-shovelling job before breakfast.

Girls of this age, especially when together, alternate between extreme ladylike behavior and the roughness of a tomboy. Stops at the girls' washroom at school become increasingly longer because of the meticulous hair-combing ritual. As the girls file out, classmates are still putting the finishing touches on each other. Ten minutes later, on the playground, running with wild abandon, dodging boys and balls, all thoughts of neat grooming have fled.

Though the children of the intermediate age group have great loyalty for their classmates, they have not overcome their childish bickering and petty squabbles . . . and tattling. Often arguments arise between members of the same sex. More often boys and girls are pitted against each other. From my observations of many classes of children of intermediate age, I believe that most hostility between boys and girls occurs at this age. In the primary grades, girls and boys mix happily . . . usually. They do not have fixed boys' or girls' games. At junior high age levels they go their separate ways, or begin to have some special interest in the other sex. In the middle age group, the sexes cannot play the same games—boys are far too rough, girls are such sissies—and whether they try to play together or try to leave each other alone, they quarrel. Yet they keep trying to play games with each other. When I was on playground duty one day after a particularly lovely snowfall, the fifth graders asked if they might have a snowball fight—boys against girls—a kind one, with soft snowballs and no face washing. I relented to their pleading faces; but ten minutes later I was called back to the battlefield, and found four girls in tears. Red faced and bruised, they sobbed out their story of mean boys who aimed for their eyes, of face washing and unfair play. As I strode toward the camp of the enemy to hear *their* story, one of the girls timidly pulled on my coat sleeve and whispered, "Don't go. We had it coming. We were just as rough as they were. We'll make up." And I sighed an intermediate grade sigh. For they must be taught that covenant children must obey rules—home rules, school rules, and playground rules.

Peer pressure in these grades is probably at its peak. There is a certain way to act, and each child does his best to live up to this standard. Girls *must* walk arm in arm, preferably giggling; otherwise whispering. Boys cultivate the art of taking big steps without sprawling; as one class goes on into the next, they exchange one book for another with as much noise as they dare make. Although they are interested in the art projects and bulletin boards of brothers and sisters in the lower grades, they often pass the works of art with studied disinterest and a forced show of boredom. Certain subjects are taboo when boys of one age group are together. A fourth grade teacher told me one day that when she came to school with a brand new diamond ring on her left hand, the boys gave it a passing glance; they further hinted darkly that they would never consider attending her wedding, if invited. It was too sissy. They could not be bothered with such things. But privately and individually each made an excuse to examine the ring more closely; and almost all of them asked, "Is it sissy to go to a wedding? I'd really like to go."

Characteristic of these middle-group children is that sometimes they try to put on a certain sophistication for which they are not nearly ready and which they certainly do not feel. When they forget the facade, they are unaffected and interested young children, bubbling over with spontaneous enthusiasm.

Along with the rest of the mixtures and incongruities which show themselves during these years is a certain maturity coupled with naiveté. They *are* maturing. But they are still such babes in understanding the world about them, full of openness and trust, that they expect everyone to be. They *want* to mature, too. Sometimes life can hardly pass swiftly enough for them in order that they may reach their goals and ambitions of the future; their aims give them the desire to develop, and all during their developing they are ready to learn, eager to discuss, quick to question, and willing to work.

These characteristics which I have gleaned are general, of course, and I base them not only on textbook research, but, more concretely, on close observation of these children through many years. Not all children—not all covenant children—show all these characteristics, and some show very few. Usually, however, these are the qualities which stand out and which make associations with children of these ages a pleasant experience.

Although we have already hinted at some problem areas, we will want to examine them more closely. Probably petty bickerings and complaints will demand much of our attention, because they occur so often. Easily ruffled, quickly outraged, and highly injured, these children know how to weave eloquent stories of injustice, complete with drama and tears. By the time we have heard the whole story, and everyone else's version of the current argument, however, feelings are soothed, grievances are minimized, wrongs are forgiven, and the tempest in the teapot is over. But very shortly another highly serious argument is certain to develop. It always does.

The swaggering independence of the boys, who try to show their superiority with rough braggadocio, is sometimes the cause of these pre-adolescent clashes. Wanting to be grown-up, and trying to act important, these youngsters are so wrapped up in their own physiological growing up and the way they have patterned themselves to act, that they are callous in their consideration toward others. Of course, we know that we never view these quarrels and self-centeredness as stemming only from peculiarities of their age, or from physical or psychological phenomena, although these factors help us to understand why youngsters behave as they do. Central to all their acts is their relation to God, a relation of love and obedience, or one of rebellion and disobedience. Never do we excuse their wrongs —though we can often see *why* they act as they do—but always we make them recognize their spiritual responsibility before their God.

Especially is their spiritual calling accented in another problem area, that of their misuse of language. Both boys and girls want to show that they have outgrown the "childishness" of polite or precise replies; they much prefer to use the coarser "huh?" or "yeah!" or "ain't got none." They have more opportunities than when they were younger to hear crude or even foul language; and their sinful nature tempts them to imitate it, at least in private, and often not only in private. We parents begin to have problems with their misuse of language to us, to their brothers and sisters, and with their talk about others.

We will be obliged to observe the bad sides of their growing up. They will listen less willingly, for they let us know that they are learning things themselves as they grow up, aren't they? The last thing the girls want to be is babyish, and the boys despise a sissy. Usually children of this age do not have a defiant, "know-it-all" attitude; but in many, if we leave this attitude unchecked, we will be able to identify the beginning of this tendency toward a wrong kind of independence from parental control.

Though there are probably many more characteristics which we could list and surely more problems which will arise (for the problems will be as numerous and diverse as the children), these are some of the highlights of the children's lives at this age. These characteristics provide the setting for the life which we will share with our child in his intermediate years. For into the background which we have just detailed Timmy fits.

He is older now. But he is still the same Timmy: tall, lithe, with blond hair and blue eyes which merrily twinkle; he is still our talkative boy, mischievous and impulsive. His personality has not changed. It will not, either, even though it may be refined in later life. Our principles in handling him have not changed, either, although we may be adapting our methods to his understanding and needs as he grows older. Always we will build on the Scriptural principles of training we have established so far in his life: the fear of the Lord is the goal of our training, and is basic in all areas of our son's training; the love of God motivates all our authority and all of his obedient response; an atmosphere of relaxed, yet controlled discipline prevails, which is undergirded by a deep spiritual foundation of mutual trust and true happiness. This is ideal. Scripture's admonitions always point to the ideal, so that "the man of God may be perfect, thoroughly furnished to all good works," II Timothy 3:17. But it is not easy—not for us, not for Timmy. Sin gets in the way, and the details of our daily mundane life in this world give us a mere horizontal vision; and we neglect to heed the admonition for the vertical perspective of Scripture: "With my whole heart have I sought thee; O let me not wander from thy commandments," Psalm 119:10.

Now that Timmy is almost ten years old, we need not spell out all the details of his behavior so fully anymore. For his physical wants and care he has achieved a great deal of independence. Though he still looks back on it with a certain nostalgia, Timmy has outgrown his "party" snacks; instead, he knows where to go when he comes home from school, famished. He cuts himself a thick slice of homemade bread, and allows himself ample butter and strawberry jam, and finds the biggest glass in the cupboard for his milk. He no more dependently asks, "What must I wear?" But he still asks, "May I wear my new blue pants today, Mom?" If he does not say it in proud defiance, we agree with him when one day he blurts out, "You know, Mom, I can really take care of myself now." What he means is that, up to a point, he can take care of his personal, physical needs.

What he does not realize is that he is yet so helpless in filling all his other needs. He still needs so much parental help and guidance, and will for so many years to come. Because we recognize that he is gradually weaning away from dependence on us, we increasingly respect his privacy during these years. This is the time when he has a secret drawer or a secret box or a secret hideaway or all three. Filled with elaborate old rusty locks, or rigged with special strings, his hiding places house such precious treasures as the badge his friend got for box tops and gave to him and dad's cast-off keys. Timmy hoards the choicest of his pants-pocket collections, and arranges and rearranges his special stones and arrowheads and bubble gum wrappers. These treasures are only for Timmy's eyes—and probably Scott's, once in a while. But even Tim will recognize that not the *contents,* but the *idea* of his secret is the important element to him. As wise parents, we know this.

We know the difference between *prying* and *caring.* When we oversee his progress in school, for example, we are *caring.* A teacher-friend of mine was once telling me about an intermediate boy somewhat like our Timmy, appealing and impulsive, whose letter grade in geography dropped from a "B" to a "D-". His parents were shocked. "They told me," my teacher-friend said, "that they had no idea he had been doing poor school work. They didn't know he failed two tests and that his map work was barely acceptable. His father is really going to give it to him! No television for two weeks. See if that will teach him not to be slothful!"

How about it, parents? Would that be our reaction, too? Is this a good way to handle the failings of this child? If our answer is yes, many questions arise. Why did we not know about his poor work before his report card came home? How will two weeks of no television teach him diligence? . . . But probably our answer is no. I hope so, because if we are dutiful parents we will know when he is going to have a "horrid" geography test. "How was the test?" we casually ask after school. If he has done well, we know that most likely we will see the paper as soon as he bounces into the house on the day the paper has been returned to him. If he is indefinite or hesitant about getting his test paper back, we know that it is hidden in his desk, or dropped into the classroom wastebasket. *This* is the time to ask questions and insist on knowing the results. *Is* he a good steward? He *can* be. We ask for his daily papers. At a glance, we detect careful diligence or sloppy indolence. And watch him when we ask, "What country are you studying in geography now?" His face lights up because we are interested. If he is in the mood to talk about school work, he knows we will discuss it and help him with it, because we care. He knows that there is another reason for our question, too. We are checking up on him because we demand that he use his abilities to the fullest measure; we are not the kind of parents who believe the story, "My teacher hardly explains at all, and then expects us to know it, and she doesn't give fair tests." If, however, somehow he slips without our knowledge of it, will we say that two weeks without television is the remedy? Going without television may be part of the chastening, but the important remedy is reproof. We will come to him with words of the Lord, "Go to the ant, thou sluggard; consider her ways and be wise," Proverbs 6:6, and "Take fast hold of instruction; let her not go: keep her, for she is thy life," Proverbs 4:13.

There will be times during these years when we are called to make decisions: to allow or not to allow. Timmy will ask permission to do something which is not necessarily wrong in itself. Permission or nonpermission would be a matter of wisdom and discretion. He may ask, for example, whether he may go to the home of his friend down the street for dinner and over night. We hesitate. The home is very permissive, of questionable religious principles, but not a wholly "bad" home. Would it be good to let Timmy see how others live, and expose him to a broadening experience? Shall we let him watch the television programs which that home allows and we do not? Timmy wants to go, of course, and we would rather say yes than no; it is easier to say yes, and Timmy would be happier, for the moment, at least. Still we hesitate. We are uneasy about letting him go; and we remember the advice of an old minister: when in doubt, err on the side of saying no. It is better than saying, "I wish I hadn't."

So we tell Timmy no. Even after our explanation, Timmy may have trouble understanding our strictness, or he may not try to understand it. If he wants to talk back or argue our decision (and he does) he needs to be reminded, curtly, that as a covenant child he obeys promptly and cheerfully. He still may want to sulk and feel injured. That is wrong. We feel sorry for him and even think we should plan a nice surprise for that night, to make up for our refusal. That is wrong, too. We may plan a surprise, of course, but not on the basis of a refusal. Our decision stands on its own merits and our child is called to obey it without pouting or rebelling. If he does rebel, he must be chastened for it.

Timmy knows all the little arts and tricks of avoiding dutiful obedience. If, on a certain day, we discover that he has left his toys, books, and possessions all over the playroom floor —contrary to rules—we will remind him after school that before he goes out to play he must take care of his neglected chore. "Aw, Mom," he protests. (Shall we let him go now and let him pick up later?) Or he says, "Okay, Mom." Then all we hear is silence as he goes to his room; supposedly he will change his clothes and then clatter away as he clears the playroom. Investigating a while later, we discover him slowly unbuttoning his school shirt, reading his library book. "I was going to get to it, Mom, pretty soon." (Do we think that it is all right if he gets to it eventually?) Does this behavior conform to our standards of *prompt, cheerful* obedience? Oh, we can argue with ourselves that he may be tired, that we must not be too hard on him; but the stark fact remains that he has not given us obedience. Not for our sakes only do we make our words stick and our standards remain. We do it much more for Timmy's sake. When he protests, "Aw, Mom," or when he reads his book, he is not comfortable; he knows that his chore is hanging over his head, and he knows that he is doubly disobedient. He was slothful first and a procrastinator now. Because he is a covenant child, he knows how wrong it is, and it bothers him. If it does not bother him enough to make him promptly obedient, we step in and prod him. For it is our duty to teach him that an obedient child is a happy child, and *only* an obedient child is a happy one.

Earlier in this chapter we noted Timmy's changing language patterns. Surely, we would not want him to continue his early primary patterns. We want his language usage to develop. But only too often we detect development in the wrong direction. Timmy likes to mutter his "yeah's" and "huh-uh's" to us; we hear him call his teachers by last names only, or by "ole lady Smith" and "dumb ole Jones." And, if our ears are sharp, we hear him talk about "my ole man." Why does Timmy begin to talk this way? Imitation of what he hears elsewhere? Partly. But a much deeper reason lies inside Timmy. As he grows toward maturity and independence he rationalizes that he will not respect authority overmuch. Parents and teachers had better realize that he is a person and he has his own rights, too. That is sinful rationalization, of course, and contrary to Scripture's precepts.

How, then, do we change Timmy's rude speech? By changing Timmy's sinful thoughts about his independence; by instilling now, more than ever before in his life, the virtue of *respect*. Respect toward one another is not just a polite word, framed with a smile. Respect is a matter of the heart and a way of looking at our neighbor. Scripture does not teach us to respect each other for our *person's* sake, "for there is no respect of persons with God," Romans 2:11. But Scripture tells us over and over to give honor to those in office, to respect them for the sake of their office. "Honour all men. Love the brotherhood. Fear God. Honour the king," I Peter 2:17. "For as we have many members in one body, and all members have not the same office . . . be kindly affectioned one to another with brotherly love, in honour preferring one another," Romans 12:4, 10. When we learn to have a high regard for those in authority over us because it pleases God that we do, our language will follow the dictates of our hearts. And the dictates of our hearts tell us that, for the believer, *respect* is a way of life laid down for us in Scripture.

What about those who are our classmates, brothers, sisters, friends? The apostle John says, "My little children, let us not love in word, neither in tongue; but in deed and in truth," I John 3:18, and "Beloved, let us love one another: for love is of God," I John 4:7. When we love others in deed and in truth with the love that comes from God we will show it as it radiates from our inner being. Thus, respecting others is a solid Biblical principle, and a foundation for our lives, not only in word and in tongue, but clearly visible in deed and in truth. If we can teach Timmy to respect others, especially those in authority, for God's sake, the problems with his crude language will diminish, if not disappear. The Europeans in certain countries a couple of generations ago understood respect when they taught their children to say, when addressing them: "Does Mother want this? May I get Father a cup of coffee? Will Rev. Smith sit here?" To us, with our informal styles of speech, this may sound stilted. But the principle is right. The very phrasing of the conversations of the children to their elders bred an aura of high regard. We in the *now* generation in America may be less formal, but let us not be less respectful. As we have taught our child when he was younger to show his love and obedience by the *way* he responded to us, also now in his years of development we insist—quietly but firmly—on this expression of high regard for us. For if we do not insist, our child will lapse into the coarse, disrespectful, God-defying language of our age.

I am sure that all of us have heard both these kinds of answers in the covenant sphere: either "Okay, Mom," and "I will, Dad, right away," or "Yeah -h -comin," or "Hold it, will ya, till I'm through with this." Certainly the mere repetition of respectful phrases will not in itself make our child respectful, we will all agree. But our child is not just any child who mouths polite phrases. He has been taught from infancy to love and respect us for God's sake; he shows it by his words and actions; and in these years when his mouth *could* run wild, we continue training that mouth in the principle of respect. And his heart will respond. Or is it the other way around? Will his lips respond to his heart?

When Timmy sins during these years, what is the best way to chasten him? He has long outgrown the "no-no's" and taps on his fingers. Generally, we find it necessary now to chasten less often, but usually more severely. Our child will react differently to chastening than will our neighbor's child, for he has a different character; and we will not chasten all sins in the same way. Just as the philosophy in the worldly courts is that punishment shall fit the crime, so our chastening will fit the transgression. One more word of caution: we are not parents or teachers who punish inanely. We have all seen examples of it—too often. If, in school, a child raises his voice when he should not, an inane punishment would be to have him shout nonsense phrases at the top of his lungs in the gym for ten minutes. If he shoots a paper wad during math class, and the teacher strews the floor full of paper-punch dots and makes his pupil pick them up one by one, is he chastening that pupil sensibly? If Timmy comes tramping into the kitchen with muddy boots, and we give him an old toothbrush and a dish of water to clean it up, are we training him well or provoking him to wrath? We can all see the folly of these methods.

What, then, do we do with a boy at this age? Before we make concrete suggestions, we remember the purpose of chastening: correction, leading to repentance . . . done in love. Now, if our son speaks loudly out of turn at home or at school, we will not provoke him to wrath by having him make a fool of himself. If it is a first offense, we will probably only talk with him. If he is given to frequent loud-mouthed interruptions, we may ban him—with the Bible—and ask him to study James 3. Or we may ask him to memorize a pertinent portion of Scripture, or write a paragraph of his own thoughts about the undisciplined use of a loud mouth. Then we will keep the paragraph, which ends with his promise to fight and forsake his sin; and if he repeats his sin, we get out the paragraph and ask him to read it to us. From there, we can discuss the promise he broke, have him write more on his disobedience, ask him for an hour of thoughtful silence, or whatever we deem would be the most fitting chastening for our son at this time. In the same vein, if he thoughtlessly messes up the freshly cleaned kitchen floor, he must clean it up, but not with a toothbrush. If he remains thoughtless, we may ask him to volunteer for another clean-up chore so that he may learn consideration for the property of others. If he shows ill-will or meanness to a playmate, or if he loses his temper, we remember the rod of correction. For he is not too old for the rod.

If, when we chasten, we never lose sight of the purpose of our chastening, namely, to *teach* and *correct,* we will have less difficulty finding an appropriate method. We will not lash out and administer the first form of discipline that enters our minds. Rather, we will weigh the offense; and if it is a "big mouth" which has offended, we will remember that we are not chastening a big mouth, but a covenant boy who is using a big mouth. The answer we next seek is where we want to lead this boy with a big mouth; and the answer will be either to repentance, or to a sanctified use of that mouth . . . or both. Finally we arrive at the "method" question: how can I best accomplish this purpose, as a covenant parent, in harmony with God's Word? How can I best teach him to control his temper, to be more considerate of others, to fight his impulsive mischief harder?

How can I best chasten, not only negatively, so that he is sorry, but positively, so that he seeks grace to overcome his sins? The answers to these questions are not easy. But by now we do not expect them to be. The answers are not a series of pious sermons delivered to a passive child. But we will think about the answers, read Scripture with our problems on our soul—it always speaks to us, we know—and pray about it. Then we will act with firmness, and often with sternness, and always with love.

* * *

Timmy's growth in spiritual life and understanding shows itself in his knowledge of Scripture. No longer does he view it as "Bible stories," or even a *series* of Bible stories. Now he is able to see the whole Bible, from Genesis to Revelation, as the revelation of our sovereign, triune God. Now he sees God's hand leading one covenant people to glory: he can trace a line through the Old Testament right on into the New, the line of believers and their seed; he can conceive of God's plan of salvation as being executed in historical settings and sequences; he can begin to understand that the New Testament is the fulfilment of the shadows of the Old; and he can respond to the lessons he learns from the lives of the saints in the line of salvation. In church, catechism, and school he learns these truths formally. We teach him informally at home, in connection with daily Scripture reading, sermon discussions, or whenever he wants to know what we think about some aspect of our lives as God's people.

And although Timmy now is ready for an understanding of the concept of "guilt," "atonement," "sanctification," and the like, we still stress an emphasis on *knowledge* of the Scripture. He must still be busy developing a background of factual knowledge, on which he can always draw for reference in later life. Timmy of intermediate age will enjoy playing twenty questions, with Bible characters as the answers. So will we. We can use the refresher course ourselves when we decide on "Nehemiah" as the man to be identified by our son's twenty questions. Let's see: did he live before or after Jeremiah, during the captivity, whose cupbearer was he, who were his contemporaries? Perhaps we need the Bible first, so that our son won't uncover our ignorance. He has just studied it in school. Or, if Timmy suggests a game, we may want to play Bible category. At the top of a sheet of paper we write four or five letters of the alphabet, and on the left side we choose various categories, such as men or women mentioned in Scripture, cities, countries, rivers, etc., and we find a name for each category beginning with each letter we have chosen. The object is to find a name we think no one else will have. Bible quiz cards or books of Bible games are fun, challenging, and instructional for us all.

Another way to teach Timmy Scripture and to teach it, not as a solemn, imposed duty, but as a spontaneous, integral part of our lives is to allow him to interrupt Scripture reading during our mealtime devotions with a question. (We will qualify that questioning, so that it is not questioning for the sake of asking a question.) During our New Testament reading, as we go through the difficult book of Hebrews, and we read of Melchisedec, that he was "without father, without mother, without descent, having neither beginning of days nor end of life," Timmy will surely ask, "What does that mean, Dad?" And perhaps his questions will send us scurrying to sources for answers. Using this method, we will not read such a long Scripture passage during each devotion, but we will try to understand what we read, and take the time, or *make* it, to discuss what we have read. By our attitude more than by what we say about God's Word, we are telling Timmy that nothing else in the world is so important to us, that this Word is the source of all truth, and the basis on which we build our lives. That is why we do not find ourselves saying, "We're in a hurry tonight. Should we just skip devotions?" Rather, we show Timmy, by faithful family devotions, that only God's Word *really* matters.

The basic spirituality of our home, our readiness to ask, "Lord, what wilt Thou have us do?", and the underlying peace and contentment in which we rest are testimonies to Timmy about our outlook on all of life. Our own conduct is probably the most eloquent sermon we could preach to Timmy. Yet it is not enough. We will be talking to him and teaching him, at this age and until he leaves our home, to view all of his life and all the world around him from a spiritual, Scripturally oriented view. And we will not do it artificially in little pious lectures. But we will do it as we meet situations head-on, and must decide what to do and how to guide Timmy in making decisions—right ones. When, for example, he wants very much to watch a certain television program, he lets us know that Scott and a half dozen others in his class may watch it. He will ask, "Just this once? What's wrong with it?" Right here is our opportunity to teach him. First, we point out that his questions are all wrong. Will God condone a "just once" watching of an objectionable, man-glorifying program any more than a "more than just once" viewing? Shall we first ask the positive question, "What is right?", instead of asking what is wrong? Timmy, the boy who likes excitement, and who revels in the tense drama of gun battles, may not want to accept such a "narrow," Biblical view of his program. But neither we nor our son may be nonchalant or flippant about our sin. God's Word stands. And our word stands, too. So do our standards of discipline. Without being domineering, dictatorial parents, we tell Timmy that argument is out of the question, and that he must give us the cheerful obedience of a covenant child. Timmy is not always ready to obey cheerfully. He may mutter, "I still can't see . . . ," or he may stamp out of the room in anger, or he may march sullenly to his room. None of these are the answers of the obedient child. Right here we will have to stop Timmy again and tell him that he not only asked permission to watch something a covenant child in our home is not allowed to watch, but he is adding the sin of disobedience. As we continue talking with Timmy, we reinforce what we have always taught him: that he obeys not merely because we tell him to, but because God calls him to. But today, our talk is not enough. Timmy still wants to argue and challenge our decision. Then what? Probably today he needs the kind of chastening that takes further thought. We will send him to his room with the Heidelberg Catechism and ask him to meditate on and memorize Question and Answer 104: "What doth God require in the fifth commandment? . . . " Or we might give him paper and pencil and ask him to write his thoughts on Ephesians 6:5, 6. And then, after all is quiet as he is settled in his room, we ask ourselves, "Was all this necessary? Did we have to go to all these lengths just because he could not rest in our decision? Would we not also be disgruntled if we were stopped from doing what we wanted to do?" But to ask these questions is to answer them: yes, we were right; Scripture says so. Scripture is much more stringent about our duty to educate our child in the commands of the Lord than we, by nature, want to be. Consider again Deuteronomy 6:6, 7: "And these words, which I command thee this day, shall be in thine heart: and thou shalt teach them *diligently* unto thy children, and shalt talk of them when thou *sittest in thine house,* and when thou *walkest by the way,* and when thou liest down, and when thou risest up." It is the difficult way. But we know that already, do we not?

One of the most important things we will be teaching Timmy in these years is the proper perspective. He needs to learn how to interpret world events from a Biblical perspective as he reads the headlines in the newspapers. Closer home, he must learn how to view the incidents that arise in his daily life. When the boy next door seems to be very happy shooting baskets in his driveway on a Sunday afternoon, and Timmy wonders if he may put on old clothes for just a little while and go over to play with him, we must make him see that the Sabbath is the *Lord's* day, and that Timmy must want it to be different from other days—to be filled with the service of his God.

Or when one of his friends asks him to go roller skating or to a football or basketball game on a Saturday night, and promises to have Timmy home by ten o'clock, what do we say? Do we believe that going to sports activities is a proper way to prepare ourselves for the Sabbath? Do we want to imitate the world's Saturday night? What do we want Timmy to learn about his Saturday evenings? The answer of the devoted child of God is to put first things first, and to teach our child to do that, too. Physical and spiritual preparation—as a covenant family—is our calling. We will teach Timmy that, too. He will learn, then, by our words and example, to want to stay at home: to review his Sunday School memory work, to study his catechism, to play a quiet game with us, to go to bed early so that he is physically fit for the Lord's Day.

Sometime Timmy may come home with school gossip that hurts a classmate, a fellow member of the body of Christ. No matter whether the story is true or a lie, a fellow saint is suffering from the sword of Timmy's tongue. Timmy is not the only one who uses his tongue sinfully. He often hears us slander and backbite our brethren in the Lord. Together we will remember that "Love worketh no ill to his neighbor: therefore love is the fulfilling of the law," Romans 13:4. And we will make it a rule in our home—one that is often broken and repented of—that we will not talk about our fellow saints if we cannot say good about them in the love of Christ.

The examples of applying Scripture's principles to our lives are as numerous as life is diverse. The important element to teach Timmy when we show him how to view all of life from a Christian perspective is that, in each situation, he must come to a judgment. Always he has two or more possible alternatives, which he will be able to recognize. Next, he must fight his natural, sinful nature, and exercise his sanctified will so that he will come to the only right decision, the one that is godly. This is an instance where the *will* of our child, mentioned in chapter two, comes to the fore. Timmy makes a judgment —intellectually and spiritually—on the basis that we are *different,* and then, through the power of God's grace, he *wills* to carry out that judgment. He must get accustomed—and this is where our instruction comes in—to use the principles of Scripture as the spectacles through which he looks at what others do and what he does. Thus he will begin to have a Scripturally oriented way of looking at life.

In a sense, he has had that Scripturally oriented viewpoint on life ever since he was a baby. The atmosphere, or the home environment, with which we have surrounded him has influenced him immeasurably. Go with him and Scott, if you will, to the music store and hear his answer when Scott asks, "Would your folks let you have this record?"

"No."

"Ask them anyway. How do you know?"

"I just know. I don't have to ask."

How does Tim know? It is true, we have not denied him that record. Not in words. But in our lives we have. By the tone of our lives we have taught him that a covenant child has no ears for music portraying the lust of the flesh.

This is one isolated example. We could expand it as far as life is broad, and Tim would guess our answers to almost any questions he could ask us. He knows the basic undercurrent and the bounds which Scripture has set for our lives. He really knows by the mood of our home and the tone of our lives how we will react. This mood and tone has also become Timmy's. And it is of inestimable value for him to know how to look at life around him. Psychologists call it his "philosophy of life." We prefer to call it "training in the way he should go," with some of the training unconscious and incidental on our part, and much of it the fruit of our active, diligent teaching.

By the time he has reached sixth grade, we will have had many opportunities to teach him a viewpoint which looks past the immediate situation into future implications. For example, he may come home from catechism, grumbling, "I can't see why the minister couldn't change catechism for just next week. It's the only time the whole season a game falls on catechism day, and he won't change our catechism day even for once." Here is a choice opportunity to teach Timmy to look beyond next week's catechism day (or football game). Would we be saying something like this to him? "Timmy, if the minister changes it for football now, he may be asked to change it for baseball next spring. And if he changes it for the boys' football game, won't he feel obliged to do the same for the girls' bazaar, if it falls on a catechism day? Besides, Tim, think what the minister would be saying if he cancelled catechism for the game: catechism is not so important, at least not important enough to interfere with a football game. Or maybe he would not be saying something quite so strong. Maybe he would be saying this: catechism is important all right, but it won't matter to make exceptions to its importance once in a while. By his action of cancelling catechism he is teaching you that you may choose which is more important, the ministry of the church or a football game. If he lets you choose for the game, is he leading your life in the right direction—in *God's* direction? Tim, he is teaching you early in your life always to look for your spiritual nourishment *first,* to "covet earnestly the best gifts" (I Corinthians 12:31) and to see your bodily exercise as profiting little (I Timothy 4:8). He is leading you beyond the fun of next week's football game to your outlook on the rest of your life."

Perhaps Timmy's vocabulary will not yet allow him to use the term *priority* freely, but he will be developing priorities, whether he realizes it or not. He develops them first of all by watching *our* priorities, whether we like it or not. If it is very easy for us to stay home from a church service, to skip society or other church meetings, to choose a shallow entertainment instead of a spiritual treat, to procrastinate or postpone duties and fill our time instead with light pleasures, it will be easier for Timmy to do the same; for he not only follows his naturally lazy inclinations, but imitates our bad example as well. But we won't do that, will we? When we as godly believers—and parents at the same time—have a choice between bowling and Bible study group, between a travelogue and a Biblically based lecture, between a basketball game and a catechism class, we don't choose the spiritual food from a sense of *duty,* do we? We do it from the depths of a joyous heart, don't we? Our son will see the difference. How will he face these choices when he grows older?

When we talk about priorities with Timmy, we will be talking about putting first things first. And since his life at this age still centers so much around his schooling, we will emphasize the proper priorities in his learning. How? By stressing scholastic excellence. We are realistic enough to know that all our covenant children are not "A" students, and certainly not in every area. We are not even unduly concerned about a mere report card grade, for much more is involved in learning than a letter grade. But when we consider what wonderful creations our intellects are, and the fact that we seldom use more than a mere fraction of their potential, together with the deplorable reality that our son does not use his will to try to work to the peak of his ability, and we do not use our authority to prod him into doing it, are we not ashamed? Before God, **Who made** us His stewards? Let us not smooth over the hard edges of our calling and say that not everyone is the studious type. The question is still waiting to be answered: are we all working to the *utmost* of our powers? We are too quick to excuse ourselves and our son, to be satisfied too soon. In this age, especially, we have lost the fine art—and calling—of hard mental exercise.

One day I met a minister as he came from teaching a catechism class of intermediate age children, and he sighed such a long, loud, discouraged sigh that I asked him what the trouble was. He sighed again and said something like this: "When the children are little, they learn their lessons well and eagerly. They can hardly contain their enthusiasm in retelling the previous Bible stories. But already at this age their written work becomes careless and sloppy. They either cram their memory work right before class, or they read the answers from books on their laps. Because they are not prepared they can't—or won't—discuss. I've *told* them that they aren't learning their catechism to please *me*. *I* know it already. I showed them that this instruction is the basis for their future life, their only *real* future life. Don't their parents see the priceless value of catechism instruction? Don't they discuss and supervise and prod? Aren't they interested anymore?"

Are we?

From all of the above we must not get the idea, of course, that all we may do is walk around with a Bible under our arm and wear a face long enough to eat oatmeal out of the end of a gas pipe—a metaphor an old minister I once knew was fond of using. The joy in our hearts will spill over into our work. We can *will* to enjoy it, and so can Timmy. He can *will* to study hard and to tackle the difficult scholastic hurdles.

Even in our relaxation we will be good stewards, and we will encourage Timmy to take an interest in a worthwhile hobby as one phase of his relaxation. Does he like collecting things? Timmy surely does. Probably he will welcome suggestions of coin or stamp or plant collections. Or he might like woodworking or gardening or painting with water colors better. If our intermediate child is a girl, she will be asking sometime if she may learn to sew. An experience of long ago still rises occasionally in my memory to amuse me and to warm my heart. Let me share it. When one of my own little girls wanted to make an apron for her very first sewing project, I set aside a summer afternoon, and helped her with each step. While she was busy concentrating on the intricacies of seam allowances and bias tape, I sat nearby sorting out my recipe box. When the thread knotted and the seams were crooked, we straightened them out and plodded on, step by tedious step. At dinner that evening she wore her new apron, and then wore it outside for all the neighbors to admire. When she went to bed that night, she sighed happily and said, "I'm so glad. . . . "

"So am I," I interrupted. "Now you can sew."

"That's not what I'm so glad about," she said seriously. "I'm glad I learned how to teach little girls to sew. All you need is a recipe box that you're not very interested in, a happy face, and a *lot* of patience. I'm going to teach my girls *just* that way when I get big."

For this little girl, learning the intricacies of her new hobby was a pleasure, for it combined diligence and happiness on the part of both teacher and pupil, and lasting benefits for both.

After these three years of our diligent instruction, Timmy begins to learn to ask the right kinds of questions. He doesn't always ask them with a pure heart. If he did, our teaching would be over. But he *begins* to reject the negative, "Why may I not?" and "What is wrong with it?" and tries to ask, "How close can I stay to God's Word?" For Timmy is showing that he loves the Lord, that he loves His worship and His praise, and that he wants to live most of all for His glory. He is showing that he is a covenant child, happy in his blessings of salvation.

We expect, in our Sunday noon discussions, that he will understand more concepts in the sermon we have just heard. He may ask (or one of his teachers may ask) to take a written sermon report. If he can do it in good order, without disturbing his fellow listeners, we let him try it. And again we learn something about Timmy when he reads it to us afterward. What does *he* deem the important elements? Is he judging well?

Each evening before we say good-night, we listen to his

prayer, and give him further instruction. He is not old enough to pray unsupervised yet. We have much more to teach him. Through these years he progresses from simple petitions to some of the beautiful prayer concepts mentioned in Scripture, which he gleans from the prayers of the heroes of faith or from the songs of David. Now he knows and understands that these saints had the same needs that he has—the need for humility, repentance, and forgiveness. With them, he knows that he needs to be covered by Christ's blood, so that he can have a thankful heart, so that he will praise God's majesty, and will know that he can be righteous only in his Lord. For, "Little children, let no man deceive you: he that doeth righteousness is righteous, even as He is righteous," I John 3:7.

NOTES

1. Arthur I. Gates, *Psychology for Students of Education* (New York: Macmillan, 1930), pp. 411, 412.

12

THE EARLY ADOLESCENT

Thou, therefore, my son, be strong in the grace that is in Christ Jesus.
—II Timothy 2:1

Entering seventh grade is a major event in the life of our child. Tim—he is not Timmy anymore . . . after all, he's in seventh grade, isn't he?—alternately views it as a challenge, a hurdle, or an uncertainty. Most of all, he is afraid. Seventh grade seems to be such a big leap from sixth grade, he says. And everyone says that junior high school is different and hard. Getting used to all those new teachers is no joke. Then think of all the homework! Some of the eighth graders say that the teachers up in junior high treat you as if you were grown up already.

Tim's fears about his junior high school years are only a part of his total fear and uncertainty. He is leaving his young childhood and starting his "growing up" years. What will it be like? As he grows older, he will become strong: he will be strong physically, for youth is the time of physical strength; if he applies himself well, he will be gathering strength intellectually; and, surely, if he is one of the Lord's chosen sons, he will become strong spiritually during these years. John says, "I have written unto you, young men, because ye are strong, and the word of God abideth in you, and ye have overcome the wicked one," I John 2:14. Our son forgets to be strong sometimes. In fact, he cannot be strong all by himself. He needs the reminder that Paul gave Timothy: "Thou, therefore, my son, be strong in the grace that is in Christ Jesus," II Timothy 2:1. He needs God's grace above all. For these early adolescent years will not be easy years for him. Not for us, either. At times it will seem to us that he delights in showing all his worst traits and all his failings to the whole world. Often we will be at a loss to understand him. In fact, he is often at a loss to understand himself. These are the *bokkige jaren:* the picturesque Dutch term, from the stem, *bok,* meaning he-goat, describes these "he-goat" years as those of uncivil, surly, rude, churlish behavior. The negative is not the whole story, we know. These are also precious years, positive years of the fruits of our training, just as all the years of our growing child have been.

What are the phenomena which make the early adolescent such a unique individual? In the next few pages we will outline the characteristics which a child in the junior high school years generally possesses, and which clearly distinguish him from children of other ages.[1]

Not very many people who work with these early adolescents enjoy the physical change and the trauma which accompanies it, least of all the young people themselves. It is the period of puberty. Their bodies are fast becoming the adult bodies they will have for the rest of their lives, and they cannot get used to it. Girls especially are awed and mystified by the new cycle in their bodies, and are often saddened by the monthly discomfort and inconvenience. Boys feel their voices dropping lower, but still catching a high tone when they least want it. Sweat glands seem to work overtime, and both boys and girls are embarrassed by the odors they struggle to control . . . or don't deem worth the effort or bother.

Many children are still growing; some have their height, but they look like spindly beanstalks. Arms too long, feet too large, hands not nearly large enough for the loads they want to manage, they stumble up and down stairs and crash into doors or walls or each other. In school corridors a classic jun-

The Early Adolescent / 273

ior high expression is: "Whoops, sorry!" And it becomes almost second nature for us fathers and mothers to say, "Take it easy. Don't fall down the stairs; not *up* them, either. Don't *drop* that jar!" Their feet come down too hard and too noisily, especially when they must clatter up risers for a public choir performance. Their ungainly arms and unpredictable legs make them uncomfortable in public.

Probably because of their lack of physical coordination and also because of the vehement exuberance of youth, they enjoy making excessive noise. At school, if they are not checked by a diligent teacher, they slam books on desk tops with exploding violence. Locker doors are slammed with resounding bangs. Boys shout, "Hey!" with triple volume, and girls shriek at ear-piercing levels. A proof of sincere friendship is a resounding thwack on the back, especially if the friend is at the drinking fountain. At home, we don't have to be told that our children are home from junior high. We hear the screen door bang hard, the clunk of heavy feet across the floor, a series of loud thuds as school books slide off the table one by one, cupboard doors opened and shut with unrepressed force, another thud as the knife full of jelly clatters down, followed by a sudden bellow: "Hi, Mom! We're home!" These children like to have noise around them, too. Two companions will talk loudly to each other, only to be interrupted by a third friend who shouts loudly enough to be heard easily above both. They like the blare of music from the radio, powerful fanfare on the piano, preferably accompanied by uproarious conversation.

Along with their strong desire to be surrounded by sound is their passion for physical vehemence. Watch a group of these early adolescents when the bell signalling the end of the noon hour recess rings. If no teacher stops them, they run pell-mell for the school door, pushing, shoving, tripping, shrieking; if no one in the corridors prevents it, they kick off their footgear with a violent fling toward their lockers, toss hats, scarves, and mittens in a generally accurate direction, meanwhile ducking the tossed snow that some schoolmate has scraped from his mitten, while one friend shouts, "Hey, watch out!"

and another elbows his way through with a brazen, "Clear the way!"

One more illustration will further prove that they seem to enjoy vehemence bordering on violence. One day, as one of my own children was dressing for her annual spring junior high outing, I casually said, "Looks as if you'll have a nice warm day. I hope you have a good time."

"Oh, we *will!*" she answered promptly. "We finally got permission to take our squirt guns."

Afterward, I heard about it. Never had they had a better outing. Everyone was drenched before noon. And it was such a warm day and the creek was so clean, they even got to dump each other in. It was, as I heard it, a riot, a blast. The only drawback was that they might not use their guns on the bus. And as they filed dripping, muddy, and bedraggled into school at the end of the outing, they were exuberantly happy.

Why is it that children, especially in their junior high school years, delight in such forceful, noisy, physical expression? Why is this vehemence often accompanied by a certain crudeness, a joy in pestering without considering the feelings of the victim? Is it because they want to test their strength? Or show that they are growing up? Is it the thoughtless exuberance of youth? Is it, in part, defiance? The answer may lie in a qualified affirmative to all of these questions. Probably more elements enter in. I do not know. Should we accept these peculiarities as characteristic of their age and let them go unrestrained? This question we will answer later in the chapter.

Tim and his friends have traits, very definite traits, other than physical, which are peculiar to their young adolescent age. Before we go on to discuss Tim's further life and problems, we will look briefly at several of these characteristics. One of the most important is their insistence on fairness. Though their dealings with one another are at times shoddy, they are very unhappy if they do not get a "square deal" themselves, especially at the hands of those in authority over them. One of the highest—if not the highest—standards of judgment by which they measure is, "Is he being *fair?* Was that a *fair* assignment?" Listen as they stand in small knots discussing the vital affairs of their day-to-day life. Indignantly one of Tim's friends blurts out, "It wasn't *fair!* He let *them* use the gym, but when it comes to *us*—oh, no!" Or, "Our coach is really a fair guy. He gives everybody a chance, not just the good players. He knows what fair play is—he's all out for everyone of us." Despite the fact that Tim and his friends may not interpret the quality of fairness properly at this stage in their lives—what is fair and proper may not *seem* fair and equal to them in their position of submission to authority—and despite the fact that they will learn all too soon that "fairness," as they think of it, is hard to come by, yet they are rigidly insistent that they be treated fairly.

Probably the trait most evident to us who are parents and teachers is their challenge of our authority over them. Sometimes it comes in mild questions concerning a minor detail in their life; other times it is revealed in open defiance of some of the basic rules governing their lives. The very phrasing of their objections shows their reasoning: they say, "Why should I have to do that?" or "What good will it be to *me?*" These growing children are especially self-centered and self-seeking in this period of their lives. It does not seem to occur to them to look around them to see how they can serve toward the best interests of others. Rather, they tend to look inward, to their own budding independence; and, with a wrong view of the idea of independence, they want to question the extent of our authority over them. Then, if we see what Scripture says about youth, we parents can better understand why our young teenagers resist us, or at least question the scope of our authority. Proverbs 22:15 says, "Foolishness is bound in the heart of the child . . . " and Ecclesiastes 11:10 tells us that "childhood and youth are vanity." We will say more about this trait later. Right now, there are more characteristics to notice.

Because they are so unsure and erratic, these children are poorly self-controlled and highly self-conscious. If they are not trained in the discipline of self-control, and if parent or teacher does not insist on the orderly discipline which is the result of having oneself under control, children of the ages thirteen to fifteen are prime examples of unbridled autonomy. For many years I have watched the junior high students assemble for choir. What happens if they are not diligently supervised? The girls giggle and laugh, with wild outbursts of hilarity and shrieking; boys swagger in boisterously, full of noise and bluster. It is too much work to walk around to the aisles and file into the rows; how much easier—and apt to get more attention—to climb over the back of one chair, stand on the seat, proceed over the next back, until one gets to his seat. And if someone is in the way, . . . well, . . . *shove*. We see it at home, too. Sometimes it seems to us parents that our children of this age enjoy the flagrant disregard for the niceties and refinements of life, and revel in behavior bordering on boorishness.

At other times, however, these children are very self-conscious. They detest standing before a class in English and making a speech; and they have undue problems with their hands and feet. This is a blushing age, when they feel as if everyone is watching, ready to criticize, when they recite in class. They are touchy, too. Boys who have not had their growth spurt don't want to be called "pint-size" or "small stuff." They are self-conscious about having their errors pointed out to them, and reluctant to be corrected.

Another trait peculiar to junior high school youths is their addiction to extremes. Observe the walk of junior high students. Either they slouch and amble lazily along or they dash wildly with bounding steps to their destination. Seldom do they walk with an even gait at an even pace. How can they? Aren't they either bubbling with exuberance and the vibrancy of the happiness which surrounds them, or declaring with sorrowful melodrama that they don't know where to turn in a life that is not worth living anymore? When their moods are rosy, their tests are easy and their chores at home are a breeze, but when their moods change to black darkness, the teachers pick on them, and they have to do all the worst chores around the house. In their personal appearance, too, they are fastidious to a fault or unspeakably slovenly. At this age, all the passing fads have appeal. If casual conformity is "in," everyone of the teenagers want to wear faded jeans. If skirts are short, the girls want to wear them as short as they are allowed to—no happy medium for them!

The reason for some of their taste for extremism is that they want to experiment, to try the new. The whole adult world lies just ahead of them. Without the caution which comes from experience, the young teenagers eagerly plunge into the new. Perhaps they will like it. If they don't, something else for them to try will soon be along. During these years the girls first experiment with make-up, comparing and trying one another's, more or less secretively, in groups on the playground or in the girls' room at school, or at a friend's home. Boys experiment with smoking, clandestinely, they hope. Getting caught does not seem to hamper their urge to try the new or the forbidden. Some, in the ninth grade or even earlier, look longingly toward dating, even if it is only walking a girl home from school. They can hardly wait to try the things that belong to the adult world.

We have already observed that when our junior high children are not on top of the world, they are hopelessly buried in despondency. Thirteen- and fourteen-year-olds (the average eighth grader) find that life seems almost always to be against them. It has never dawned on them, of course, that they, before their own consciousness, set themselves against the world around them. Do we know many eighth graders who *like* school, who think teachers are *great,* who heartily endorse their parents' decisions? Do they *gladly* do their math, rake the leaves, wax the car, or dress up? Usually these children are hard to find. But when we ask them *why* so many things in life are distasteful to them, we find out that the fault always lies somewhere else than in the eighth graders themselves. It's the teacher's fault, or their classmates got them into trouble, or parents don't even try to understand them. They claim with utmost candor that they *do* want to be pleasant and happy. But how can they when everything is against them? And while they feel that everything is against them, they still sincerely want to be popular, to have the feeling of being liked, or at least accepted by their peers. That is why they are such conformists: it is of great importance to be one of the group.

These teenagers of rapidly changing extremes can tease one another mercilessly and pester brothers and sisters until the tears roll. One year the junior high students were particularly offensive in their language to each other; names like "goose-hump," "bird-legs," and "puff-cheek," not always uttered good-naturedly, flew over the playground. In an editorial in the school paper that year, I thought "Consideration" would be a timely topic, and I hoped that they would read it, and wished that they would awake to their faults. But I was not at all sure they would. A couple of gangling ninth grade boys came to me soon after the paper came out and said, "We liked your editorial. You really hit us. We had it coming, though. Thanks a lot for helping us." Their candidness and their sincere compliment caught me off guard. It should not have. By experience I should have known that covenant young teenagers often react this way. In fact, this is the way they *should* react. And both their language and kindheartedness improved.

I am sure that we have not exhausted all the characteristics that mark this period in the lives of early adolescents, but we have seen enough to know, generally, what to expect from them, to know what problems will most likely arise. Not all of these traits are as exaggerated as I have illustrated them, and some children of junior high school age have only a few of these characteristics, or they have personalities in which these characteristics are not accentuated. Yet, they all will have their problems. For, though these children are highly idealistic, they seem to take a perverse delight in exposing the negative sides of their characters.

Based on a survey of young students, the following traits ranked highest in the list of their ideal behavior for students in their own age group: dependability, the knowledge that one's friend will keep his word; sincerity—these teenagers have an uncanny knack of spotting a "phony"; unselfishness, and the good sportsmanship which accompanies it; honesty—they want to trust their friends; the will to speak well of others; cheerfulness, even when things go wrong; and self-control, so that they have neither sudden outbursts of temper nor days of moodiness. These ideals, viewed from a formal point of view, would probably be ours, too. So far we have not mentioned the distinction between these characteristics and ideals as mere moral discipline and as means by which we can better live in the fear of the Lord, and to His glory. We see our teenagers, who have the same natural tendencies as any teenagers of this world, in the light of the Word of God and the distinctive perspective of the Reformed faith; and we show our covenant teenagers how to fight their weaknesses through prayer, to channel their energies in the service of their King, and to direct their ideals to the glory of God and the love of their neighbor. These goals we will spell out in detail farther on in the chapter.

* * *

Now that we have drawn a sketchy background of the teenage child in general, we will watch Tim's development through his years of thirteen to fifteen. This is a transition period for him, a transition from childhood to adulthood, from dependence to independence. In a sense, he lives in a no-man's-land. He does not belong, and does not want to belong to the childhood he has just outgrown. The pleasures and wishes he had in sixth grade seem childish, and in the remote past. But he is far from ready to assume the role and responsibility of the adult. He is too dependent. Yet he wants to be independent. And, being still an immature child, he has the wrong idea of his independence: he wants to become independent all at once; and he somehow wants to equate independence with a freedom from parental authority. When he gets a part-time job and proudly shows us his earnings, he assumes that he may do what he wants with his money. It is his own money—he earned it, didn't he? And he implies that we have no jurisdiction over it. Right here he must be taught that his becoming independent is a gradual process, and that even the money he earns is not his to spend foolishly. Because *he* is under our authority, so is his *money;* he must be taught how to use it wisely and that he must ask permission to spend it. In his surging independence and rising self-importance, he does not like to hear that his possessions, in a sense, belong to him, but are under our control; but he understands it better when we tell him that we are also stewards under God's control of what He has given us. As we teach him how to be a steward of his money, and as we call him to account for it, we do not do this as rigid, legal overseers. When birthdays come, or spontaneous occasions for little surprises, we enjoy his little splurges with him, and, by our reactions, guide his judgment on the next giving he plans. We can teach much by our reactions. We know that. Without crushing his enthusiasm, if he asks whether $4.95 was quite a bit to spend for little sister Sarah's toy, we can either heartily endorse his purchase or say, "You probably went overboard a little this time. Next time. . . . "

In these years of transition, we parents often find it hard to understand Tim. The violence of his outbursts often mystifies us. When the mailman delivers the model he sent for many weeks ago, we suddenly hear an alarmingly loud whoop of joy followed by the crash of the planter he knocked over in his exuberance. Then he is sorry: "I didn't mean to knock it over, Mother. I was just glad." He cannot seem to be glad quietly. It is not so difficult for us to understand his boisterous reaction. We consider the careless and carefree joy of youth. At the same time, we guide Tim in the way of a more moderate, self-disciplined response.

However, when he teases Sarah and she teases back, and when he keeps up his teasing until he provokes her to tears, one of us parents will have to intervene.

"Aren't you overdoing it, Tim?" we ask.

And then comes his outburst: "She's always right and I'm always wrong. I can never have any fun around here! I always get picked on and blamed for everything!"

With stamping feet he turns to go to his room, and we wonder, open-mouthed, why his temper flared. We don't continue wondering. After we have given him time to calm down, we ask him. Sometimes we find out that he was irked by something else, and vented his anger on us. Sometimes we never find out. He is sorry that he blew up, but doesn't know, himself, why he did it.

And then there are the senseless things he does. One day we get a call from school telling us that during choir period Tim has pulled a chair away from one of his friends who was ready to sit down; and this friend now has a very sore back. That afternoon a very sober Tim walks in.

"I honestly don't know why I did it. And I truly wish I hadn't," he says.

He already knows all the things we are going to discuss with him—kindness, consideration, thoughtfulness, obedience to school rules—and he has disregarded them all.

"How could you be so thoughtless?" we finally ask.

"I wish I could tell you, Dad," he replies sadly.

In his early adolescent development, Tim begins to understand adult concepts. But he always seems to fall short of understanding completely the basics and the relationships which the mature mind can grasp. His concepts seem to be arranged loosely, so that he has difficulty sorting through his intellectual loose ends, and coming to the proper conclusions. He may say, for example, "In civics we were talking about inflation. Boy, if I were the president, I'd put price controls on everything—just like that. How come he doesn't, Dad?" Then, as Dad relates one chain reaction in the economy after another, and the far-reaching results of a drastic decision such as Tim would make, we see him slowly shake his head and say, "I never thought of all these things." As he accumulates facts and the knowledge of the broad range of world affairs and the complexities of the life of his time, he does not yet fathom all their interrelationships nor the steps to proper solutions. He still has too many pitfalls in his logic, and he lacks the experience of the adult world.

But he craves these experiences and usually begs for new responsibilities. Eagerly he scans the ads for part-time jobs. And almost always he takes his first lawn jobs seriously. Our girl of this age prizes the pay for her baby-sitting jobs, but often values the responsibility and experience more. Tim and his friends may gladly forego a family outing or a trip to the beach in favor of working. There is something adult about saying, especially to a younger sister, "I can't make the outing. Gotta work, you know." He enjoys being on committees for church or school outings and usually is very serious and diligent about his duties for the cause for which he is working. For though Tim may consider himself rather grown-up and important sometimes, in many—perhaps most—areas of his character and life he is an enthusiastic, unsophisticated child, eager to help and to learn more.

Along with Tim's increased responsibilities come new skills. Through maturity and practice he has begun to refine many delicate skills. Tim may know more about tinkering with electronic gadgets and computers than we do; he is able to construct a delicate or complex science project for the annual junior high science fair, and enjoys the challenge. During these years Tim's talents in the fields of the arts often reveal their potential. These talents are far from reaching their peaks, but the aptitudes are showing themselves more clearly. These are the years during which his band instructor asks Tim to play the solo part and afterwards suggests that Tim take more advanced lessons on his cornet.

Or, during conferences with his teachers, we may learn that he has been showing a free-flowing literary style; his teachers remind us that the ability to express oneself well is a talent which the Christian is especially privileged to use. Think of teaching, preaching, writing. And his teachers urge us to encourage him to use his talent and accept opportunities to express his ideas in school papers or youth periodicals.

If Tim's talents are not those of music or verbal expression, nor of intellectual excellence, he may have talents with the use of his hands. To our amazement, he discovers the problem plaguing his radio and repairs it before we know what he is doing; he takes an interest in gears and motors and stubborn lawn mowers and, with fingers that know what they are doing, coaxes them back into running order. He may prefer wood and hammer and nails, or paints and palette. Whatever he likes to do he begins to do well, and we see signs of a lifelong hobby.

Another area of talent which we often neglect to recognize is our child's use of his God-given personality. He may have a tender-hearted and compassionate nature, the kind of person classmates come to when they need help. Or he may be able to use good judgment in assessing clashes among his friends, and soon come to be known as the arbiter or peacemaker. If we parents see these traits and help our son to see them and use them well, we may be helping him to decide in which direction he will go in choosing his vocation.

Though he needs parental guidance and answers to his questions as he grows nearer to a choice for his life's work, we know that we can be only guides. Often we parents secretly—or not so secretly—want to cast our child into a certain mold. He should be a doctor, or teacher, or lawyer. But Tim knows that he should not. He is a unique individual; and through all the years in which we have been training this individual, we have kept in mind his uniqueness. As we have tried to mold all his being in the service of the Lord, the last thing we have wanted is a stereotype. We have recognized that Tim has a distinct individuality, and we have enjoyed it. But, especially with a personality like Tim's, we see the danger of his individuality running foolishly wild; so we reckon with all these factors, and guide our unique son the best we can in the fear of the Lord. On the one hand, we are rigidly insistent on obedience to the whole of God's law; on the other, we let him have his own likes and dislikes, his own methods of expression, and his own goals —under obedience to God's law.

Now that he is a junior high student, does Tim need a different kind of guidance than he did when he was four or five years old? I suppose that, basically, he does not. But common sense and experience tell us that Tim has much different wants and needs now, as well as much more training and development. We build on that. God's Word says that our standards remain high; so we will follow our general pattern of discipline with Tim, even though we will vary our methods. Guiding Tim through his junior high school years is possibly the most difficult kind of guidance we will experience. Perhaps we parents make the most mistakes at this time in his life. His life seems to be fast-paced and packed with the unpredictable. So are his reactions—fast and unpredictable. And we are taken aback. Is this puzzling child our son? How do we handle the tragicomic events that erupt around us so unexpectedly?

The following five guidance rules may help us. First, our guidance will take more thought than ever before. Usually our young teenager will want an answer *now*: yes or no, why or why not. Yet, deliberately we set ourselves to allow time for thought or discussion with our spouse, if we are not sure of a good or wise answer. We can shape for ourselves an unhurried frame of mind which tells our child, without words, that no calamity will befall us for allowing an hour or two for contemplation. Soon he will get used to our saying, "Let me think *that* over for a while!" When admonishing him for doing wrong or for being foolish, we stop first to consider our approach. For if *he* doesn't know why he has done it, how can *we*? Sometimes saying, "We'll both think about the problem for a while," will prepare a more calm atmosphere for all of us. A thoughtful preparation for handling the problem will go a long way toward solving it.

The second guide is patience. All our life with Tim we have asked God for grace to have patience, to bear with his weaknesses. Now he seems to exaggerate his weaknesses. Sometimes it seems to us that when Tim clatters through the house, bangs things around, drapes himself and his possessions over the furniture, and is glum and stubborn, too, he is trying... and succeeding... to exasperate us. We need patience to reprove Tim in love, to correct him, to guide him to proper conduct, and probably to see the humorous side of his adolescent problems. It will surely cheer *us* and probably will give him a better perspective on his immediate troubles. Yet our standards remain high. Patience is not sighing and looking the other way, or failing to enforce our rules. That is slothfulness.

Third is tact. Already we have learned how sensitive Tim and his friends can be. How easily he blows small incidents out of proportion or misinterprets a word or an action! We also have already explored all the other extremes of behavior of Tim and his friends. When we use tact with Tim, we do not necessarily use the kind, sweet, and mild word at every turn. Tact is much more than that. It is the ability to assess the situation and then to use the proper method and proper words. For example, Tim comes home and says, "Our history teacher said he wouldn't ask questions on chapter twelve on the test, and then he went right ahead and gave us a whole section on it on the test." Tact would *not* be to say, "Well, everyone was in the same boat," or "Who said life was fair?" Tact would be to hear him out on all the details and suggest how he approach his history teacher about his problems with the test. At times tact may not even employ words. Merely pointing at his books, jacket, and baseball glove lying on the forbidden area of the dining room table might be the most tactful—and effective—way of telling him to take proper care of his possessions. Tim often feels lonely, I think, and by turns alienated from us, his friends, or his teachers. Saying the wrong words in the wrong tone of voice only increases his feeling of alienation. The right word, with the voice of love, shows that we're not so far from each other, after all. We use caution here, however. Tact is not smoothing over his faults, looking the other way, or fearing to cross him. Our tactful words always proceed from our standards of the proper relationship between God-fearing parents and God-fearing child.

The fourth guide is fairness. At first glance, this may seem to be belaboring the obvious. Would we try to be *unfair* to our child? However, if we remember how conscious our teenager is about fairness, we, who have always tried to treat our child with fairness, will try to demonstrate it more concretely than ever during this period in his life. An example will serve to highlight this principle. Once, in my brief tenure as grade school principal, a few junior high students came to me and said they had a complaint about Mr. X.

"Have you talked with him about it?" I asked, before I listened to the complaint.

"No, but. . . . "

"Go to him first and tell him," I told them.

They hesitated, and then one girl finally blurted, "You know we can't do that, and you know why. He's against us and we know it. You're strict, but you're on our side. You're fair."

Again, I was surprised at the girls' candidness. I hadn't thought of it that way. I think I had supposed we were all on the same side. Then I began to think of something Mr. X had said to me a day or two earlier. "If those eighth graders think they're going to put something over on me, they can guess again. I'll win this one. My strategies are stronger than theirs, and I'll come out on top." Maybe he was right. Eighth graders may not be left undisciplined. And basically he was on their side because he insisted on obedience. But, probably unknown to himself, he was pitting himself and his authority over against his students, and the students heard the battle cry.

Do we hear the battle cry in our covenant homes? We should not. We will show, by word and action, that we are on the same side, and that we parents are doing our best, with all fairness, for our child's good.

Finally, our guidance will be godly. We have always tried to make it godly. Now, as our problems with our son grow more serious, or when we must guide him to decisions which affect his future, we continue to ask God to order our lives in the way of His Word. Our son will see our godly attitude in the way we reprove him, in the way we guide him to make decisions based on spiritual values, and in the way we ask ourselves and him, "What does the Lord want us to do?" By our godly walk with him we are leading him in the way eternal.

Neither of us can walk the godly way by ourselves. We fail and he fails. When we stop to consider that we are sinners instructing sinners, we almost become afraid. We would have every reason to be afraid—to the point of despair—if we could not go to our Father for help. We desperately feel the need for God's grace for ourselves, but we also pray for grace for our son. For so often we show him the right way time after time, we reprove him for the same fault repeatedly, we help him battle his besetting sins day after day . . . and we don't see a lot of improvement. We tell him, "That's not right to act that way," and he says, "I know it, and I'll try to do better," . . . but he is a sinner, and he repeats his wrongdoing. And then we have to say to him, "You're not walking in the way that we taught you." And we have to keep on teaching him.

Let us take a brief look at some of the main aspects of that instruction during these three years. Paradoxical as it may seem, we *en*courage and *dis*courage independence. Tim must pull away from the hands that do things for him, and the minds and hearts that decide his course through life. As Tim pulls away, we increase the slack so that he can use his own hands, and his mind and will and heart. But we still hold the rope. This is the independence we encourage. For example, this summer Tim wants the whole care of the family garden, from preparing the soil, planting and cultivating, to harvesting. Do we say, "Go ahead, Tim. You're on your own"? We *might* not have crops this year. Instead, we increase the slack by giving him detailed instructions, careful supervision, cheerful encouragement, but no actual labor. If he listens well this year, and if his gardening is successful, next year we let go more rope, and let Tim do the gardening, with only a few reminders.

If our child is a girl, and she comes home from her first few baby-sitting jobs crestfallen and discouraged because other homes have situations she has never encountered and cannot cope with, and the children do not respond as she had expected, our girl needs instruction for her independence. Step by step, just as when she was small, we try to help her and show her how to handle her new responsibility. Giving her some wise and practical hints will help, but she will still have many "what if's." So we further our instruction in independence by teaching her how to think in an unexpected situation or emergency. But our helpful hints will be only that. Her blossoming independence will force her to make judgments of her own. And then we will find out that we still hold the rope. She will ask us if the decision she made was wise.

As we slowly let out more slack, we encourage our teenage boy to try odd jobs around the house, and our teenage girl to make that casserole from a new recipe. If Tim asks us our opinion on an issue or a situation, such as, "What would you do if . . . ?", we often turn the question back to our child and say, "What would *you* do?" Then we have a good springboard for discussing wise and foolish evaluations, while at the same time we teach him to think out his solution independently. This is the kind of independence we encourage. *We* still hold the rope.

Almost every day in the life of our teenage child we encounter the kind of independence which we *dis*courage. We see it in its most blatant form when our teenager tries to cut the rope. He will say, "I just don't agree with you, Dad. I can't see why you won't let me listen to *some* rock music. Here's why. . . . " Or he says to his teacher, "Why must we study *literature?* Literature will never do me any good anyway. Take shop, now, or electronics. . . . " When Tim says things like this, he is asking us to drop the rope, abandon our authority, and let him be free to decide issues for himself. This kind of independence which we discourage is called *defiance* or *disobedience.*

What do we do when Tim talks this way? Explain, discuss, argue, or tell him, "Because I say so"? Immediately we will throw out the possibility of arguing. That we will never do. To argue would put us both on the same level and would presuppose that the best logician wins. Sometimes we will explain and discuss the issue with him. We will give him our reasons why rock music is not good fare for the godly, why literature is necessary for a well-rounded education; we will, instead of inviting his argumentative "buts," ask him to cite his own (or Scripture's) reasons why we are right. Psychologically and spiritually, this approach often works. In the final analysis, it always produces right responses in the covenant child, because he is spiritually receptive to the words of Scripture and the voice of authority. But Tim is sinful, and in his stubbornness often perversely carries his questions and arguments to the point of absurdity and disobedience. Then the time has come for us as parents to enforce our God-given authority, and curtly tell him, "Because you are called to obey." Then we enforce our demand of obedience.

Often—and we must be aware of this "often" and rejoice with our child in its positive fruits—our child diligently and cheerfully obeys us. He obeys us because we are his parents and he wants to obey for God's sake. He tries hard to do his best in the task at hand. He studies hard because that is his calling as a student. He cooperates with his neighbor. Dozens of times a junior high choir student has come to me dry-mouthed and wide-eyed before a concert and gasped, "I'm so worried! Do you think we'll do all right?" Afterwards, besieging students swarm around, asking, "How did we do?" They are concerned. They tried. Probably they are not always concerned for God's sake; there is always the earthly pride and self-reward for which we all foolishly look. But one example will serve to show the unseen, lasting spiritual benefits that come when a covenant child does his best, also his spiritual best, in his work. For many weeks one season we had drilled on all the details of polishing a particularly beautiful arrangement of "The Lord's Prayer." After an intense rehearsal and a totally satisfactory rendition by the junior high choir, a ninth grade boy lagged behind, straightening chairs, and generally loitering. When we were alone in the room, he finally said, "That is the most beautiful song I ever sang. You know, after we've sung it this way, the Lord's Prayer means more to me than ever before." Through the means of choir, with its mechanical and technical aspects, he had, with his covenant neighbors, responded with sincere praise to God.

But, alas, neither we nor our child stays long on a high and happy spiritual plateau. Our corrupt natures so feebly fight our sin and depravity, and we are back on the old battlefield of sin. Tim is pulling too hard at the rope again. This time his will to be independent takes the form of sneaking the forbidden. He knows that he is too young to begin smoking and he knows the effect of cigarettes on his body; he also knows that we will not allow it. But he wills to be independent, and to decide for himself whether smoking is for him. So he smokes secretly, he thinks, alone or with friends.

He also decides that we parents are too strict about the television programs he watches. Independently, wrongly so, he watches what he wants when we are away from home. And then, amazingly, Tim is shocked that we know all about his secret transgressions. How in the world did we find out about it so quickly? He does not fully realize that diligent parents know all about the temptations of youth, and they know *Tim!* Usually, if we have sharp eyes, and ears tuned for the subtle nuances of life, we find out. A neighbor child innocently tells that Tim and his brother can smoke now, or the school principal alerts us that Tim is one of a group of boys suspect for clandestine smoking, and he asks us to watch for it, or Tim does not act quite natural, is not quite at ease. Sometimes a sort of sixth sense makes us mention, in passing, the name of the forbidden program he watched while we were gone; often his startled reply is, "How did you know?"

We know because we are parents and because we care. We care enough to find out and then to talk to him, to chasten him, to pull in the rope again and show him his duty to obey his covenant parents. We talk with him much these days about priorities; he must be made to understand that his priorities exist only under the rules governing our home. He has no choices, no independence, outside those rules. Tim does not always welcome this kind of tether. *"Must* I always ask permission? Why can't I start thinking for myself? You've taught me so far, and now it's time for me to do the deciding," he complains. Sometimes we are tempted to go along with his thinking, and let the rope out all the way; then we remember *our* priorities. We know that we may never abdicate and give the reins to our child; we are the authorities and the guides while he is under our roof.

Besides, this is the prime time to guide his thinking toward choices which will affect his future outlook on life. Take, for example, his view of recreation. Tim discusses baseball, football, basketball, with friends at school. He comes home and says, "What a good night *this* will be! No homework, and the best game of the season on T.V. Say, Dad, what say we go to the big game Saturday?"

Probably dad will go with Tim. But dad and mother will conscientiously watch Tim's talk. Is he preoccupied with sports? Is there a danger that it will become a controlling interest in his life? A priority? If so, we will steer his priorities into proper channels, those of good stewardship of his time and talents, of diligence in his calling as student; we will teach him to leave his love of sports at the periphery. In this age group of extremes, Tim is no exception. If baseball is his interest, the batting averages or the starting lineup of his favorite team takes precedence over his list of intransitive verbs or the sequence of Paul's missionary journeys. When this happens, we insist on first things first.

The matter of priorities involves Tim's whole life. It always has. The difference is that, having achieved some independence, Tim is putting his system of priorities into practice for himself. Sometimes they are in the right place. Sometimes not. Priorities involve the stewardship of his finances. "How much must I put in the collection, Mom?" He asks this question with no ill intent. Yet . . . how about that "must"? Without preaching, with a lighthearted tone, we ask, "How much do you *want* to give, Tim? It's all the Lord's, you know. You can't give anything back to Him. He just lets you take care of it; so put His kingdom causes first, and be generous. Always." In the use of his time—"Do I have to go to that meeting at church? It's so hot, and the kids want me to practice softball"—we show him that this also is a matter of priority. In his relaxation—"No,

I don't want to read, and I don't want to finish making my bookends. I want fun"—we alert him to the danger of craving fun for fun's sake.

This placing of first things first, we know, is not a system of externally imposed, artificial rules. These priorities come from the heart: from *our* hearts first, and then, as Tim learns, from *his* heart. But they do not pop into our hearts from nowhere. We find them in our Guidebook: "Seek ye *first* the kingdom of God and His righteousness . . . , " Matthew 6:33; and "Thou, therefore, my son, be strong in the grace that is in Christ Jesus," II Timothy 2:1. When we find guidance in Scripture, we ask God for grace, for us and our son, to live up to those Scriptural ideals, and to have them govern all our thoughts and all our lives.

Although the early years of puberty are often hard ones for Tim, and trying ones for us, yet they are joyful ones. Because of the nature of a child, our son can easily forget his sorrows and replace them with the joys of youth. For that is one of the properties of youth—its quickness to forget trouble and to plunge ahead. Tim, talkative, enthusiastic, impulsive, has not lost any of the characteristics of the personality he revealed as a child. To these characteristics he has added excessive physical exuberance. Tim is one of the teenagers who does nothing quietly, and very little orderly. Not only does he whoop with delight and bellow out the news to Sarah when we announce that dinner is served, but he also strides much too fast on legs that are longer than they were last week, and jolts the table as he crashes into his chair. Water glasses teeter, gravy sloshes over the edge of the boat, Sarah scolds, and father frowns.

Mother meditates. This kind of behavior has become a way of life for Tim. After school, he takes the four back steps in one leap, shoves the door open with his knee, slams it resoundingly, jumps up and touches the ceiling as he bounds into the kitchen, drops his books with an ear-splitting bang into the corner, says "Hi," and takes the steps three at a time upstairs to his room. How can throwing a jacket on the bed make so much noise? On his way down, he propels the top half of his body forward, so that his fingertips touch the ceiling break as it meets the landing, five steps up. Braced by his fingers on the ceiling, he jumps the five steps in one swoop, and is busy shouting, "Yeow! Mom! The instructions for those new bookends came!"

What do we do? Should we let it go? Is this physical exuberance a stage that will pass? We know that he is clumsy and awkward right now, and we know how carefree a boy is in the days of his youth. But then we wonder if we should allow *all* of his exuberance, or if we should leave most of it unchecked. Can it be that also this exuberance is exaggerated? He carries so much of his life to extremes these days. And as we wonder, the thought comes to us that possibly there is an element of defiance in all his actions. Tim was brought up in an atmosphere of controlled flexibility in which he was taught order, neatness, consideration for others, obedience to his parents. Is he subtly—or not so subtly—disobeying these rules, under the guise of the natural foibles of youth? If we carefully watch Tim's behavior, we will soon be aware that many times Tim is flagrantly disobeying all these rules. Then we realize that his exuberance is sinful, insofar as it defies authority.

Now it is our duty to call Tim's attention to his irresponsible conduct; we will guide him in the proper and orderly use of his body, and also of the material possessions God has given him. This means setting down rules for orderly and considerate behavior when entering or leaving the house, for mealtimes, and at any other time we think necessary. We take care, though, that as we tell Tim that he can and must learn to behave more quietly and orderly, we do not become rigid authoritarians who demand unyielding obedience to precept upon precept. We are loving and understanding parents. But we still have problems with our understanding of Tim; we are often puzzled, to the point of consternation, to know whether he is youthfully happy or defiantly play-acting. Where does the natural buoyancy of youth end and the defiance of the rules of our home begin? We know there is such a point, but we cannot always recognize it. Sometimes we laugh, often we shake our heads; but always we stand ready to reprove and correct. Our standard remains true to Scripture's: "Train up a child in the way he should go; and when he is old, he will not depart from it," Proverbs 22:6.

Many of our decisions about Tim in his teenage years will be the clearly discernible ones of the stark difference between right and wrong. Many more will concern matters of wisdom and judgment. These are the hard decisions to make; but when we do make them, we consistently enforce our decisions. Especially in these growing up years we keep our atmosphere of easy communication and quiet trust of one another. But neither the communication nor the trust means that we blindly accept Tim's stories, the likely and the unlikely, without being skeptical and without investigating. We let him know, if he informs us that Scott's mother has called to invite him at the last minute to spend the night sleeping over at Scott's house, so that he can help with the babysitting of younger brothers and sisters, that we suspect Scott's mother had probably already left when Tim got the telephone call (from Scott); we remind him that we know about Scott's smoking habits, and we hazard a guess that Scott's mother will be quite surprised to see Tim in the morning. Then we investigate.

We would rather not be suspicious. We would rather not watch Tim very closely, nor check on his stories. But we are aware of the poison of sin in his life. We know from experiences in our own lives that "the good that I would I do not: but the evil which I would not, that I do," Romans 7:19. And we know that as long as sin rules in all his members, that sin has dominion over him. If we love him as only covenant parents can love him, we *must* guard him from plunging into more sin. This is Scripture's only premise for us in the training of our son—to train him in the love and fear of the Lord. Proverbs 5 says, "My son, attend unto my wisdom, and bow thine ear to my understanding; that thou mayest regard discretion, and that thy lips may keep knowledge . . . lest strangers be filled with thy wealth; and thy labors be in the house of a stranger: and thou mourn at the last, when thy flesh and thy body are consumed, and say, How have I hated instruction and my heart despised reproof; and have not obeyed the voice of my teachers, nor inclined mine ear to them that instructed me!"

In a sense, all of Tim's life is religious in perspective. We have trained him as a covenant child, and he knows and loves Scripture. He knows, too, that he may not disagree with Scripture's rules for his life, and that in every area of his life God's Word is his guide. But in a narrower sense Tim's life has an area for special religious development. In this sphere, he develops mentally and spiritually as he responds to the teachings of the doctrines of Scripture. G. Brillenburg Wurth, in his book *Christian Counseling*,[2] has an excellent chapter titled "Pastoral Care in Connection with the General Religious Development." Although Dr. Wurth writes specifically about pastoral care, he devotes many paragraphs, well worth quoting, to the general religious development of the child. In the first paragraph of the chapter he repudiates the philosophy of the naturalists and the humanists. He says of them:

> Religious growth was considered to be closely connected with the biological development of man. This explains the special interest in religious life in puberty, the natural period of growth.
> The Scriptures here show us a different way. They represent spiritual development and growth within the sphere of the Church of Christ, above all as 'growing in grace.' This implies that according to the spirit of the Scriptures this process of growth already starts before puberty, in the life of a very young child. These children are already the children of the Covenant and the objects of the care of divine grace, though mostly in an indirect sense, through their education in the family.
> A child may share in the divine grace in Christ, but still in a childlike manner. He has not yet reached spiritual independence. His whole existence as a child is still embedded in the family relations, especially those to the father and the mother. His religion is still characterized by childlike dependence. The element of choice or decision is not apparent. He still leans strongly on outward authority. God's authority as our Father in heaven is still closely bound up with the authoritative Father-figure—with very great advantages if his father on earth is a sensible and loving father, but also with very great dangers if he is not.
> Spiritual growth in the life of grace will have to be manifested in puberty in the acquisition of greater spiritual independence, in the conscious believing acceptance of what

was promised us by God in his Covenant of grace before we knew about it. The question is in what way this acceptance will take place. Will it happen by gradual growth or are we to pass through a crisis?[3]

We know that in Tim's life it happened by gradual growth. Wurth puts it more picturesquely: "They are youngsters that impress us as, like flowers growing towards the sun, they turn to God without any sudden break through."[4]

What the author says next about *pastoral* care could as well be applied to *parental* care:

Also with respect to pastoral care, Christ's parable in Mark 4:6-29 is relevant. He speaks of the grains of wheat that 'fell on the ground and sprang and grew up and we know not how,' because 'the earth bringeth forth fruit of herself; first the blade, then the ear, after that the full corn in the ear.' In other words, pastoral care should refrain from forced activities which lack the courage to leave a great deal to the silent and hidden work of the Holy Ghost.

This does not mean, however, that Reformed pastoral care should above all avoid speaking of conversion. For the development of grace in the life of God's children is not merely a natural process of growth. It never lacks the element of 'a crisis' in the Biblical sense of this word. Without rebirth and also without conversion, nobody can enter the Kingdom of God (John 3:5). In every human being something is pulled down and replaced by something new. Every human person's old life must die in order that the new life will break through. This development is not exclusively restricted to the sphere of the unconscious, though it no doubt has its unconscious side. But these things must and will also be consciously experienced. They demand something from us that can only be designated by the word 'decision.' A convert surrenders unto death in order to be resurrected to a new life.[5]

Perhaps we would prefer the word "dedication" to "decision."

Next Dr. Wurth speaks of pastors and teachers as *examples*. Certainly, this would include us parents.

> In puberty, . . . exterior imitation will be replaced by an inner following in the footsteps of others. An adolescent is in need of people embodying his ideals and feels the urge to identify himself with them in inner freedom, in order thus to come to himself spiritually. He wants to see himself and to find himself in the mirror of others.
>
> Happy are the young people who at this age find what they are looking for in their spiritual counsellor. He may often be a strong support in their spiritual crisis and a stimulus to conversion, and to making an independent spiritual choice in life.
>
> . . . After this there is still a great deal to be done before he has reached spiritual maturity. His development after that comparatively critical stage may become more and more gradual, but this does not mean that from now on there will be no more 'ups and downs,' i.e., spiritual heights and depths.
>
> There may be times when there is a 'failing of the grace of God' (Heb. 12:15), spiritual alienation, desertion, also of a temporary relapse into the life of sin. Youth has its spiritual dangers, but maturity, senescence and old age are no less beset with dangers. And it is high time for spiritual care to devote attention to these more than it has been accustomed to do.[6]

With that we heartily agree.

Concerning Tim's growth toward spiritual maturity, H. Hoeksema says:

> In this connection (instruction in doctrine, i.e., in the principles of Reformed truth as it is based upon Holy Writ) we may make the following remarks.
>
> This instruction should not only be doctrinal, but also spiritual and practical. The purpose of this instruction must not be lost sight of, i.e., to lead the children of the covenant to the conscious confession of faith. The instruction, therefore, should be adapted unto this purpose. It should show

to the children of the covenant the way in which they may expect the assurance of faith and of their personal part in the salvation of God in Christ; and it should encourage and admonish them to walk in that way.[7]

We, as Tim's parents, together with his pastors and teachers, are leading him toward taking his place in the active life of the church, as a professing believer of the precious doctrines of Holy Writ as they are embodied in the Reformed Creeds. Tim has made spiritual strides toward this point of maturity, but his strides have often been halting, slow, and weak. So were ours. We know we could never make progress in our own strength. That is why we always have come to our son with the admonition, "Thou, therefore, my son, be strong in the grace that is in Christ Jesus," II Timothy 2:1.

NOTES

1. I am indebted for much of this information to Engle, *op. cit.,* pp. 183-195, and to H. Sorenson and M. Malm, *Psychology for Living* (New York: Webster/McGraw-Hill, © 1949), pp. 151-166. Used with permission.
2. G. Brillenburg Wurth, *Christian Counseling* (Grand Rapids, Michigan: Baker Book House, 1962), p. 165.
3. Ibid., pp. 165, 166.
4. Ibid., p. 167.
5. Ibid., p. 168.
6. Ibid., pp. 170, 171.
7. Unpublished Catechetics Notes, p. 38.

13

THE HIGH SCHOOL ADOLESCENT

Rejoice, O young man, in thy youth; and let thy heart cheer thee in the days of thy youth, and walk in the ways of thine heart, and in the sight of thine eyes: but know thou, that for all these things God will bring thee into judgment.
—Ecclesiastes 11:9

Tim is going to high school now. His silky blond hair has turned darker and thicker; he is probably not quite as tall as he will be in a year or two, when he has his total growth, but his voice has become deep and manly. Some of the clumsiness of his junior high school years is gone, and the bluster and boisterousness of those years is replaced by cleverly laid plans for pranks on teachers, classmates . . . or parents. Tim, still talkative, full of fun, rejoices in his youth. He enjoys his high school years, studying—not too hard—working, relaxing with his friends. The text at the heading of this chapter encourages Tim to rejoice, to let his heart cheer him in the days of his youth, to walk in the ways of his heart and in the sight of his eyes. Then the text comes with its admonition. It calls on Tim to remember that in all the rejoicing of his youth he must have in mind that God will bring him into judgment. Now, this is not a morbid dampening of Tim's cheery heart. Scripture never does that. Rather, Tim rejoices and walks in the ways of his heart with the idea that the judgment is coming. This judgment, for Tim, is not a fearful trial before a wrathful, condemning God, but a just vindication of Tim (and all of God's own) through the blood of the Lamb, under which Tim stands. If Tim stands covered with Christ's blood, his rejoicing, and the ways of his heart, and the sight of his eyes will all be in the fear of the Lord. As a covenant child, Tim knows that the only true rejoicing he will ever experience is rejoicing in the fear of the Lord.

But—and surely by now we know it well—Tim sins so much. His sins are as many as his character is varied and his nature is depraved: stubbornness, pride, greed, jealousy, slander, lying, dishonesty, hate. However, even more than during his junior high school years, Tim's besetting sin seems to be resistance to authority. In his early teens he put out feelers for his independence from parental rules. He tried to take up the slack in the rope of authority; and we pulled it tight again, time after time. He knew, deep in his heart, that he was quite dependent. He did not always want it that way.

Watch Tim as he goes through high school. He is getting as much education as his parents may have had. Driver's education, a permit, and a license are soon upon us. His part-time job gives him money for gas and for little luxuries. Girls are looking his way, and he is looking theirs; suddenly he knows that he can have more fun on outings *without* his parents. No, he assures us, he does nothing really wrong with his friends. (We believe him, too.) It is just that he does not need parents anymore; he is his own man now.

Go with me, if you will, through the typical thoughts of the high school adolescent; discern his views on his independence, some foolish views, some unsanctified. Tim says (or if he does not say it, he thinks it) that now that he is almost grown up he is his own boss. Insofar as he is independent from us, he need not obey us, either. There comes a time when we are equals in the home; we're all intelligent, mature individuals, and we should sit down at a family council together and vote on the affairs in our lives. Furthermore, since we have trained him so well up to this point, we can rest assured that the groundwork will pay off. Now it is up to him to make the decisions on his personal appearance, smoking, entertainment. He has rights in the home, too, he says, and tells us *where* he is going, *when* he needs the car, and *when* to have dinner ready. Now that eighteen-year-olds are considered legally of age, Tim is looking forward to that birthday. He will be of age, also at home. The state considers him of age. No more submission to rules at home!

Let us follow more of Tim's rationalistic ideas. After all, education is more sophisticated in these days, and he has been under the influence of wise teachers long enough now to know how to go his own way. He can map out his high school program and his first year of college, if necessary. He is not sure he wants guidance in the choice of a career; his parents are good, solid, devout Christians, but—let's face it—some modern-day careers didn't even exist in *their* younger years. The last thing he wants to be is a stereotype, a plumber or a teacher because his father is a plumber or a teacher. He *must* live his own life the way he thinks he should live it. Speaking of parents, however, we know that Tim is apt to put their early instruction of him to the test of a skeptical mind. There were times, he judges, that they were too strict. Fanatic, you might call it. In a sense, they were rigidly bound by the traditions they carried along with them and the customs that were their heritage. Provincial, Tim would say. Often they were carried away with their idealism and their high spiritual standards. Non-realistic, if you will.

Tim is still thinking improper thoughts of independence. These are thoughts without foresight. After all, he reasons, youth is a carefree time. Pleasure and good times belong to youth. So do money, a nice car, and a girl who is full of fun. Youth truly appreciates its pleasures, and there is nothing really wrong with a good time, is there?

Although Tim does not express all of these thoughts audibly, our ears are honed to the tones and moods of the words he does use. Our eyes are quick to catch facial expressions, actions of defiance or disgust. For we do not agree with Tim, and we will not let Tim go on, unchecked, thinking these thoughts.

Sometimes the occasion calls for the offhand approach, with a bit of humor mixed in, sometimes the talking-it-over method, and sometimes the curt demand of obedience *now*. Let us take a covenant parent's look at Tim's thoughts.

When Tim philosophizes that soon he will be old enough to vote, to take alcohol if he wishes, that at eighteen he will make up his own mind about issues, we may jolt him by retorting, with a wry grin, "And on that day we cease being parents?"

"Well, no, I'll still live with you, even though I'll be independent in the eyes of the state."

"Independent from obeying us, Tim?"

"Sort of, I think. You see, Dad, I can be tried as an adult, and if I'm an adult, I'm equal. Right?"

We tell him, "Wrong," of course. His thinking has proceeded from the wrong starting place. So we take him to the right place. Probably we will start by showing him Proverbs 23:22, "Hearken unto thy father that begat thee, and despise not thy mother when she is old." From Scripture we demonstrate to Tim that we will always be his parents, and as long as he is under our roof his calling is to be obedient and submissive; even though he will soon be eighteen, he still remains a child in our home. The sphere of the state may never encroach on that of our godly home. Even after he leaves our home, he still respects us as parents, and listens to us.

While we are talking with Tim anyway, we might as well clear away some more of his erroneous ideas of independence from our authority. Just as we told him when he was a lad in junior high school, so we tell him now again that our authority is the same as it was in the cradle, but we use that authority with the sanctified Christian judgment for which we daily pray. We tell Tim that we know that he is growing away from us, and that never again can we take him by the hand and set him where we want him to be. That in itself is good, and the way we want it to be. But our relationship of authority and submission still stands. Our authority now takes on the form of guidance—some of which guidance he *must* follow, and some of which he *should* follow, if he is a wise child of God.

If Tim, the impulsive, the experimenter, wants to find out what kind of beard he can grow, how he looks with shoulder-length hair, bare feet, and patched jeans, we frown. As we frown, we are quick to assure him that Christianity and a godly life do not reside in hair lengths or the material of our clothes.

It resides in a much deeper principle. So we ask him, "Whom are you imitating? The youth of today? The social radicals? The rebels? The flouters of the institution of the church? If so, why? Do you want to be close to the ungodly world, and the drug culture and the social revolution they promulgate? Do you even want to *look* like them? Or do you want to be different—one of a minority—and show in your clean-cut appearance that you are not ashamed to look different from the rebels? Let them imitate *you,* if they wish."

Tim may want to argue with us, and to say that there is nothing wrong, as such, in going along with the styles and customs of our times. And we will agree. In the same breath we will assure Tim that if the customs and styles of this world show, by their association or by their immodesty, that they come from Babylon, then the people of Jerusalem may not share them. We will not waver, as did one mother I know, when a fellow believer brought to her attention that her high school daughter's dress was immodestly short. "I know it," wailed the mother, "but my daughter will cry if I make her wear a longer one." This mother was a covenant parent; but she had not only given up her authority, she had also failed to instruct her daughter to reject the dress of the lust of the flesh, the lust of the eyes, and the pride of life.

As long as Tim is a teenager under our roof, the rules of our home stand as they always have stood. He never *tells* us that he is going somewhere or doing something; nor does he let us know about his problems with an "I need. . . . " Tim, as a child in the home, still asks permission. We, as covenant parents who love him, will grant him that permission, if we can. Many times we cannot give that permission—or rather, we may not. Again, we will err on the side of not being too permissive. He wants to go to the beach overnight with a group of his friends, tenth and eleventh graders. What will they do, unsupervised? Is this too much freedom for so young a boy? In this instance we will rule that it is, and hold the ropes fairly close yet. When he wants to watch the drag races at suicide alley, do we want him to be party to those risking their very lives for a purse . . . or fame? Again, we will decide that this is not godly fare for Tim. Many times we will say no to Tim; and we will not be hesitant or ashamed to say it. God's Word calls us to reject much—yes, most—in this sinful world.

Because we must refuse permission for many of the requests which our child makes, we will try to arrange our lives so that we are able to say yes to those requests which are not wrong. We recognize that our child's will to be independent is right and good; and we do not want to suppress his wishes, if they are not evil wishes. In fact, we encourage him to cultivate habits and hobbies, and a whole life style, which uniquely fit *him*. In the area of his likes and dislikes, we give advice and guidance if our child asks us. We are interested, but not domineering parents.

Once a sad-faced mother sighed and said to me, "I've tried so hard, so *very* hard to train my son right. I tried not to preach mere wordy sermons to him, but I did not permit the wrong, either. I came to him with God's Word, in love. His father and I taught him sincerity, consideration, honesty, trust, and all the rest. We talked to him since he was a babe about living in the fear of the Lord. Sometimes we led him gently, sometimes firmly, always with prayer. He listened, but not the way he should have. He always wanted to go his own way.

"Now that he is growing up, he finds it harder to listen. We keep talking to him, and witness to him with Scripture. And while we talk, he doesn't rebel. He just goes his own way afterwards. Oh, the things he does are not the horrid, hideous sins of an unbeliever. But when we tell him to drive carefully, he gets a ticket for speeding or reckless driving. He gets caught at a questionable 'beer' party. In short, when we tell him one thing, he may very well do the opposite. And we didn't train him that way. We've trained him to fight his disobedience. Why does he do that? What did we do wrong?"

Probably nothing. Probably there was nothing more these devout parents could do. They cannot change the heart nor the nature of their child. All they can do is to keep talking to him and pray, and ask their child to pray for grace to listen to them. That duty never ends.

But there is often more here than the mere questioning of his parents' decisions and their authority. He, along with many of his friends of high school age, has even more serious problems and questions. And they strike deep, even to the foundation of his religious training.

When Tim sits with his biology or world history text open on his lap while he stares into space, we can see by his frown of concentration that he is pondering some problem. Suddenly he asks quietly, seriously, "The days of creation *couldn't* have been longer than twenty-four hours? Did you ever wonder about that, Dad? You know, because of what science says about it. Do we have something good I could read on the subject?" And we parents look up from our newspaper in amazement. Ever since he was small, we all expressed faith in a literal interpretation of the beginning of Genesis.

He reads the newspaper and asks us questions about Christians cooperating with world agencies in humanitarian ventures. He questions our decisions on amusement. Or, at Sunday noon dinner, with the morning's sermon fresh in his mind, he asks, "Dad, are we *sure* that every detail of the Reformed doctrine of Christ's atonement is right?" His whole outlook these days is one of questioning the faith, or questioning the implications for his practical life stemming from it. He is not questioning flippantly, but apparently sincerely. Why?

It is urgent that we ask ourselves the *why*. If we do not, we may be led to panic, and consign our son as bent on the road to apostasy. Or we may take a hands-off attitude, fearful that whatever we say may be the wrong thing. We bear in mind that when he was younger, he accepted what we said, also in his religious training. That is the nature of a child, to believe his teachers and accept what they say. But we know that Tim realizes that now he must make these principles his own confession. He must live by them. And before he can live by them, he must know that he understands and trusts them fully in order that he may stand on them. He must be *sure!*

This embracing of the fundamental doctrines of Scripture as his own is a process, sometimes a long process, a part of the whole process of Tim's becoming independent. He realizes that the time for asking dad and mother the answers to all his spiritual problems is coming to an end. He must soon do battle on his own. Is he *sure* that the traditional, "old-fashioned" views of his parents are right, the *only* right ones? On the one hand, Tim believes the doctrines in which he was instructed, because, by faith, he is convinced they are true. On the other hand, at school or at work someone throws a convincing argument his way, his faith wavers, and he has questions again.

And this struggle is not all bad for our teenage son, as long as he talks to us about it. He thinks and reads and discusses, and through it he is strengthened in the faith, even though we do not always see visible evidences of it. True, this period of spiritual development is not always so pleasant for Tim, for he is truly troubled, plagued with doubts and seemingly in the throes of a spiritual crisis. Some of the arguments and temptations for Tim to leave his sure foundations are so convincing and appealing that Tim's nature yearns for them. The pastures outside those of the narrow confines of the covenant sheepfold seem so pleasant. He is torn, and runs to us for help.

For us, this time of spiritual crisis is an unhappy one, too. When our own child begins to ask hard questions that lead to the heart of Scriptural truth, when he questions the very faith, and seems to be forsaking the truth, how do we help? First, we always remember that *we* cannot put faith and trust in Tim's heart. But God can. So we take him to God's Book. And we talk to him patiently and understandingly. We can tell him that the devil and his cohorts are working hard to trouble Tim, for they would like nothing better than to cut loose from his spiritual moorings a Christian young man in the early prime of his life. When we talk with Tim, we will not scold or accuse, or rant that he is already adrift from the faith. Nor will we argue, back him into a corner, or insist that he agree with us right now. But we will tell him that we understand his problems and questionings, even though at the same time we don't justify them. Then we use Scripture to try to dispel his doubts.

Often we will not be able to see that either Tim or we have benefited from our discussions. But we have planted seeds, and Tim will think about what we have said. The rest we leave to the Lord. He will work faith in His own, and clear away doubts. And if our son continues his questions or becomes perverse, we never stop admonishing him.

If our high school child views his place in the family in the proper light, he will not go off and make his own career plans, independently, and high-handedly. Certainly, the final decision is his, and the decision affects the rest of his life. But our child loves us, trusts us, and confides in us. I think he knows that we are the only ones in the world fully able to see the whole child, to know his nature, his capabilities, and his aptitudes. On that basis we may suggest, advise, and guide him toward a choice. Sometimes—and I say this with great caution—when he is undecided, we may influence him. But we will take care that we do not dictate or mold him according to our own predetermined pattern, and that our child understands that we influence him for his best interests and in line with his talents and personality.

Even though Tim has gained a measure of independence, we are not finished training him. In order to establish proper independence, he must learn foresight. In handling his money, we teach him how to weigh the immediate over against the long range, the spending versus the saving. We tell Tim about foresight in choosing his life's work: a job right out of high school, or college and more learning first, with a better job later. Especially we try to instill foresight when Tim begins dating. A rule of our covenant home is that he may never date a girl he could not marry. This eliminates any street "pick-up," and unbelieving, godless girl. Even before he dates, even when he puts on a show of indifference, we teach him how to look at a girl, and where to look for one. For, as high school teachers are fond of saying, "Many students have more hormones than brains." Tim needs more than hormones and brains, however, when he begins to look seriously for the girl with whom he will share his life. He needs spiritual eyes. And, as his spiritual counsellors, we will help him use those eyes to look for a girl with a covenant background and a spiritual beauty. He may date several before he finds the one he can love for life; but his choice is limited, and he knows it, and he wants it that way. For most important to Tim is that his mate be spiritually compatible.

Throughout Tim's high school years we watch new abilities arise. As Tim is saddled with more responsibilities, he has become more self-assured and poised. Physically, he is not so clumsy or boisterous. His exuberance is not gone, and we would not want it to be. But psychologically and emotionally, he has learned to develop a balance, a more even keel; he does not have as many "ups and downs," nor are they so high nor so low. Many high school students are exceptions to this rule; they have not been able to settle down to a measure of maturity. At times Tim also proves to be an exception: he still ranges easily from being angry to cantankerous to silly. But his balance seems to return more easily.

Tim's intellectual abilities have expanded. Now he is able to understand more concepts than he had ever thought possible. Certain skills, which he has shown in earlier years, emerge with striking vividness. God has given the student of high school age a great ability to master thoughts and concepts. The pity is that Tim and his schoolmates do not use nearly all these abilities; their other interests—leisure, cars, sports—are overwhelming. And, in passing, I might mention, and high school teachers will bear me out on this, that high school age is often an age of indolence. Shame on them . . . or shame on us?

When Tim takes on new duties, either at school, church, or at a part-time job, we discover that in many respects he is still a child. When he fails at a task, he is quick to come to us and ask, "What did I do wrong? What would you have done? Can you help me?" We are glad to. Our years of training are not yet finished.

Yet, Tim finds out that his past instruction has molded his way of thinking, his standards of right and wrong, and his viewpoints. *We* find out when Tim relates, with high enthusiasm, an argument with a classmate or other friend about an aspect of his belief or Christian walk, or when he comes to us for what we call "continued parental guidance," and he calls "ammunition" for his argument.

He reveals the fruit of his training in his discussions with us at the dinner table, in his reports about school, and his reactions to the events of the day. Often he talks about school rules . . . and complains. "It isn't that we don't need rules over there," he says, "but why do they give us so many 'don't's' and so few 'do's'? Don't they know that we resent the negative approach just as much as we did in grade school—maybe more? They tell us that the girls' dresses are too short, the boys' hair is too long, that we may not do this, that we may not act that way . . . and they're right. But then—wham—comes the penalty. You know, Dad, I've been thinking: we still need a lot of correction in high school, but why doesn't it follow the lines of our training when we were younger; we're covenant young people now, and I wish they'd guide us by a positive spiritual motivation at school. After all, the only kind of school that can guide us that way is a Christian school like ours. Right, Dad?"

We dads and mothers understand that Tim is trying to say that the time for saying no to the forbidden never ends in this earthly life. But in his years of maturity, he wants to be taught a forward-looking spiritual perspective so that when he says no to the wrong he can, with his whole heart, know why he wants to say yes to the right. Tim knows that as he approaches the years when he must make his own decisions, he will rely on his background of training; he will need reasons, based on sound principles, for what he decides.

Now that Tim nears the time of his complete independence from us, he is both eager and afraid. Because he is one of God's own covenant children, he does not say, with the masses of modern-day teenagers, "I don't know *where* to turn. I see no future for me." Tim understands that his life will not be easy. He will understand it better a few years hence. But he knows that the covenant child stands only when his Father holds him up. Then, though it is hard for him, and he has many falls, he walks the path of the antithesis. But he often finds it difficult to say no to so many pleasures his sinful nature loves. His friends tempt him, too, and he does the wrong. We parents find out about it, and show him how to fight harder: by a diligent study of the Scriptures, and through prayer for God's Spirit, His grace and wisdom to rule Tim's life. It's the same old struggle, all over again, on another level.

Tim is gradually becoming our forward-looking teenager. As yet unstable in some respects, he comes to us with his problems in this age of intensive preparation. More than we realize, he draws on the resources of the godly training of his youth. Lest we burst with pride that we have done a fine task of rearing our child, we will quickly bow on humble knees, and give glory to Whom it is due—to our covenant God. Using His rules as our guide, and His grace in our hearts, we were only the tools He used to bring Tim to maturity, also spiritual maturity. Only God could cause him to say, "With my whole heart have I sought thee: O let me not wander from thy commandments," Psalm 119:10.

In his years of immediate preparation for adulthood, he has scores of questions to answer: school or skill; fun or future; a monied career or kingdom work; a helpmeet or a playmate. All of these questions he answers with common sense and with grace. Not all covenant children can be scholars; not all are qualified for full-time kingdom work. But all must begin a serious search for lasting qualities based on Scripture's standards. We counsel Tim to take as serious a calling as his abilities allow. We urge him to look for a beautiful wife—beautiful as Sarah and Rebekah were. We send him to young people's society, and urge him to use his expressive talents in youth publications. And we guide him toward making one of the most important steps in his growth in the church—public profession of his faith in his Savior, and a place as full member of the church of Christ, a partaker of the Word and sacraments.

We all rejoice, and Tim most of all. He has a text to carry along with him for many years: "Rejoice, O young man, in thy youth; and let thy heart cheer thee in the days of thy youth, and walk in the ways of thine heart, and in the sight of thine eyes: but know thou, that for all these things God will bring thee into judgment," Ecclesiastes 11:9.

This judgment, through Christ's blood, is his only comfort.